THE
REAL
F. SCOTT FITZGERALD

THIRTY-FIVE YEARS LATER

THE
REAL
F. SCOTT
THIRTY-FIVE

FITZGERALD
YEARS LATER

BY SHEILAH GRAHAM

GROSSET & DUNLAP, INC.
A FILMWAYS COMPANY
Publishers New York

ACKNOWLEDGMENTS

My thanks to Scott's daughter, Scottie Fitzgerald Smith; Mr. Alexander Clark, Princeton University Library Rare Books Department, and his former assistant, Mrs. Wanda Randall; and to Professor Matthew J. Bruccoli.

Certain letters of F. Scott Fitzgerald, Zelda Fitzgerald, and Scottie Fitzgerald printed by permission of Harold Ober Associates, Incorporated. Copyright © 1976 by Frances Scott Fitzgerald Smith.

Excerpts from *The Letters of F. Scott Fitzgerald* reprinted by permission of Charles Scribner's Sons from *The Letters of F. Scott Fitzgerald*, edited by Andrew Turnbull. Copyright©1963 Frances Scott Fitzgerald Lanahan.

To my daughter, Wendy W. Fairey, Ph.D.,
who helped so much with the organization of this book.

Other books by Sheilah Graham

GENTLEMAN CROOK
BELOVED INFIDEL
THE REST OF THE STORY
COLLEGE OF ONE
THE GARDEN OF ALLAH
CONFESSIONS OF A HOLLYWOOD COLUMNIST
A STATE OF HEAT
HOW TO MARRY SUPER RICH

CONTENTS

THE
REAL
F. SCOTT FITZGERALD

THIRTY-FIVE YEARS LATER

1.

WHY I AM WRITING THIS BOOK

IF EVER THERE was a Jekyll and Hyde character, it was F. Scott Fitzgerald, a man of two completely different personalities.

One Scott was kind; the other cruel. One was completely mature; the other never grew up. One wanted to be loved and admired; the other wanted to be despised. One tried to make people better than they were; the other tore them down. One was careful to the point of hypochondria; the other reckless of his health and safety. There was Scott the considerate husband and Scott his wife's oppressor; the proud father and the father who embarrassed his daughter. The Scott Fitzgerald I knew best was the mature man, although Jekyll sometimes turned into Hyde. It was, of course, his drinking which brought on the transformation, when even his usually wan and self-contained expression changed into flushed anger.

"Which is the real you?" I once asked him. And he replied, "The sober man." I believed him, maintaining my faith that the drinker, however terrible, intruded only passingly and without aftereffect on our life together. Then, too, the fact that Scott was completely sober during his last thirteen months led me, after he died, to cherish the image of the tender man I had known and to resent the biographies with titles such as *The*

11

Disenchanted and *Far Side of Paradise* that stressed his fall from grace.

My first book about Scott, *Beloved Infidel*, written and published eighteen years after his death, was to set the record straight—my obligation to the man with whom I had been so much in love—that he was not a defeated alcoholic when he died on December 21, 1940, but a sober and serious man who was diligently at work on *The Last Tycoon*, which Edmund Wilson believed would have been his best novel.

This I still believe. Yet I also recognize that *Beloved Infidel* was a romanticized version of my love for Scott, not fully exploring our story's complexity. It gave the facts as I viewed them in 1958, looking through the discreet haze of the times and the gloss of my experienced collaborator, Gerold Frank. When the book was reviewed by Arthur Mizener for a British publication, he hoped that "one day Sheilah Graham will write her own version of Scott Fitzgerald, to give the real man."

I had thought that *College of One*—my 1966 account of the two-year education Scott planned for me—would be my last work about him. But it has been impossible for me to be quiet in the flurry of recent publications about the two Fitzgeralds, Scott and Zelda, with all the misconceptions and errors that have not only persisted but bloomed in size—especially the last few "true accounts." Apparently, there is to be no let up in the avalanche of Fitzgerald memoirs, and, again, I feel obliged to tell the accurate story, this time without the obscuring gauze of the 50s, but as it was, what he himself told me of his whole life and what I remember personally. Perhaps with a more probing analysis of his whole personality and mine, and a fuller account of our relationship, I shall finally dispel some of the irritating errors that have been printed—and spoken —about Scott and about me in connection with him.

The worst error that continues, even though one of the chief ideas of *Beloved Infidel* was to correct it, is that Scott went drunken into his grave. Aaron Latham, whose recent book *Crazy Sundays* deals with Scott's life and work in Hollywood, speaks in his preface about the "recurring bouts during

Fitzgerald's Hollywood years, 1937 to his death in 1940, when all his days seemed to be turned into Crazy Sundays, when he seemed to be caught up in a drunken party which would not end." This simply is not true of Scott's last year. And it has always angered me that people continue to make this mistake, as if they wish to see Fitzgerald—even at the expense of truth—as the beautiful, gifted but doomed, artist who squanders life and talent and dies in dissipation.

As persistent as Scott the drunk is the image of Scott the exhausted dying man—such a wrung-out figure as he had made Dick Diver in *Tender Is the Night*. Scott, himself, contributed to this impression with "The Crack-Up" pieces and with the complaints that run through his late letters of diminished vitality. But my feeling is that part of his world-weariness was a pose. And certainly to view him throughout his last three and a half years in Hollywood as a dying man, as some writers who were with him at M-G-M have done, is a distortion. They all describe him as looking so pale. *I* thought he was pale, but he looked okay—sometimes he seemed rather jaunty. Whatever vitality he lost, enough remained for him at forty to delight me as the most vibrant, enthusiastic man I have ever encountered. Perhaps in retrospect, it is tempting for others to look back on him as wasting away before his death.

Given such a notion of Fitzgerald, there is a tendency to see me as the nurse figure of his declining years—a view that is unfair to both of us. When Latham writes that "to help the man get through the night, there was the woman, Sheilah Graham," even sex sounds medicinal. And anyway, I didn't help Scott through the night. He never slept through the night, and we could never have shared the same room because of his insomnia and restlessness. I was a very good sleeper until he died, and then I too needed sleeping pills.

Even more absurd is the account that when Scott, in his drinking periods, "began to run a low fever and to sweat his bed wet at night, Sheilah would change his sheets two or three times before morning." Except during the daytime I never went into his bedroom. Scott would tell me in the morning that the nurse had had to change his sheets or that he had changed them two or three times. And once, very dramatically, he reported that he'd changed them five times in one night, and his pajamas as well. But that was his TB, he said. Well, one doesn't know if the TB was real—not all the time —but he certainly wouldn't call me in to perform the chore of changing his sheets. This would have been the last thing. He was a fastidious man, also proud. He wanted my respect, not my solicitude or pity.

He did have my respect. I cared for him (rather than took care of him) as the man who expanded all my capabilities for loving, for anguish, for honesty, for joy, for unselfishness. And because he touched me so deeply, it has also depressed me to have our time together reduced to "an affair." The extreme deprecation came from Anita Loos, famous in the 20s for her book *Gentlemen Prefer Blondes,* who told Paulette Goddard, "You know Sheilah Graham writes these books, but she hardly knew him!" Was she prompted by some kind of jealousy? Perhaps she felt *she* could have written a book about Fitzgerald. Or could it be that here was one gentleman who certainly preferred blondes—his wife was blonde, I was blonde, and his daughter was blonde . . . but Loos was a brunette!

"He died in her arms" is another malicious error that has caused me some anguish. This canard was, I suspect, told by a disgruntled agent to a Hollywood trade paper gossip columnist, because acting on the plea of Scott's daughter and his executor, Judge John Biggs, Jr., I thwarted the possible film purchase of a novel, suggesting rather openly it was about Scott. It was I who made known to the studios Scottie's threat to sue if this cruel, one-sided portrait of her father was bought for a film. The result: no sale, and the item in a trade column was something like "Sheilah Graham, who was so shocked by———. . . is a fine one to talk . . . when Scott Fitzgerald actually died in her arms."

Since then, "he died in her arms" has been repeated *ad nauseam* in print. And just recently in a Fifth Avenue bookshop, the salesman, not knowing who I was, when I asked for the paperback of *Beloved Infidel,* told me the same old story.

"How do you know?" I asked him.

"*Everybody* knows," he replied.

"What does it mean, 'he died in her arms' "?

"In bed."

As Scott's serious biographers have printed—with corrob-
orations from the friends who flooded my sitting room when
he died there that sunny afternoon in December 1940—death
came to this great American novelist, interrupting his reading
the *Princeton Alumni Weekly*. He started up from the green
armchair where he was sitting, clutched the mantelpiece, and
fell to the floor with a fatal heart attack. He did not die in my
arms, that is, in bed, sex having in fact been out of the picture
since his first heart attack three weeks before. Loving him, I
was hesitant to resume it even though the doctor told us his
condition was improving.

I think I suffer from the false gossip about his death not only
because it is inaccurate but because it violates my sense of
respectability. When I was a girl in the East End of London, to
be respectable, or seem to be, was the be-all of a girl's life.
Also, sex was never discussed, or if it was, I didn't understand
it. Imagine, at the age of fifteen, I asked my mother how babies
are made and she told me never to ask that question again. I
soon after learned the facts of life from a co-worker at the
Addressograph Factory, then in Shoe Lane off Fleet Street,
and at first couldn't believe such an amazing explanation. I
learned, too, that if you did allow your feelings to run away
with you, you *never* told anyone.

Thus, when people spoke of Fitzgerald dying in my arms or
referred to me as his mistress in books read by thousands, I felt
humiliated and exposed. I even started a book author's talk in
1966 for the Long Island paper *Newsday* with a definition of
what a mistress was. I looked it up in the dictionary, and I told
the audience that a mistress was someone who had a longish
affair with a man, who in return supported her, usually lux-
uriously. Because of my upbringing, such a position carried a
stigma. I envied Du Barry and other great mistresses of kings.
But I also knew that I could never carry it off because of my
longing to be respectable and respected.

In terms of the dictionary definition, I was never F. Scott Fitzgerald's mistress. Not only did I always keep my own home and pay my own bills, but our relationship—except for one drunken time—never had such an overtone. "You were not his mistress," Edmund Wilson assured me when I told him of my distress. "You were his second wife."

I have also been accused of "trading" on my relationship with Fitzgerald. Two books and a couple of random chapters about a great writer by one of the few people left who knew him intimately—I knew the best and the worst of Scott—is that trading? Professor Matthew Bruccoli has written several books about Scott, ditto Professor John Kuehl, and so many others. "Write about what you know," Scott always told me, when neither of us knew that he was the subject I would know best, or that I would be humiliated because I was his girl, rather than his wife, when all that was required to become the latter was the most gentle push.

In this book I shall do my best to present an objective picture of what Scott Fitzgerald was really like, seeing him partly through his own eyes and also judging him from my present vantage point. I think I can do this clear-sightedly because I am no longer the young woman mesmerized by his love for me and mine for him. My hypnotic devotion has faded somewhat in the last few years when so much has been written about him and Zelda—perceptive as well as error-ridden commentaries—and I have learned to look at and accept the more cruel part of his nature that I earlier rejected. I still like and admire him enormously, but I can see the man more as he was.

Rereading his books and the best of his short stories, I am more and more aware that he was a magnificent writer. But how good was he as a man? And how good was he for me? Did he treat me badly, as Helen Hayes stated to one of his recent biographers?

When I first saw Scott on July 14, 1937, I didn't know that I was to be just a three and a half year experience in his total life of forty-four years and that everything that had happened to him before we met would minimize a great deal of what was happening to him then. It was like jumping over a cliff with my eyes closed. But in terms of experience I have always been a bit reckless.

In many ways my time with Scott was strange. And today, remembering some of his escapades before I met him, and his drunken bouts during our time together, I am appalled at my involvement. How was I able to keep on loving him so unquestioningly? It is plain to me now that my time with him was not always beautiful; it was marked, as Scottie observed to me in a recent letter, by "nightmarish episodes."

But however I reevaluate my love story, I will always remember Scott as the only person before or since to give me such a compelling relationship. He remade me in many areas so that I am still more honest with myself and don't rationalize my misdeeds. And however badly he may have treated me when he was drunk, the pluses of our years together—his love for me, the education, and the marvelously happy times we had between the binges—were much more than the anguish of the drinking quarrels. As long as I live I will be grateful for my time with him.

2.

IN THE BEGINNING

WHEN SCOTT FITZGERALD advised me early in 1940 to write my own story and gave me a ledger in which to record everything I could remember, he wrote on the title page, "The Book of Lillith." At the time I thought this was a play on my real name, Lily. Scott often indulged in such affectionate puns—for example, he changed Dante Gabriel Rossetti's line, "and the lilies lay as if asleep along her bended arm" into "FSF and Lily lay along his bended arm as if asleep."

I did not think further about Lillith until recently, glancing through a dictionary, I saw that Lillith, the first wife of Adam, flew away from him and became a demon. So, as Scott had conceived my story, it was to be the story of a demon, of a witch.

This discovery aggravated an old doubt. I was thoroughly confident that Scott had loved and respected me. But was there also a part of him that despised me?

Right after his death I had received a tremendous shock when I took the photograph I had given him of myself from its frame. Scrawled across the back was the inscription, "Portrait of a Prostitute." I was terribly hurt and also reminded of a party at Malibu Beach in the summer of 1938 when Scott, very

18

drunk, had spoken of me to Nunnally Johnson as his "paramour."

I knew that "Portrait of a Prostitute" was also a drunken commentary. He must have written it on the photograph after the first of our two bad quarrels in 1939 when he was drinking so heavily. We had struggled for his gun, I had slapped him —the first person in his life ever to do so—and as I walked out, I had delivered a harsh exit line, "Shoot yourself, you son of a bitch. I didn't raise myself from the gutter to waste my life on a drunk like you."

This was hysterical and somewhat theatrical, as first of all I had never been in the gutter—my family was poor but respectable; my father, who died when I was a few months old, was an educated man—and secondly, I didn't really consider my time with Scott a waste. Perhaps he wanted to retaliate with an insult equally cruel and outrageous. But nonetheless, his comment—which I discovered when I was powerless to challenge it—reflected the puritanical streak in him that rebelled against his falling in love with me.

Did he feel guilty, as some writers have suggested, about his dual commitment to me and to Zelda? Or did he mind that I was a girl, as he describes me in the poem "Beloved Infidel," "with eyes made bright by other men"?

Scott's ambivalence toward me began, I think, after he asked me how many lovers I had had—he was always curious to know about people's lives. At this point I did not know him well, but I was pleased at his interest and happy to answer his question. "Eight," I told him flippantly. This struck me as a good approximation. There might have been more, there might have been less. This was 1937 and I wasn't a baby. I had been married and had been on the stage and had worked in New York.

But Scott was visibly shocked. His own life, for all its exhibitionistic wildness, had been more sexually conservative. In 1925, while they were in the South of France, Zelda had had one notable affair with a French aviator, and Scott had been unfaithful to her only after 1930, when she lost her sanity and was in an institution. I am sure that his Hollywood fling in 1927 with Lois Moran was not consummated, for she afterwards visited him—and Zelda—at Ellerslie in Delaware. Scott's loves and heroines in the past had all been flirts. But a woman such as myself who casually acknowledged earlier lovers was not within his experience.

Perhaps it is true, as the literary critic Leslie Fiedler has observed, that American authors tend either to idealize women as virgins or damn them as whores. At least this generalization holds somewhat true of Scott. My past obviously disturbed as well as intrigued him, and at times he found it easiest to cope with by villifying it and me. He knew that I was a working woman who, from the age of fourteen, had always earned her own living. In fact, I was the only woman, as he wrote of Kathleen in his notes for *The Last Tycoon*, "whose life did not depend in some way on him or hope to depend on him." He knew I stood alone and could stand alone, as indeed I have all my life.

Yet why did he cast me in the image of the prostitute? Working at M-G-M on the script for *The Women*, he draped Joan Crawford, portraying the kept woman, in a silver fox jacket—the very coat he had bought for my birthday in September 1937. And an even more blatant insult—though I did not recognize it at the time—was his writing out a check to me for $2,000 after our fight in Encino, in early 1939, as though paying me off. Then I looked on it as a present for the time I had spent with him. He had said late in 1938 that because it might be impossible for us to marry, he would give me several thousand dollars a year for every year I had spent with him —to have something for that time in my life.

His solicitude had touched me, though I did not wish to place any further financial burden on this man who already had so many obligations. I took the money, however, after our fight, because at that moment I hated him and was glad that he should be out of pocket. And after we came together again, instead of giving it back to him, I kept it in my savings bank. But I always felt that the $2,000 was his. When he was so hard up in the few months before his death, I planned my letter to Max Perkins, suggesting that I would send Scribners $2,000 if they would add another $3,000 and give the $5,000 to Scott as a further advance on *The Last Tycoon*. My share in this scheme—proposing it and contributing to it—I insisted, should be kept from Scott because I knew his pride would be offended.

He died before I could send the letter, but my penciled notes for it are still among the papers that I donated to Princeton University. After his death, going through Scott's checks and records, Scottie asked me about the $2,000, but I told her it was a private matter. I think she assumed that I had loaned her father that money and he was repaying it.

It has recently occurred to me that Scott may, himself, have felt enmeshed in a type of prostitution and that his anger at me may have had something to do with his own sense of weakness and frustration. Hadn't he prostituted his talent, writing what he recognized as inferior stories—full of "trashy imaginings"—in order to make the quick money he always needed? And at the end he ran out of time in which to complete the work of integrity—*The Last Tycoon*. Scottie, writing to me three days after his death, felt that the unfinished novel was "almost the greatest tragedy" of the situation. "It would have meant so much to him and to his career and to his reputation in the future."

Scottie's letter also thanked me for my involvement with her father. And at a time that I had just been jolted by the discovery of "Portrait of a Prostitute," she helped to remind me of all the warmth and dignity of my years with Scott:

> Dear Sheilah,
>
> I know it seems somehow absurd, but I did want to write and thank you, however inadequately, for "everything." It must be a comfort to you to know that you were the main factor, and, as far as I know, the only factor, in making Daddy's last years comparatively happy. You have always been so kind to him and to me, and saw him through on so many occasions when someone else would have walked out on him. . . . He told me often how very devoted he was to you and how very much he respected

you. Of course it's unnecessary to dwell on this point
since you realise it all, but I just wanted to tell you
how grateful I am. . . .

> Love, Scottie

I do realize how devoted Scott was to me and how he
respected me. But, looking at it coldly thirty-five years later,
how ought I to deal with his ambivalent treatment of me?
Perhaps I should try to regain my earlier trust and believe
Scott's own explanation of his behavior. After our second and
final fight at Encino in early November 1939, he wrote me two
letters, both bidding me a contrite and loving good-bye, but
also intent on winning me back. His cruelty, he explained, was
but the inconsequent mumbling of a drunken madman. He
had said "awful things," the letter acknowledges, but

> . . . they can to some extent be unsaid. They come
> from the merest fraction of my mind, as you must
> know—they represent nothing in my conscious and
> very little in my sub-conscious. About as important
> and significant as the quarrels we used to have about
> England and America.

The rest of the letter expresses his contrition:

> I don't think we're getting anywhere. I'm glad you
> no longer can think of me with either respect or
> affection. People are either good for each other or
> bad, and obviously I am *horrible* for you. I loved you
> with everything I had, but something was terribly
> wrong. You don't have to look far for the reason—I
> was it. Not fit for any human relation. I just *loved*
> you—you brought me everything. And it was very
> fine and chivalrous—and you.
>   I want to die, Sheilah, and in my own way. I used to
> have my daughter and my poor lost Zelda. Now for
> over two years your image is everywhere. Let me
> remember you up to the end which is very close. You
> are the finest. You are something all by yourself. You

are too much something for a tubercular neurotic who can only be jealous and mean and perverse. I will have my last time with you, though you won't be here. It's not long now. I wish I could have left you more of myself. You can have the first chapter of the novel [*The Last Tycoon*] and the plan. I have no money but it might be worth something. Ask [Leland] Hayward. I loved you utterly and completely. I meant to send this longhand but I don't think it would be intelligible.

Scott

In the second letter (handwritten), a couple of weeks later, there is no further talk of his own dying; the tone is more subdued. But Scott again laments that he violated my trust:

I wrote down a lot of expressions of your face, but one I can't bear to read, of the little girl who trusted me so and whom I loved more than anything in the world—and to whom I gave grief when I wanted to give joy.

And he again insists on the insignificance of his lashing out:

Something should have told you that I was extemporising wildly—that anyone . . . should ever dare to criticize you to me. It was all fever and liquor and sedatives—what nurses hear in any bad drunk case. I'm glad you're rid of me. I hope you're happy and the last awful impression is fading a little till some day you'll say, "he can't have been that black" . . .

Well, I have never thought he was very black. I understand better now how much he needed me—he was a man with a great talent and need for quiet intimacy. But when he was distressed with his own life, he hated his intimates as well. Then, too, these letters he wrote me show how well he could idealize a woman—who must necessarily often fall short for him of such perfection. I am happy that in our final year together, with the drinking all behind us, he seemed to reach a more balanced acceptance both of himself and of me.

When I first met Scott on July 14, 1937, neither of us was looking for a relationship of such intensity. He had too many other responsibilities. I was engaged to the Marquess of Donegall—who died recently—and planning a New Year's Eve wedding to be followed by a honeymoon cruise around the world. Part of the unwritten marriage contract was that I would give Don an heir as soon as possible, and a doctor had told him that the swaying of a ship was conducive to pregnancy. Yet despite Scott's commitments to the past and mine to the future, there must have remained in each of us a receptiveness to new romantic risk and experience.

Scott's arrival in Hollywood followed what was undoubtedly the lowest period in his life. The years 1935 and 1936 had seen him debt-ridden and drinking heavily. In 1935, he had strained some shoulder muscles in North Carolina, attempting a show-off dive. And in 1936, after Michel Mok's interview with him appeared in the *New York Post*, he had tried to gulp down an overdose of morphine pills—if rather safely in front of his nurse. The Mok piece bore the headline, "Scott Fitzgerald, 40, Engulfed in Despair." Scott always insisted to me that this was a cruel distortion. Yet wasn't he in despair—convinced that he had exhausted his vitality and written himself out? He himself announced his condition in the three "Crack-Up" essays. But they are nonetheless extremely well written. "Your best writing," I comforted him.

That Scott could write so beautifully about "the dark night of the soul" shows the detachment he had toward all his experience that helped in pulling him through the worst, the most hectic upheavals. Just as he was both the flaming youth of the 20s and the cool, analytical observer of his youth, so a part of him stood outside his despondency. And when he had to, he was able to pull himself up by the thin rope he never quite let go. Although I didn't realize it then, he would never be completely intact—there would always be a soft, deteriorated side to his nature that could not be repaired because it had been destroyed. But he *was* able to carry on. He never forgot, as Zelda observed in an unpublished story, "The use of making an effort."

So when Harold Ober arranged for him, in 1937, to go to Hollywood on a six-month contract at M-G-M for $1,000 a week, Scott stopped pitying himself, went on the wagon, and grasped this opportunity to clear his debts, provide for Zelda and Scottie—they were his deep-gut responsibility—and perhaps reactivate his career in a spectacular way.

It was typical of him that no matter how defeated he had been feeling, any new opportunity aroused all his enthusiasm and optimism. He was a very enthusiastic man. And setting out on his third and most determined attempt to make good in the well-paying field of script writing, he shows his excitement in a letter to Scottie: "Given a break, I can double this contract within two years." By careful behavior he was sure he could bring the Hollywood tycoons to respect him as a screenwriter and to allow him to do his own work, free of the interference of bosses and collaborators.

It was an impossible task he had set for himself—to change the entire system where the goal was what he later described as "a practiced kind of mediocrity," where originality was suspect, and where you needed more stability or dullness than Scott possessed to keep your footing on the factory treadmill. But, in July 1937, he was hoping for the best in terms of both financial and artistic achievement.

Some of his Eastern friends had preceded Scott to what was then the film capital of the world: Donald Ogden Stewart, whom he had known in St. Paul, Minnesota, and advised to become a writer, was now earning $5,000 a week; Ben Hecht and Charlie McArthur doctored scripts at $10,000 a week; the late playwright Eddie Mayer was in the $3,000–$4,000 a week bracket for the movies he wrote for Marlene Dietrich and Gary Cooper—Eddie had been brought to Hollywood after the success of *The Firebrand*, his play about Cellini; Ogden Nash, Edward Paramore, Jr., and Nunnally Johnson. The two latter had written one good book each and were now reaping a fine financial harvest. There was also Robert Benchley, whom

Scott had patronized in the early 20s when Scott was the golden youth of the Jazz Age and Benchley simply a New York critic and editor; Marc Connelly; Dorothy Parker, who always treated Scott with deference, even when he was drunk; John O'Hara, his devout disciple; and many others. Hollywood was full of prominent literary names in the late 30s and especially after the start of World War II with the influx of the famed European refugees, among them Thomas Mann, Aldous Huxley, and André Malraux.

Scott spent time with these other writers, particularly in his first and most gregarious year in Hollywood. But he was a man who needed more than the companionship of friends. The center of his life always had to be a woman—Ginevra King, Zelda, me. I sometimes try to analyze why I was the one in Hollywood toward whom he felt such instant attraction. Was it the look of Zelda that he describes in *The Last Tycoon?*

> Smiling faintly at him from not four feet away was the face of his dead wife, identical even to the expression . . . the eyes he knew looked back at him, a curl blew a little on a familiar forehead; the smile lingered, changed a little according to pattern; the lips parted—the same. An awful fear went over him, and he wanted to cry aloud.

I did not know that I had reminded Scott of his wife until he read me this passage from the novel. Part of his charm was the ability to make a woman feel as if she were the most special person in the world—a goddess from an enchanted country. I believed that he looked on me as the most beautiful girl in Hollywood, and, as in the past, he always had to have the most beautiful.

That I was so confident of my allure must have also attracted him. That first time in Robert Benchley's bungalow at the Garden of Allah where I was celebrating my engagement to Donegall, he was sitting quietly in a corner of the room, very pale, wearing a blue suit, a jaunty bow tie, his ash-blond hair shining under the lamp. He was smoking and looking at the more exuberant celebrants through the haze of his cigarette.

But what did he see? Not only a woman who bore an eerie resemblance to his wife, but one who was at the center of the party, radiating the sense of her own beauty and importance that is a part of every Fitzgerald heroine's nature.

When later he questioned Eddie Mayer as to who I was and learned of my engagement to a Marquess, this can only have whetted his interest further. He always admired girls whom other men were in love with. It pleased him that men were in love with Zelda, though, of course, he didn't want her to have an affair with any of them. In my case he must have been delighted in the challenge to woo me away from a nobleman. I wonder if it occurred to him that he was reversing the "droit de seigneur," whereby the rich and aristocratic could claim the beautiful girl, that he had written about in "The Crack-Up."

Scott's first remark to me when we were dancing at the Clover Club about ten days later, brought together by Eddie Mayer, was, "I hear that you are engaged to marry a Duke." I laughed and corrected him, "Not a Duke, a Marquess." "Is a Marquess higher than a Duke?" he asked, smiling, his head on one side, and taking me in. "No, no." And I proceeded to give him the order of British titles—"As you know, King and Queen come first. Their children are Princes and Princesses, and sometimes Princes become Dukes. After the Dukes come the Marquesses. Then Earls, then Viscounts, Baronets, Honorables—children of the plain Lords—then Knights." He seemed fascinated by my account.

Our attunement to one another, however, really had little to do with society and its echelons. It was something instantaneous and without calculation. We danced and danced, waiting on the floor for the music to begin again. The rest of the people at the Clover Club seemed to be murals, as Scott describes Stahr and Kathleen dancing in *The Last Tycoon*. When the orchestra stopped, we returned reluctantly to our table, but with eyes only for each other. Again, this is described in the novel:

> Stahr's eyes and Kathleen's met and tangled. For
> an instant they made love as no one ever dares to do

after. The glance was slower than an embrace, more
urgent than a call.

This was Saturday. We made a date to dine on Tuesday.

In the next couple of days I thought a good deal about Scott,
enjoying the afterglow of our evening. But I did not intend this
involvement to be serious. Although my engagement to
Donegall struck me as something of a fantasy, it was a fantasy
that I was eager to cling to for at least a while.

I did not really believe I would marry Donegall because,
although he was kind and gentle, he moved in the most
urbane upper crust society, and I felt the pretense of keeping
up with him would be too great, the burden too heavy. He
knew nothing of my humble past, and that worried me. I
thought, I can never marry this man, some of whose titles had
been originally conferred by Queen Elizabeth I, for services his
family had rendered in Ireland.

Still, I could almost convince myself as I fingered my temporary engagement ring—Don had bought it on Hollywood
Boulevard, promising to get me a much better one in London—that I would soon be giving up my job as an unpopular
gossip columnist for the regal splendor of life as a Marchioness, with an imprinted coronet on my notepaper and lingerie.
I disliked the gossip, sensitive that I was intruding into other
people's lives, although my determination to be a success
pushed me on to write as sharp a column as I could. The stars
barred me from their sets, and I, in turn, tried to look on them
as paragraphs, not people. It was not pleasant work.

Later Scott told me it was marvelous that I was still in
Hollywood when he arrived there. I had gone to London in
June 1937 to obtain my divorce from Major John Gillam,
D.S.O., to be free to marry Don. A few weeks before I left
California, never to return as I thought, an Eastern advertising
man had called on me, offering me a five-minute spot on a
variety radio show that would emanate from Chicago. I was to
be cut into the program from Hollywood with the latest gossip
about the movie stars. He offered me $100 a week for the job.
"Oh no," I told him. "I'm leaving Hollywood for good. My life

will be in England from now on." But when he went to $200, my venal streak could not resist. I have a terror of poverty, and $200 added to the $160 a week I was then receiving for my column was substantial money.

I made a quick trip to London, returning to Hollywood at the end of June. I could always give up the column if Donegall was serious. And in any case, I had to wait six months before my divorce was final—I might as well be working. My titled suitor followed me to Hollywood to settle the engagement and slip the temporary diamond on my finger, then flew away to win his mother's consent to our marriage.

So there I was, in the middle of July, looking to a future in England with Don, yet also preparing for my added career as a radio broadcaster. As I now look back, I see that I was covering all bases—preparing to leave Hollywood and, at the same time, preparing to stay. My intentions were confused. But whatever they were, I did not expect Scott Fitzgerald to interfere with them—however attractive I had found him.

Scott, too, after that evening at the Clover Club, was retreating from our involvement. Thinking matters over, he considered it wiser not to see me again—he had too many responsibilities. He sent me a telegram; we could not dine because his daughter was coming into town.

I was surprised at the intensity of my disappointment—a feeling as though the sky had become suddenly drab. I called him at the Garden of Allah. "Why don't I have dinner with you and your daughter?" I asked. He was embarrassed but after some hesitation consented with a not very enthusiastic, "All right."

We went to the Trocadero on the Strip, then the most fashionable place for dining and dancing, where he corrected Scottie without ceasing, and I wondered what had made this middle-aged, nagging father so attractive to me.

I was sad when he drove me home, after dropping Scottie off at the Beverly Hills Hotel where she was staying with Helen Hayes, who had brought her to Hollywood. What a pity. I had liked him so much, and I didn't want to lose the fascinating man I had danced with. We reached my home, and I had already opened the door and was preparing to say good night politely. But when his face came close to mine, pale under the outside lamp, I couldn't bear to let him go, and I gently pulled him inside. That was the beginning of our involvement.

I have often tried, and failed, to describe the charm of this extraordinary man. Physically, except for his face, there was nothing remarkable about him. He was on the short side —about five feet eight or half an inch less—with the strong shoulders of a bantam boxer and a dwindling torso inherited from the potato-famine McQuillan ancestors of his Irish mother. His hair was thinning on top—he was careful to comb the strands over the bald patch, and I was careful to refrain from noticing it. But it always made me feel rather sad that he minded.

Also in all our time together, I don't remember seeing him naked. But I was just as shy about my own body. However, this modesty did not prevent us from having a good time sexually. We satisfied each other and could lie in each other's arms for a long time afterwards, delighting in our proximity. It was not exhausting, frenzied love-making but gentle and tender, an absolutely happy state.

I would sometimes lean on my elbows, looking and looking into his face, absorbing the love in his eyes. Was the charm there, in the wide-apart green-gray-blue eyes, a color which I have always described as rain-washed? Was it in the expression, varying from admiration, compassion, delight, tenderness to fun? I learned to laugh with Scott, a quiet laughter, as though we possessed communicable secrets that brightened our days and comforted our evenings. Was his charm the ability to make a young woman feel that he was completely absorbed in her, that she was at the center of his world? Perhaps it was all of this, and something else I still cannot describe. But it made me his slave.

Had Scott been drinking at the time I met him, I don't think that I would have been drawn to him. I could never have fallen in love with an alcoholic. It would have clashed with my nondrinking, nonsmoking, tennis-playing life style. And then, too, my entire poor class upbringing would have been against it. Nice girls did not drink or consort with drunks—you hurried past them when you saw them staggering outside the pubs. Nice girls ran away from trouble.

But there was no trouble with Scott in those first few months—it was a gentle, courteous man I saw in the Benchley bungalow and met later with Eddie Mayer at the Clover Club—the man I went to football games with at the Los Angeles Coliseum, who explained the various plays and rules to me while the people around us smiled at his enthusiasm and my naïve questions. And if his hand shook when he lit a cigarette, I did not notice it.

It now occurs to me that part of my value to Scott was that I knew nothing about his past. And though I was later enchanted with the line from "The Crack-Up"—"In the dark night of the soul, it is always three o'clock in the morning"—I really understood only my own strong, healthy reality. That Scott was not fully a part of it never occurred to me, especially in those first months when our time together was always delightful, never dark. It was so easy to fall in love with the boyish, collegiate-looking man who seemed so much less than his forty years in the dim light of the restaurants we frequented. The sad lines on his face when I saw him in the daylight simply made him seem more interesting.

Thus, while neither of us was aware that it was happening, the immediate attraction we had felt toward one another slowly took root. At first we both continued to spend time with other people. Scott visited the homes of such people as King Vidor, Norma Shearer, Joan Crawford, and his writing friends. I was not with him when he met Ernest Hemingway at Lillian Hellman's in mid-July 1937. Ernest had come to Hollywood to raise money for the Loyalist cause in Spain. "We had nothing to say to each other," Scott told me afterwards. Later I would meet Hemingway at a Sunday breakfast in Benchley's bungalow, where I remember him asking about Scott—who would not come with me.

On my return home, Scott asked eagerly, "How does he look? What did he say?" I was able to tell him that his idol was planning to divorce his second wife Pauline to marry Martha Gelhorn. And Scott said sternly, "Don't put that in your column." He was fascinated with all the news I could bring him about Ernest. But he did not want to see him. "Not really friends since 1937," he wrote on a 1940 scrap of paper about the people he had known in his life.

As for my life apart from Scott in the summer and early fall of 1937, I was still dating Eddie Mayer, Benchley, John O'Hara, and also Arthur Kober, well known to readers of *The New Yorker* for his Bella stories. He was at M-G-M writing for the Marx brothers. Then, too, there was Donegall, whom I broke with in late September. Scott notes the event, perhaps with a touch of smugness, in a letter to Scottie: "The poor man was about to get on a boat, but it was a sort of foolish marriage in many ways."

I shed a small tear for my lost title and then forgot His Lordship until after Scott died and Don sent me a cable asking me again to marry him. He was sorry that my "friend" had died, but I should settle up my affairs and come to England —he had the marriage all arranged. Having become a more honest person and better educated, I would then have been a better wife for him. But by this time I knew the difference between liking a man who could keep me in comfort and make me a Marchioness and loving a Scott Fitzgerald, who could do nothing materially for me except give me everything in my life I had never had. A complete adult love.

With Scott it was the things we did together, smiled at and laughed over together that put the concrete into our relationship, and day by day the love grew more solid. There came a moment—and I can remember it exactly—when I realized how important he was to me.

It was just after I had broken with Donegall and shortly before our trip together to Chicago where I was to learn the horror of his drinking for the first time. I was in his bungalow at the Garden of Allah taking a bath. Scott came into the bathroom carrying a little pillow, which he placed carefully under my head without looking at my submerged body. He then slipped out to leave me to my comfort and to my deep appreciation of this small gesture of tenderness and consideration. It bound me to him—forever. No one, I felt, had ever cared for me so much.

3.

"SAT WE TWO, ONE ANOTHER'S BEST"

WE WERE FACING each other on a settee in the living room of my Hollywood home on King's Road, north of the Sunset Strip, where I had lived from early 1936. It was now September 1937. My bare feet were in Scott's lap and his were in mine. He told me that by gently bending the toes back, you could stretch the nerve ends and that this was very relaxing. It was a good time for talking, and as I was entranced by whatever Scott said at this early time, I was content to listen to him while I played with his toes and he played with mine.

"As a child I had a mysterious shyness about showing my feet," Scott mused. He told me how on a trip with his parents to Atlantic City, New Jersey, he had refused to take off his shoes and go into the ocean. He let his parents assume that he was afraid of the water. "In fact, I was longing to take a swim, but was held back by this strange Freudian shyness about my feet." "Perhaps," I giggled, "it was jealousy of seeing your father's feet too close to your mother's." Scott laughed at the idea. All the time I knew him, he always refused to take off his shoes and socks on the beach.

Having myself been raised in an orphanage, I was intrigued by Scott's account of a home where both parents so wholeheartedly devoted themselves to their son. His mother, in particular, had overindulged him, fussing over him when he was ill and making him stay in bed for the slightest sniffle. Scott readily admitted that his mother had spoiled him. Two sisters had died shortly before he was born in St. Paul, Minnesota, on September 22, 1896—stricken in an epidemic. Then came Scott, another girl who died, and finally Scott's sister Annabel who only slightly deflected the mother's intense attention from her son. By that time, Mollie Fitzgerald—described to me by a Fitzgerald relative as "the most awkward and the homeliest woman I ever saw"—was so much in love with her beautiful, blond, blue-eyed boy that she could deny him nothing. As far as she was concerned he could do no wrong. "No matter what awful thing I did, I was just a bad brownie," Scott explained. It is my belief that in all the drunken escapades throughout his life, he maintained the image of himself as the little bad brownie, whose charm could always win a woman's tolerance and forgiveness.

The indulgence of Scott's mother did not, however, endear her to him. In my time with him he considered her a fool—not because she loved him but because she did it with so little style. He was ashamed of her terrible clothes and ghastly manners. Her sleeve cuffs were always dipping into her coffee; her high buttoned shoes—in themselves unfashionable— were unbuttoned at the top to give her swollen ankles relief; and her *faux pas* in St. Paul were legendary. When she and the wife of a very sick man were riding on the same streetcar, Scott told me, the latter asked her obviously pensive companion, "What are you thinking about?" Mollie Fitzgerald replied, "I'm trying to decide how you'll look in mourning."

Scott was understandably eager to distance himself from this mother whom other children used to joke about. When she wanted to visit her son at summer camp, he made all sorts of excuses to prevent her coming. One letter from Camp Chatham, Orilla, Ontario, dated July 18, 1907, reads:

Dear Mother:

I received your letter this morning and though I would very much like to have you up here, I don't

think you would much like it as you know no one
here except Mrs. Upton and she is busy most of the
time. I don't think you would like the accommoda-
tions as it is only a small town and no good hotels.
There are some very nice boarding houses but about
the only fare is lamb and beef. Please send me a dollar
because there are a lot of little odds and ends that I
need. I will spend it cautiously. [If only he had held to
that resolution in later life!] All the other boys have
pocket money besides their regular allowance.

Your loving son,
Scott Fitzgerald

Scott's future ability to charm and flatter was showing in his
use of careful diplomacy to get what he wanted. When he was
older, however, he would be less careful about hurting his
mother's feelings. One of his anecdotes concerned her be-
musement at Disney cartoons. She couldn't understand how
birds, animals, and other cartoon characters could move in the
Disney films. "How can he make those birds fly?" she demanded of her famous author son. Scott tried to explain, then
lost patience. And when his mother complained that he did
not love her, he retorted, "No, I don't," whereupon she wept.
When Scott told me of this incident, I lectured him, "There are
times when it is better to lie. If you had said 'Yes,' you loved
her, it would have pleased her and not harmed you." His
reaction was to look away from me. (I wonder what she would
have made of television!)

While Scott could not forgive his mother for being so grace-
less, after her death in September 1936, when he went to pick
up her bits and pieces from the Washington hotel where she
had been living her last few years, he felt a rush of sympathy
with her life's struggle. In a letter to his sister Annabel, he
explains:

Mother and I never had anything in common except a relentless stubborn quality, but when I saw all
this it turned me inside out, realizing how unhappy
her temperament had made her and how she clung to

the end to all things that would remind her of moments of snatched happiness.

Scott acknowledged that his energy derived from his mother and his McQuillan grandfather, who in 1843 had migrated from Ireland to America, still a boy with his parents, and by the 1860s was making his fortune in the wholesale grocery business. But in reviewing his lineage, Scott preferred to dwell on his gentle, courteous father's descent from an old Maryland family, established in America since the 1600s. He liked having such roots to offset the rootlessness he recognized as the affliction of post-World War I society. And he liked the historical and social connection with Francis Scott Key, author of "The Star Spangled Banner," whom Scott said was his great-great-grandfather, though in actual fact Key was his great-great-great-uncle.

Scott always liked his father, who, despite his failure in business, maintained a certain moral authority in the family. Scott remembered that it was the cultivated father, and not the energetic mother, who, when discipline had to be applied to him, did the thrashing. The childhood crimes that lingered in Scott's memory most vividly were tormenting two little black companions, tying them up with ropes, and pushing a little Jewish boy around. He explained to me, "We were Catholics. My mother went to mass every day. I'm sure she believed that Christian boys were killed at Easter and the Jews drank the blood. She was a bigot but my father was not."

The worst beating came after Scott, age six, wandered away from home on the Fourth of July and spent the day with a friend in a pear tree, oblivious that time was passing. The police were called in, the parents were frantic, and Scott watched the fireworks that evening with his pants still down and his behind smarting from the thrashing that had greeted his return. Scott was, himself, to suffer the anxiety of the parent the time he telephoned from California to chat with Scottie at Vassar and discovered that she wasn't there. Scott was terribly disturbed, our weekend was ruined, and of course his daughter was all the time safely, happily with her friend Peaches Finney in Baltimore. Scottie was not physically beaten. Her punishment was worse—a halving of her $30 a month allowance. I received piteous letters from her, imploring me to intercede with her stern parent, which I did.

Scott's own father actually sounded less harsh than Scott could be toward his daughter. Certainly, like all kind parents, Edward Fitzgerald always regretted beating his son. And Scott, who even at an early age could guess at the feelings of others, would comfort his father, asking him to tell again the story of how he had watched the armies of the North and the South during the Civil War fighting and retreating across the "dark fields of the Republic."

Scott's heritage gave him certain sureties—the sense of belonging to a country and its history, the conviction of being loved. But in the three and a half years that I knew him, I was also to hear of all the important incidents in his life that he had found unsettling. There were those early years of insecurity, of moving to Syracuse and Buffalo and back to St. Paul, due to his father's changing jobs as a salesman in the grocery and cosmetic fields. And he never forgot his terror as a twelve-year-old boy, overhearing that his father had lost his job with Procter & Gamble. "I thought it was the poorhouse for sure," Scott told me. I understand such fears very well from my own childhood.

"I don't know what would have become of us if my mother had not had her inheritance from her father," Scott told me. She kept them going, though as Scott with his keen eye for exact social nuance explained to me, "We were comfortable, not rich—always on the lower edge of where the rich lived. I was aware that we were poorer."

James Hill, the railroad magnate, and his family were wealthy St. Paul neighbors. With money and position they seemed to be made of different cloth. They were looked up to—literally, since their home was situated higher up from the Fitzgeralds' at the fashionable end of the street. "As a child, you never know what drives you," Scott said, "but subconsciously I yearned to be as rich and important as the Hills."

By consciously placing the Hills above himself, he created his own sense of inferiority that in later years prompted his drunken boasting. I was so startled when in October 1937 I first heard him vaunt to perfect strangers on an airplane who he was and how great he was. I think that Scott's early admiration for the rich and powerful was to color his behavior most of his life. But one must be clear that it was never the possession of money in and of itself that he admired. As he defended his outlook in a letter to Ernest Hemingway, after the latter in "The Snows of Kilimanjaro" had ridiculed Fitzgerald's kow-towing to the rich, "Riches have never fascinated me unless combined with the greatest charm or distinction."

Scott wanted to associate with the best and to be the best as well. If as a child he knew he wasn't rich, he at least could strive to be charming. He was a bright boy, his pretty looks were much admired by ladies of all ages, and he loved to show off. After his father taught him to recite, "Friends, Romans, Countrymen," he spouted it everywhere to admiring groups of mostly middle-aged women, often without being asked. "Once I started, I wouldn't stop." He so enjoyed being praised that if the compliments were not forthcoming, he'd turn cart-wheels or make funny faces to obtain them. He yearned for applause, wanting it all the time. It was mother's milk to him. He had to be noticed. But there always seemed to be one boy who could do things better than he could, whom he envied and longed to supplant.

The opportunity to shine without competition came at four-teen when Scott wrote his first play, "The Girl From Lazy J." The admission money went to a local charity, and there were write-ups in the local newspapers. But it was too much for the ambitious boy and, as he wrote in the Basil stories, he became insufferable, the freshest boy, and was disliked by the girls as well as the boys. He alienated Marie Hersey, with whom he was infatuated. Scott showed me his scrapbooks in which she figured prominently in the early pages. Marie was the model for the pretty, unattainable girl, Ermine Gilberte, or Labouisse Bibble, commonly known as Minnie Bibble, in the Basil stories. Reuben Warner became Hubert Blair—the boy who could do everything better than Scott-Basil.

Already it was an obsession with Scott to have the best girl, the one who was most sought after. He confessed to me that he considered himself a failure unless he got the prettiest, the most desirable girl. But, as when he succeeded with his play, he couldn't control himself once the girl was won. He would strut about, offering unsolicited advice as to how his friends might emulate his success. The other boys would turn against him, and then the girls. He always went too far.

I've since thought that Scott was curiously unsure of his own worth. Though people in St. Paul praised him for his precocity and his good looks, he had no inner sense of confidence. Because, if you need to associate with the prettiest, the loveliest, the richest, it suggests that you feel deficient in yourself and that you hope to shine in the glow of the person you consider superior to yourself.

Such dependence on someone else, however, can be precarious. Scott was inevitably disappointed when the girls failed to live up to his impossibly high ideal. The fear of disillusionment grew to be almost an integral part of his romanticism—a fear that the spell people had for him, that he actually wove around them, would break with too much reality.

A few months after I met him, he had the chance to see Ginevra King, whom he had found so lovely when she was sixteen. Ginevra, long since married to multimillionaire John Pirie of Carson, Pirie, Scott, the great department store in Chicago, wrote to him that she was visiting in Los Angeles and Santa Barbara and would love for them to get together. He was very reluctant to meet her, dreading the prospect of what she would look like and be at thirty-eight. Like Anthony in *The Beautiful and Damned,* who is afraid to see the older Gloria, Scott feared that he would find Ginevra haggard and decayed.

To risk the encounter with "the first woman I ever loved," he started drinking again. At least this is what he told Ginevra. Concerning the same drinking bout, his account to me was that it began because of his jealousy over a date I had with Arthur Kober. But however suspect his excuses for the drinking, they indicate how much he cared that the women in his life live up to his expectations and ideals.

Ginevra, incidentally, did not disappoint him. At thirty-eight she was still a beautiful woman. Scott could retain his early dream of her intact. And somehow this made him feel better about himself and his own life. His insecurity still seems strange to me because, as far as I was concerned, he didn't need anyone else's glitter—he was always so complete in his own right.

I remember Scott telling me that the Jesuit priests would say "Give me a boy until he is seven. By then his character will be formed. Nothing afterwards could much change him." In Scott's case the early influence was his mother and her adulation that created his lifelong craving for a similar response from other people. "I want to be extravagantly admired again," he writes gaily, but not untruthfully, to John Peale Bishop in 1925. But his doting mother had not prepared him for the harsher judgments of those outside the home. And he suffered from childhood onward when the world was indifferent or hostile to him. His insecurity made him try too hard to be popular.

It was a great shock to Scott, going off in September 1911 to board at the Newman School in New Jersey, that not only did he fail to establish himself as a well-liked boy and a leader, but that he was overwhelmingly unpopular. Some of the Newman boys, he confided to me, actually hated him. Throughout the whole of his first term he was miserable, taking long walks by himself and wondering how he could make his classmates like him. There was football, of course. To be captain of the school's team was to be God. But Scott was short, and after the first try-out in which he strove to look good while at the same time saving his skin, he doubted that the applause would come from the football field. On one occasion when his fright was obvious, he was ostracized as a coward.

But perhaps because of his "relentless stubborn quality," Scott gave up on neither his popularity nor his football. During his second season he played one magnificent do-or-die game, and he was hailed as a hero. A teammate shouted "Good old Scottie," and he thought he would burst, he was so proud. "You only had a nickname if you were popular," he explained to me. In the Basil Lee stories, Basil, when he triumphs for the first time on the football field, is hailed as "Lee-ey."

Then in 1913 came Princeton, Scott's beloved Princeton. He

could barely contain his suffering waiting to know whether he had been accepted by Cottage, one of the top four eating clubs. Later he would be relieved that Vassar did not have clubs and that Scottie would be spared his experience. But, actually, Scott would not have had to worry about her. Scottie has always been a natural person, undaunted by social success or failure. It was Scott who cared so much about the clubs, convinced that you could be scarred for life if you were not accepted by the right one. He felt sorry for the few Jews at Princeton who had no choice of getting into a decent club and who, shunned by the popular men in the university, could find companionship only in huddling together.

This, of course, raises the question of Fitzgerald and anti-Semitism. "Wasn't he anti-Semitic?" a young woman asked me recently at a party in Palm Beach. That she should think so isn't surprising. In his novels, Scott uses Jewish characters to emphasize some of the shoddiest aspects of American life. The portraits of Wolfsheim with his "gonnegtions" in *The Great Gatsby* and Manny Schwartz with his obsequious misery in *The Last Tycoon* are not flattering. My feeling is that Scott was somewhat put off by Jews as a group, however much he liked Eddie Mayer and almost canonized Thalberg and had many Jewish friends in Hollywood. But the Jews, for him, were not The Beautiful People. And at Princeton he perceived them as socially disadvantaged whereas he wished to achieve as much social distinction as he could.

Scott was so excited by his acceptance into Cottage that he immediately invited Ginevra King, whom he had met in St. Paul during Christmas—she had been the house guest of Marie Hersey—to attend the sophomore prom. Ginevra, a junior at Westover, was a striking brunette, the unattainable dream girl of Scott's future fiction. College boys of Yale, Harvard, and Princeton fought for her favor, and Scott was not surprised when she refused his invitation on the plea that her mother was unable to chaperone her. How quaint that seems today. But they met again during her vacation from school, and Scott was madly in love with her, or at least convinced that he was. In love and in anguish.

He was always jealous, and he suffered when Ginevra

wrote him long accounts of the parties she had been to. It would be worse when he fell in love with Zelda Sayre. Ginevra, Scott felt in retrospect, was aware that she was teasing him. Zelda applied the torture seemingly unaware of or indifferent to the misery she was causing. But this was in the future.

Despite his setbacks in love, Princeton was paradise for the handsome young man from the Midwest, who always seemed on the point of bursting with excitement at his new discoveries of people and ideas. He could never have enough discussion of the poets and authors who interested him—Keats, Marlowe, Conrad, Swinburne. After he discovered Swinburne, he walked around the campus for days declaiming "The Hounds of Spring." He himself had been writing prolifically most of his life—poems, stories, plays, outlines of plots. And since the success of his second youthful play "The Captured Shadow," he had determined to be a famous writer.

The desk drawer in his room at Princeton was jammed with mystery and detective stories, full of heroic deeds, and of course in his imagination he was always the hero. Then when the *Nassau Lit* published his one-act play *Shadow Laurels* and his story "The Ordeal," he felt he had arrived. There were no heights to which he could not aspire. The world would soon know of him. He was burning with ego, energy, and, in turn, depression and tremendous confidence. Compton Mackenzie's *Youth's Encounter* gave him the idea of writing a novel about Princeton, a project which would develop into *This Side of Paradise*.

I believe that Princeton, more than any other time or place, incarnated his youth for Scott with all its hope and promise. For the remainder of his life he clung to his memories of the eating clubs, the football games, the proms, because he had experienced them with so much intensity. Also Princeton saw the expansion of his literary talent and the cultivation of certain lifelong friends. Among these was the editor of the *Lit*, a blond, stocky intellectual, Edmund "Bunny" Wilson, who lived by his own critical standards and unlike Scott didn't give a damn for popularity. He was what we called in England a "swot"—a "grind" we would say in America. Classmates at

Princeton thought him rather conceited. Certainly he had reason to be. Although just a year older than Scott—Bunny died in 1973 at the age of seventy-seven—he was a decade older in critical ability and assurance. Scott with his usual extravagant admiration for what he considered the best, put Wilson on a literary pedestal to which he genuflected all his life.

The friendship of the imaginative writer and the critic—always more literary than personal—climaxed in Edmund Wilson's undertaking after Scott's death to edit *The Last Tycoon*. At Princeton the two worked together on a play for the Triangle Club, the Princeton drama society which Scott had chosen deliberately as the best outlet for his writing. "My lyrics," he told me, "were praised in the cities where the shows toured. I was hailed as the new Cole Porter, and I became obnoxious again as I always did when I was successful." The humility that came with failure made him nicer. Given too much praise, he was off like an erratic sky-rocket.

Scott showed me the photograph of himself dressed as a girl for one Triangle musical, *The Evil Eye*. His bad grades prevented his appearance in the show. But the publicity photo was printed in *The New York Times*, and it was later misused by some of his detractors to prove that he was a homosexual or had some tendencies that way. This group included his own wife, Zelda, who accused Scott of being in love with Hemingway, or vice versa—she was rather confused on this point. Scott *did* make a beautiful girl. He was also a handsome man—Robert Redford at his best looks somewhat like Scott as a young man.

Scott wrote the lyrics for *The Evil Eye*, and Edmund Wilson, the book. But while Wilson was able to study in addition to the extracurricular activities, Scott neglected his courses and found himself on the edge of flunking out of school. He was saved from this disgrace by an attack of TB, which gave him the excuse to leave of his own volition. "I really had been a delicate child," he assured me at various times, "which was one reason my mother coddled me and made it difficult for me to cope with later problems." To the best of my knowledge the touch of TB was genuine, though it was strongly rumored that Fitzgerald had left Princeton because of his bad grades.

Edmund Wilson admitted to me after Scott's death that he had always believed Scott left college under a scholastic cloud. "But," he added, "I learned recently that he really did have TB." (I have this letter in Wilson's handwriting.) "That's what Scott said," I reaffirmed loyally. Scott's last doctor confirmed this to me. I was also aware that Scott would claim a flare-up of his illness to cover the effect of his drinking. In his last thirteen months of sobriety the TB rather mysteriously disappeared.

However convenient his attack in December 1915, Scott was unhappy away from Princeton and for the first time in his life he worked hard at his studies so he could return to the university in September 1916. Nonetheless, his reacceptance meant stepping down a class, and he could no longer serve on the board of the Triangle Club. But although he continued writing lyrics for the productions, he missed out being club president—the honor he had so keenly anticipated—and he was angry and depressed.

Scott still managed to have a reasonably good year—his junior year—at Princeton. In addition to his work for the Triangle Club, he submitted numerous stories and poems to the *Lit*—he had made up his mind to follow in the footsteps of Keats and Conrad rather than Cole Porter. The prospect, however, of a senior year with his original class of '17 already graduated, did not appeal to him. Leaving Princeton for the last time in October 1917, he reported to officers' training camp at Fort Leavenworth, Kansas. Thus, while he has been regarded for several decades as one of Princeton's brightest alumni, he did not graduate from the university he loved. It would have pleased him to know that one of his grandsons was a student at Old Nassau.

But just as the presidency of the Triangle Club eluded him, so did the distinction of serving overseas in World War I. "I have never forgiven fate that the war was over before I could get to France," he complained. "I was actually on the boat, several hours at sea, and we were some way out in the Atlantic when news came of the armistice, and we turned back." I have since learned that his ship never left New York harbor. As a good writer and storyteller, Scott sometimes dramatized his experiences in order to heighten their effect.

If the actual experience of the war eluded him, in imagination he lived it to a doomed and poignant end. He was sure that he would be killed, but only after he had written poetry of the same sort as Rupert Brooke, one of his heroes. My poetry section of the College of One curriculum included several of Brooke's war poems—"If I should die," etc. I believe that in Scott's fantasies he heard the whole world applauding as he went gallantly to his death. But in his farewell letters to friends and relatives, some written even before leaving Princeton, he eschewed heroic bombast in favor of a world-weary fatalism. In one epistle to his favorite cousin Cecilia—at seven he had been a ring bearer at her wedding in 1903—he forecasts with a certain perverse enjoyment:

> It looks as if the youth of me and my generation ends sometime during this present year, rather summarily. If we ever get back, and I don't particularly care, we'll be rather aged—in the worst way. After all, life hasn't much to offer except youth and I suppose for older people the love of youth in others. I perfectly agree with Rupert Brooke's men of Grantchester "Who when they got to feeling old They up and shot themselves I'm told." Every man I've met who's been to war—that is this war—seems to have lost youth and faith in man unless they're wine-bibbers of patriotism, which, of course, I think is the biggest rot in the world.

It is illuminating that already at twenty, Scott had the reverence for youth which was to make his own loss of youth so hard for him to come to terms with. It is also interesting that despite his confinement in the war to a spectator's role, he could so aptly sum up his generation's disillusionment. One of Scott's greatest talents as a writer was the ability to capture the mood of his times. The letter to Cousin Ceci is a strange combination of bravado and discernment.

The same can be said of a letter from Scott to his mother, though given his mother's feelings for him it is more cruel. "About the army," he writes distantly, please let's not have tragedy or Heroics because they are equally distasteful to me. I went into this perfectly cold-bloodedly and don't sympathize with the "Give my son to country" etc. etc. etc. or "Hero stuff," because I just went and for purely social reasons. If you want to pray, pray for my soul and not that I won't get killed—the last doesn't seem to matter particularly and if you are a good Catholic the first ought to.

To a profound pessimist about life, being in danger is not depressing. I have never been more cheerful. Please be nice and respect my wishes.

It is Scott's statement here about going to war for purely social reasons that stands out from the pose of carelessness. I sense that he equated the battlefield with the football field or the dance floor as a place to achieve social distinction. He always wanted to participate and excel in the most popular activity. And although he so often failed, at least he could always see the irony of his position and so glean material for fiction.

The army in fact brought Fitzgerald little distinction. "I hated Kansas," he shuddered at the recollection. "It was freezing and we had to sleep fifteen to a room with all our things huddled at the foot of the beds. Baby, it was hell." He did as badly as a military officer as he had as a university student, and his unpopularity with his fellow trainees, who resented his Brooks Brothers uniforms and his assumption of superiority, was reminiscent of the Newman School.

But he had been writing his novel on and off since his last year at Princeton. To be a published novelist would be a magnificent recognition. He had something to say that might not be popular with the head men at the university he loved, but he was eager to say it. The book would of course be about himself and his relation to people and events, as every future book and story would be—even *The Great Gatsby,* which he considered the least autobiographical of his works. But even there, as Scott wrote to John Peale Bishop, another Princeton friend, in August 1925, "Gatsby started as one man I knew and then changed into myself."

During the dreary months in Kansas, Scott managed to write a hundred and twenty thousand words of his novel about Princeton. He showed the work in progress to Father Fay, his teacher and friend from the Newman days, who thought it was first rate, and to his Princeton poetry mentor, John Bishop, who thought it was mediocre. Undaunted, Scott continued to write at a furious pace.

In March 1918, his novel was finished, and he settled on the title *The Romantic Egotist,* which his daughter recently borrowed for her photographic biography of her parents written with Professor Matthew Bruccoli and Joan Kerr. Scott sent the completed novel to his British author friend, Shane Leslie, who in turn sent it to Scribners in New York, asking them to hold it, even if they did not wish to publish it. This meant Scott could go to France feeling he was a successful author. As for Scott, he was increasingly impatient with the army routine of drills and marches which he considered an interruption of his life as an author. But as he explained to Bishop, "I did want to go to France, and if I survived it would have meant my next book."

Preparatory to going overseas, Scott's regiment, now part of the new Ninth Division, was ordered to Camp Sheridan, Alabama, for the final training. He was surprised and amused to find that there was still some resentment in the South against the Yankees. Also he was lonely. Ginevra King had written that she was getting married, and with his book off his hands, he was in a mood for some gaiety. He began attending the Saturday night dances at the country club. And at a dance in July 1918, the twenty-one-year-old Scott Fitzgerald met Zelda Sayre, who was not quite eighteen. The whole course of his future was set at that first meeting.

4.

ZELDA

THE SCENE IS a store in Montgomery, Alabama. Mr. and Mrs.
Scott Fitzgerald were buying shoes for their young, blonde,
six-year-old, blue-eyed daughter, Scottie. The time, late 1927.
A woman standing nearby with her twelve-year-old daughter,
wishing to chat with the famous author and his wife Zelda,
whose exploits as an adolescent in the sleepy city of her birth
had made her equally well known, strolled over and ex-
claimed, "What a lovely child!" "She's not a lovely child,"
Zelda snapped, "Look!" and she raised one of Scottie's legs.
"Look how terrible this is!" "I told her to stop talking like
that," said Scott. "She's my child as well as yours, and there's
nothing terrible about her. Zelda and I quarreled for the rest of
the day. I didn't realize then that she was ill. How could I have
been so blind?" (Actually, Scottie happens to have beautiful
legs.)

Everyone who writes about Scott and Zelda seems to take
sides—either sympathizing with Scott and blaming Zelda for
the stress of the Fitzgerald marriage or sympathizing with
Zelda and blaming Scott. For example, Andrew Turnbull, who
was partial to Scott, saw Zelda as spoiled, selfish, and unstable, a drain on Scott's energy and talent. For Nancy Milford

it is Zelda who emerges generous and courageous, and Scott who is selfish, jealous of his reputation, and immature.

Both Mr. Turnbull and Mrs. Milford are responsible biographers—both have striven to be as accurate and fair as possible. But in writing about a pair of lovers who were more antagonists than helpmates, one comes up against such questions as "Which of the Fitzgeralds can be held most accountable for the wreckage of their lives?" "Which was the most selfish?" "Which one was the other's victim?"

Trying to sort this out, their biographers seem to lose impartiality. Since boyhood, Andrew Turnbull, who committed suicide a few years ago, had been under the spell of Scott's charm—from the days when the Fitzgeralds lived as his parents' tenants and neighbors at La Paix in Maryland. Nancy Milford did not know Zelda personally but seems to sympathize more readily with the struggle of a woman to express and fulfill herself than with that of a man to preserve his reputation.

My own point of view cannot escape being prejudiced in Scott's favor. It was he who told me the story of his courtship and marriage, and I unquestioningly accepted his point of view: that Zelda had been a spoiled first family Southern belle, as tomboy Tallulah Bankhead, her acquaintance, was—one source informed me that Zelda and Tallulah attended first grade together. Zelda, said Scott, was unable to accept the spotlight shining on her famous husband; that her efforts to compete with him had climaxed in her obsession to equal him as a writer and finally in her overanxious desire to be a top ballerina; that unable to bend, unable to accept that she was too old at thirty to become a great dancer, she broke, and that he had been victimized by her selfishness and madness. As he wrote in a letter to Scottie, "I think the pull of an afflicted person upon a normal one is at all times downward, depressing, and eventually somewhat paralyzing." "The weak," he said to me, "always destroy the strong." And though I have since read accounts insinuating that Zelda was more normal than Scott and that he insisted on her insanity simply to get her out of the way, Scott at least had no doubt that Zelda was the afflicted, he the normal—however emotionally and physically exhausted—person.

In order to free himself from the paralysis of his ruined marriage, Scott seemed, when I knew him, to have achieved a certain detachment from his wife and her condition. The shadow of Zelda only darkened him when he visited her. Even when he read me her letters, his involvement did not seem too personal. She was like a case history in which we were both interested. I felt sorry for her, but he had told me that she was mad, and I knew that the best place for her was in the sanitarium.

But perhaps my acceptance of Scott as the strong partner and Zelda as the weak one was too simple. After Scott's death, friends feared that she would completely fall apart. Yet she managed quite well, staying most of the time with her mother in Montgomery, and returning at rare intervals to the sanitarium when she found she was not coping. Also, I think that Scott to the end was more bound to Zelda—dependent on her just as he claimed that she was dependent on him—than he ever acknowledged to me. They had leaned against each other and both had fallen down. Sometimes he saw himself and his wife as a couple of invalids, bound together by their common collapse.

I now realize that during the time I knew Scott, he was leading a sort of double life. I knew that he looked after Zelda, and I understood that he must. But I didn't know that he was still—certainly in the first couple of years of our association—writing her love letters. And Zelda, almost to the end, was writing even stronger love letters to him. He didn't show me his letters to her, though he did read hers aloud to me. We discussed their style. I thought there was a dignity and beauty in her sometimes extravagant prose, especially when she was describing nature. Though the lush images became repetitive, and the relentless intensity a bit exhausting, I was impressed. But when I said to Scott, "This is beautiful writing," he replied, "Yes, but it doesn't lead anywhere. It doesn't add up."

Rereading Zelda's letters later in the various books, I find that they do add up. They show a woman clinging to her past and to the man who had been her life. Her appeal, I think, touched him more deeply than he would ever admit to me. I thought then that I was the center of his life, together with his daughter, and that for Zelda he had only pity. But actually, I wasn't the center, I was somewhat off-center, because if he had turned his back on Zelda and the image of their past, he would have been denying his youth, his legend.

Scott and Zelda had worked hard at becoming legends —that was the fabric of their lives. Perhaps it was not quite real. But it was still the cloth they had made to wear. Scott had to make Zelda the most important factor of his life because otherwise there wouldn't have been much life left.

So, however Scott minimized her to me or dwelt on the experiences with her that he claimed had disillusioned him —her breaking off their engagement because he had no money, her affair in the South of France with Edouard Jozanne, the French aviator—I now understand that Zelda was his great passion, however destructive their years together.

I still accept Scott's point of view that Zelda was spoiled, selfish, and rather calculating. Indeed, it might have been better for both of them if they had never met. But to the end I think Scott was proud of Zelda and in a strange way, proud even of the chaotic waste of their lives. If he considered his wife a responsibility, it was his precious burden.

Zelda Sayre, provincial belle and pampered daughter of Montgomery's prominent Judge Sayre and his wife, was a match for the author of "The Captured Shadow" and *The Romantic Egotist*. Both felt that the world and everything in it belonged to them. From early childhood they had lived with the conviction that they were marked for a spectacular destiny. Perhaps the central difference in their expectations was that Scott always knew he would have to work for his fame and glory. But Zelda, and girls of her background in the South —Tallulah, and Mrs. H. L. Mencken, for example—did not go out to work. They expected to be taken care of—well taken care of—all their lives. Thus Zelda felt no need to discipline her talents. She was a bright student, but she never bothered with much studying—she would bring her homework back to class and finish it while waiting for the teacher to call on her. She never kow-towed to anyone. Insensitive to the opinion of others, she was her own person. And her insouciance was a large part of her charm for Scott.

It was only when things started going badly for the Fitzgeralds and he was tired of wondering what Zelda should do that Scott started reminding her that he was a worker and she was not. When Zelda tried to be a worker, with her frenzied writing and the strenuous ballet dancing, it precipitated her madness.

Scott's change of attitude now strikes me as unfair. He began to despise his wife for precisely the quality he had initially loved about her—that she was the gay, good family, spoiled, darling, beautiful girl.

When Scott first met Zelda, she had an aura of confidence and supremacy that dazzled him. Scott, who had never been excessively brave, was also impressed by her daredevil bravado. "She had no fear whatsoever," he told me. As a child she had climbed the highest trees and laughed when her frightened friends begged her to come down. She dove into swimming holes from heights that could have killed her. This was her way of saying, "I obey no one but myself. All you conventional people, what a dreary life you have." It never bothered her what anyone thought or said, that she was talked about disparagingly or envied by more normal girls.

It seems to me that in Zelda's carelessness, there was a streak of calculation. If she didn't care what impression she was making on other people, she did crave their attention. It pleased her when the local newspapers praised her dancing in a charity ballet performance and remarked on her beauty and talent. Also, like Scott, she knew how to create her own dramas. The day she calmly telephoned the fire department and said there was a girl on the roof who was unable to come down, she then climbed onto the roof and kicked away the ladder. She loved the fuss of the screaming fire engines and the startled neighbors. Perhaps a boy might have done this but not a girl. Zelda preferred to be with the boys. They were more daring, but none more than she was, and they admired her.

Hearing about Zelda from Scott, I felt both akin to her and very different. I, too, had dreamed of glory, of doing something wonderful, of trying for the best. But I did not have her careless attitude toward people and events. I conservatively followed the rules in public, although hypocritically I had always done as I pleased in private. But even in my private life, I don't believe I ever lost my sense of balance, of self-conservation.

For Zelda, before her breakdown, there were no limits. This made her fascinating, especially as she was so beautiful. She was the sun-kissed child. But as Edmund Wilson wrote of her in his January 1959, *New Yorker* review of my book, *Beloved Infidel*, "While the good fairies had bestowed on her every possible gift they could, they had omitted the stabilizing influences that could have saved her the later anguish of schizophrenia."

In hindsight it is easy to discern the germs of madness in Zelda's early behavior. I wonder that no one questioned it, especially given the mental instability in her mother's family. Minnie Machen's mother—Zelda's maternal grandmother—committed suicide when Zelda was a girl, but no one in the Sayre household ever mentioned this. Also Zelda's oldest sister Marjorie had suffered a nervous breakdown. And later on, after Zelda's own collapse, so did her brother Anthony. Finally afraid that he might kill his mother, he took his own life by jumping out a window. (In fact, Turnbull has pointed out that there was mental illness on both sides of Zelda's family.)

As for Zelda, I have seen a photograph of her when she was five, and there is a strangeness in the unsmiling face with its piercing eyes. It could be a twin for the photograph taken after she became officially insane—remarkable for the same staring rigidity.

Scott, however, had no doubts concerning Zelda's sanity before 1930—when he came home to their apartment in Paris to find her playing in a corner with some dirt. The doctor told him, "Votre femme est folle." I shivered when he described this scene. There are two things I was most afraid of—drunkenness and madness. They both have the unreasonableness of a hysterical child. They are outside the laws we have made to contain ourselves from frightening aspects of behavior.

It also seemed incredible to me that he should not have suspected earlier that she was obviously unstable. But the 20s were a crazy time, what with Tallulah and John Barrymore making spectacles of themselves, so that Zelda in its context was simply "an original." Those plunges into the Plaza fountain—today she would have been carted off to Bellevue. The undressing at the Follies—well, that at least might be countenanced today as streaking. But streakers seem tame compared to Zelda. She was flamboyantly wild in an era when even little old ladies were seen staggering across the lobby of the old Waldorf Astoria. They were still staggering in the hangover from Prohibition when I came to New York in 1933.

Scott sometimes wondered whether he might have been able to help his wife if he had worried about her sooner. But he never tried to control her "original" behavior. Instead of serving as a rock for her to lean on, he tried to be more original than she was, to outdo her in crazy pranks. The time he lay down on the road and told her to drive over him—a feat Zelda would have attempted except that the car stalled. Knowing Scott, I am sure he would have rolled out of danger at the vital second, as I am sure he had one eye open when he and Zelda slept in the stalled car on the French railroad tracks. They were both adept at playing Russian roulette with life. Only he was not crazy and she was. He could have helped her but he didn't. This tender transplant from the South needed care to survive in the reckless postwar cosmopolitan world. Perhaps if Scott's character had been more solid, Zelda might have been spared her collapse.

Zelda was the youngest of her family—at her birth Anthony was already nine, her sister Rosalind eleven, and Marjorie fourteen—and from the beginning to the end of her life, close relatives called her "Baby." Judge Sayre set himself at a rather formidable distance from his children. But Minnie Sayre —who breastfed Zelda until the child was four and standing to take the milk—was even more obsessed with this daughter than Mollie Fitzgerald was with the young Scott. All her life Zelda adored her mother. I have always felt that in her death before Mrs. Sayre's, she was spared what might have been an intolerable loss.

Mrs. Sayre made clothes to enhance the fairy-tale quality of her pretty daughter—fluffy tulle flounces spreading from the tight bodice. And she protected Zelda from ever being punished. When Zelda started smoking and going out with boys—as flamboyant a belle as she had been a tomboy—her father locked her in her room but her mother let her out. No one, said Scott, ever thought of giving the girl a sense of responsibility or of teaching her to consider her effect on other people. She took everything that came her way as rightfully belonging to her. And this included, in 1917, the young handsome lieutenant, Scott, whose air of weary cynicism alternated with his wild enthusiasm for life, especially for the beautiful, fearless belle. She had never met such an appealing man.

Scott described to me his encounter with Zelda at the Montgomery Country Club Saturday night dance. (How strange that he and I should also come together on a dance floor.) He saw this lovely, blonde, vibrant girl in a flouncy white dress—made by her mother—surrounded on the dance floor by officers. "I was immediately smitten and cut in on her. She was the most beautiful girl I had ever seen in my life. And from that first moment I simply had to have her." The handsomest boy had to have the most beautiful girl. Scott and Zelda looked fairly alike—both blond and blue-eyed. They say opposites attract each other, but more often it is people who resemble each other who fall in love—perhaps it's the reflection of themselves. Zelda was Scott's dream come true, not rich but with the insolent confidence of the most popular girl in town.

Scott characterized her to me as "sexually reckless." He believed she was a virgin until they became lovers a year before they married. But she flirted dangerously, going as far as she could without the ultimate act, claiming to have kissed "thousands of men." Scott remembered how she had teased him. It was called necking in those days, but it went further than that—in cars, on the dark grass, anywhere. Scott didn't really want to go the whole way. He respected Zelda, and well-brought-up girls saved the final yielding for the wedding night. But, he told me, "I doubt whether Zelda would have cared if she had become pregnant." She might have enjoyed it as another slap at the conventions she found depressing.

When Scott returned from his aborted war, they became engaged, Scott wishing to marry at once but Zelda more sensibly holding back. She knew Scott wanted to be a writer, but though she shared his dreams of glory, she was conscious they had not yet materialized. Scribners had rejected *The Romantic Egotist,* as Scott learned when he was out of the army, though the editor, Max Perkins, had been encouraging. Meanwhile, Scott had no money. In the army there had been his officer's pay and additionally an allowance from his family. As a civilian, out of his Brooks Brothers uniform, he had nothing except his dream of success. A job was imperative. So in March 1919, he went to New York where, after failing to get work with the newspapers, he landed an unglamorous job with the Barron Collier Advertising Agency.

While Scott created slogans for his employers at the job he hated and lived in one room in the Bronx, Zelda, back in Alabama, was flirting with every man in sight. It was as though she was playing to a vast audience, and every man in it owed her homage. As when, driving in an open car down the main street of Montgomery and seeing a group of boys, whom she had named Jelly Beans, she had thrown open her arms and cried, "All my jellies." To be a belle in a Southern town in those days meant that you could have any boy you wanted. "She used this power," said Scott, "to make me unbearably jealous, writing to me about this and that party, this and that man." In one letter she offers the consolation, "You are the only man on earth who has ever known and loved *all* of me." This wasn't at all soothing to Scott. Yet her desirability for other men was one of the reasons he fell in love with her and wanted to pin her down for himself.

What Zelda loved about Scott was his air of excitement and optimism. But when he paid her gloomy visits from New York, nagged her about her flirtations, and seemed to have no prospects of success, her faith in him wavered and she broke the engagement. Not that she was mercenary, she hastened to explain, but she sincerely believed that he would love her less without the money to give her the setting to make her always attractive to him. "I would never love her as much," Scott confessed to me. But he was still in love with the idea of capturing the prettiest girl in the South. When they finally married, following his recognition as the new brilliant author for his generation, did they love one another or were they just smitten with their image of success and glamor?

The truth about their feelings strikes me as elusive, because they were both so adept at playing a role. To hold Scott on a string when the engagement was off and to continue to make him jealous, Zelda invented an "engagement" to the famed golfer Bobby Jones. Scott always believed that she had promised to marry Mr. Jones. He told me this with conviction. But when Andrew Turnbull was writing his biography of Scott, he questioned the golfer, who denied even knowing Zelda.

As for Scott, he dramatized to everyone that his girl had thrown him over, writing to several friends of his broken engagement and heart. I am sure he suffered as much as he told me he did. The idea that Zelda might be having an affair with someone else tormented him. He desperately wanted her back. Yet a part of him was thoroughly disillusioned with her. Why not then give her up?

Perhaps because Scott so insisted on his attachment, he committed himself to being true to it. At any rate, deciding that his life was to be all or nothing, he gave up his job in July 1919 and went back home to St. Paul to rewrite his book—Max Perkins had liked some parts of it. With an untrammeled energy that he no longer had when he was writing *The Last Tycoon*, he wrote at a feverish pace in his attic room. And when the book was finished and accepted, his girl came back to him. He had been completely faithful to her, her image for him was everywhere, but he was to hold it against her for the rest of his life that she had broken their engagement because he was poor.

After *Beloved Infidel* was published in 1958, I received a letter from a lady with the pretty name of Isabelle Amorous containing a letter she had received from Scott:

Princeton, N.J.
Feb. 26. (1920)

Dear Isabelle:

Excuse this wretched paper but being a hard working literary man it's all I ever use. I hope you're a
reader of the *Saturday Evening Post,* Smart Set, Scribners etc., in which my immortal writings appear from
time to time. And I read your letter with a mixture of
impressions, the situation being somewhat complicated by the fact that Zelda and I have had a recon-
ciliation. And Isabelle, much as I like being a "strong
character," candor compells me to admit that it was
she and not me who did the throwing over last June.

No personality as strong as Zelda's could go without getting criticism and as you say she is not above
reproach. I've always known that, any girl who gets
stewed in public, who frankly enjoys and tells shocking stories, who smokes constantly and makes the
remark that she has "kissed thousands of men and
intends to kiss thousands more," cannot be considered beyond reproach even if above it. But Isabelle I
fell in love with her courage, her sincerity and her
flaming self respect and it's these things I'd believe in
even if the whole world indulged in wild suspicions
that she wasn't all that she should be.

But of course the real reason, Isabelle, is that I love
her and that's the beginning and end of everything.
You're still a Catholic but Zelda's the only God I have
left now.

But I want to thank you for your letter and thought
of it. You are a strange and rare combination, Isabelle;
a woman who is at once very beautiful and very good,
and I hope your destiny won't lead you into the same
devious paths that mine has. My friends are unani-
mous in frankly advising me not to marry a wild,
pleasure loving girl like Zelda so I'm quite used to
it. . . .

Faithfully,
Scott Fitzgerald

I showed this letter to Nancy Milford, whose book *Zelda* was published by Harper & Row in 1970. She used it, but I am borrowing it back because in addition to demonstrating the charm, truthfulness, boasting, and loyalty, so typical of Scott to the end of his life, it shows his willingness, even his pride in marrying a woman he knew might be no good for him.

Scott's feeling that Zelda was bad for him never wavered despite all his love for her. A letter to Scottie, written during the time that I knew him, explains:

> When I was young I lived with a great dream. The dream grew and I learned how to speak of it and make people listen. Then the dream divided one day when I decided to marry your mother after all, even though I knew she was spoilt and meant me no good. I was sorry immediately I had married her, but being patient in those days, made the best of it and got to love her in another way. . . . But I was a man divided. She wanted me to work too much for her and not enough for my dream. She realized too late that work was dignity and the only dignity, and tried to atone for it by working herself, but it was too late and she broke and is broken forever.

Scott's remarks here call to mind the passage in *The Great Gatsby*, where Gatsby pauses before kissing Daisy, knowing that "When he kissed this girl, and wed his unutterable visions to her perishable breath, his mind would never romp again like the mind of God." Was Scott thinking of his own experience with Zelda?

Certainly Zelda was jealous of Scott's fame. She was used to being the center of a group, and she would do anything to retain the spotlight. When Scott was the one everybody wanted to know, she rebelled against being pushed into the background. In Paris while Scott chatted with Gertrude Stein, Zelda had to talk with Alice B. Toklas, and she swore they would never go to the Rue de Fleurus again. Perhaps making Scott work for her was Zelda's way of sharing in his glory, of somehow stealing it from him. She, too, longed, as she once put it, "to move brightly along high places." Unfortunately she lacked the discipline to make this dream her own reality. But she did manage some short stories in 1930 and 1932 and published her book *Save Me the Waltz*, written during a frenzied six weeks while she was in the Phipps Clinic in Baltimore.

Scott blamed Zelda for draining him, distracting him. But in reality they were both victims of their fame, Zelda as well as Scott. The Southern gum-chewing speed and the unsure Midwesterner, two babes in the New York woods, found suddenly to their bewilderment that they were the leaders of the rebellious postwar generation. They created the Jazz Age of the 20s practically single-handedly. Whatever they did became news, and then they had to outdo themselves in order to stay in the news. They were expected to behave wildly and they did. But meanwhile they were destroying themselves —their energy, their money, and the capability of Scott Fitzgerald to work. Several of the stories he wrote at that time were mediocre. It was a miracle, in fact, that he did any work at all. But he could write all night then—sometimes for forty-eight hours without a break. With the arrogance of youth he thought he could always stay on top of the world. His recklessness seemed heroic to him. In retrospect, said Scott, it was merely foolish.

Where Zelda failed Scott—just as he failed her—was in her inability—even before the insanity—to take a firm stand when he went too far. When he told me about his crazy pranks at the Murphys' during the mid- and late-20s in the South of France—smashing Gerald's beautiful Venetian goblets, dropping a ripe fig into a décolleté gown, a lump of ice down the back of an evening dress—I was not amused, I was shocked. One great difference between Zelda and me was that I would never have condoned such conduct. But however she might protest feebly at his drinking, she could not criticize his infantile show-off pranks. She did not recognize any limits.

I think their lives also suffered from Zelda's increasing desperation as to what to do with herself. She had no idea of being a wife—shortly after they were married Scott discovered all his dirty shirts piled up in a closet—and, although she tried in the times of sanity, still less of being a mother. Her famous utterance at Scottie's birth which Scott incorporated into *The Great Gatsby*, "I hope she will be a beautiful fool," is pure whimsy—a beautiful fool is such a bore. It was Scott who proved the more realistic parent, assuming the responsibility of Scottie's clothes, her schooling, her health, her habits.

"What shall Zelda do?" was a common remark at the Murphys' in the South of France. Scott had his writing and Zelda her swimming. But what should she *do*? Her friends were relieved when she was seen with the good-looking French ex-aviator, Edouard Jozanne, frolicking on the beach and dancing with him intimately at the waterside bistros. "I liked him and was glad he was willing to pass the hours with Zelda," Scott told me. "It gave me time to write. It never occurred to me that the friendship could turn into an affair."

Scott had previously believed in his wife's faithfulness, even when in the early 20s in New York she sometimes spent several hours out and returned to their hotel without explaining where she had been. She had married him and sexually he trusted her—despite all his earlier jealousy over her suitors, and their fights about everything else: Zelda's lack of housekeeping, her helter-skelter dealing with servants, her erratic behavior toward Scottie, her competing with Scott, her jealousy.

My own feeling was that the constant quarrels must have bred resentment. I told Scott that I did not believe in quarrels, that each hurtful remark leaves a scar that grows larger with the next bout of anger. "Perhaps for women, but not for a man," he replied. "Each love, each quarrel is the first time for a man, but a woman remembers the last time and adds it to the present." Well, Zelda was a woman.

Soon everyone at St. Raphael knew about her affair with Jozanne (Tommy Barban in *Tender Is the Night*) except Scott. When he did learn of it, he told me, he was so furious that he challenged Jozanne to a duel and bought a pistol. According to Scott, they each fired a shot but neither harmed the other. While he was telling me this, I had the feeling that the whole episode was to provide material for his book, and this it did. Did the Fitzgeralds ever do anything just for the sake of doing it, and not to bolster the legend they had deliberately created about themselves or to provide Scott with episodes for his fiction?

Moreover, I have since wondered how much of the affair and the confrontation of husband and lover actually occurred. Jozanne, interviewed by Nancy Milford, failed to mention a duel and flatly denied that the romance with Zelda was ever consummated. Perhaps he was still acting the gentleman and seeking to protect her. It is so difficult to know the truth, entangled as it is in the roles the Fitzgeralds played for one another and for the world. Zelda conceivably could have lied to Scott to make him jealous. Scott might have exaggerated the affair to dramatize his sense of victimization. One thing is certain—Zelda emerged from the romance more frustrated and desperate than ever to find some way of achieving her own recognition.

"The ballet lessons, were they the cause of the ultimate breakdown?" I asked Scott. "Not really," he replied. Scott felt that Zelda's problem was her inability to recognize any limits. And her obsession to be a *première danseuse* was just one manifestation of this. It was unrealistic. She was thirty years old, too old to compete for a top place with the great ballerinas who had been studying and practicing all their lives with Spartan austerity. Certainly, Zelda had taken ballet lessons when she was a child and had been praised in the local newspapers. But she was an amateur, and it was too late to be a professional.

Scott disliked amateurs, and he did not spare Zelda's feelings in rubbing in that she belonged to this group. She was upset when he told her that, measuring herself against the great dancers, she could never be more than third rate. She might be good enough for a role in the Folies Bergères—she had the offer of a part in their ensemble and a leading role with a second-rate ballet company in Monte Carlo—but she would never get far with the best of ballet. This must have slapped her as a cruel assessment. Both Fitzgeralds always aspired for the best. Scott had admired Gerald Murphy for deliberately giving up painting when, as he told Scott, he realized he would never be a truly great painter. "But he enjoyed painting," I protested. "That was not the point," replied Scott.

Zelda's obsession with ballet caused the most bitter quarrels of their marriage. She accused Scott of being jealous of the time she spent having dancing lessons with her teacher, Madame Egorova, a former Russian aristocrat who instructed the top ballerinas in Paris. She retaliated by saying he spent too much time in the bistros with his idol, Ernest Hemingway. Zelda once described herself as sensual whereas Scott was not. I never thought he was. He was gentle, sensitive, and had all the intuition usually associated with women. There was nothing gross about him. He had a certain spiritual quality.

After Zelda's breakdown, ballet was out of the question, but she still was determined to attain artistic recognition for her writing and painting. Scott encouraged her in these efforts, as he later did me. But he also felt that a part of her illness was due to the intensity with which she tried to prove to him and the world that she could be as good as he was. Zelda couldn't abandon the idea that she merited the same attention and adulation and that the way to achieve this was to be recognized as a genius in her own right. Only then would she be as extravagantly admired as she had been as the belle of Montgomery, Alabama. Scott felt his duty was to protect her from strain and disappointment. She should write and paint and even dance, but only in moderation. If she worked too hard at anything, even athletics, the doctors had warned that she was in danger of lapsing into total madness. He was wryly amused as he told me of Zelda's reaction to a doctor at the hospital beating her at a game of tennis. She sailed over the net and hit him over the head with her racket.

Scott's concern that Zelda not overtax herself can be and has been interpreted as a fear that she might overshadow him. The articles that she wrote with minimal help from Scott he attributed to both of them and one to himself alone. But his motive was not insecurity. As Scott explained to me, his name brought in the money, so it ought to be used. And when they found themselves vying for the same material—the breakdown of Zelda's sanity and their marriage—Scott felt that, as he was the breadwinner and had the reputation, he knew how to put Zelda's undisciplined gifts into a coherent story that could support them all. I agree that he had every reason to be outraged when he read Zelda's novel *Save Me the Waltz,* covering the same ground as *Tender Is the Night,* on which he was progressing so slowly. Zelda was sharp enough to send the manuscript direct to Max Perkins at Scribners. Even so, Scott insisted on substantial cuts and changes.

I have read *Save Me the Waltz* and find it a difficult book to enjoy with its overlush, sometimes unintelligible prose and its unremitting intensity. But even though Zelda was not a writer of Scott's stature, should this mean that she be denied the freedom to tell her story? Scott encouraged her (as he did me) to "write about what you know." It seems to me, though, that Zelda was acting out of hostility in whipping out a book in a few weeks on the exact subject her husband had been wrestling with for many years. "A very shrewd and canny woman, whose motives, both healthy and pathological, can stand a good examination," Scott was to describe her to one of her doctors.

It took Scott eight years to complete *Tender Is the Night,* largely because of his preoccupation with Zelda's illness. To pay for the series of expensive sanitariums—Prangins in Switzerland, Phipps in Baltimore, Shepherd Pratt in Towson, Maryland, and Highlands in Asheville, North Carolina—he constantly abandoned work on the novel to turn out short stories for magazines. He also proceeded to drink himself close to insensibility.

In the long years of intermittent writing, *Tender Is the Night* became confused. It was really two books, Scott explained to me. The focus was always to be Zelda. Originally, Scott conceived the story of a girl who was raped by her father and became strange, with a background of the Riviera. After Zelda's breakdown this shifted into the tale of a woman cured by a charming doctor, who falls in love with her and is ultimately destroyed by her. This, confessed Scott, was his and Zelda's story with himself superimposed upon Gerald Murphy, who was initially outraged when he read the book and claimed that he was not the least like Scott. When I knew Scott, he wished to redo *Tender Is the Night,* and cut the confusion in it.

Scott often complained to me and others that he resented

the hours he had wasted writing what he considered "trash"—a favorite word—to keep Zelda in the luxury he thought she craved. Actually, after several bouts in costly sanitariums, she begged him to put her in a state asylum, to save his money which had shrunk to a dribble. But this did not tally with his idea of the right surroundings for his wife. And yet he blamed her for causing him to leave his serious work for the fast buck.

I once said to him, "There are so few people with real talent that you should consider your writing first and your wife and daughter next." He put my advice in a letter to Scottie dated June 12, 1940:

> . . . What little I've accomplished has been by the most laborious and uphill work, and I wish now I'd *never* relaxed or looked back—but said at the end of "The Great Gatsby": "I've found my line—from now on this comes first. This is my immediate duty —without this I am nothing" . . .

I may sound jealous, and perhaps I am, but I am trying to be honest when I ask: was the Scott-Zelda legend *the* love story it has been acclaimed? Looking at it coldly from the distance of Scott telling me about his life with Zelda, it seemed more like a nightmare than a love story. How restless and unsettled they were, always moving around, always renting homes, always living in other people's furniture. Scott bought books, but never, with few exceptions, a rare book or antique furniture or painting masterpieces.

Perhaps if Scott had not been raised in the Catholic faith, they would have parted in the first year of marriage, when indeed they talked of divorce. Or perhaps if they had not been such a famous couple, they would not have had to keep up their show together for a world that was watching them so minutely, or so they thought.

Zelda in the early 20s confided to her sister Rosalind, when they found themselves together at a party on Long Island, that she had never really wanted to marry Scott. As Scott felt, Zelda "might have been happy with a kind simple man in a southern garden," sheltered from the stresses her nature could not cope with. And Scott would not have wasted the years building up their legend. Zelda's experiences were of use to him in his writing, but they also destroyed the time he could have been writing.

I often wonder how Scott's career would have been affected if he had not married Zelda. She is the model of so many of his novels and stories. But if not Zelda, there would of course have been other models. And given Scott's susceptibility as a young man to spoiled, elusive women, I wonder how different from her any others might have been. But perhaps they would not have been so "original."

Possibly the suffering that Scott experienced because of his commitment to his irresponsible, wild, egocentric Zelda helped to mature him both as a man and a novelist. I think he finally outgrew his attraction to her type of woman. And his writing, moving away from "the flapper," the "rich bitch," gained in depth and power. It could be I say this because in *The Last Tycoon* he wrote about me and my coping with a harsher reality. But being as objective as I can, I find the love affair between Kathleen and Stahr the most adult, the most fully fleshed to be found in all of Scott's fiction.

The idea that I was the model for a new type of Fitzgerald heroine has been suggested by several critics. It's a notion that intrigues me though I think there is a danger of error in drawing too pat a distinction between Zelda and me. In such comparisons I always come off sounding enormously helpful, efficient, and a little lack-lustre. Aaron Latham, for example, writes:

> Zelda had been first rate, like the 20s but with the 20s' fatal flaw, burning with the bright short-lived flame of paper when set afire. She had been greatly admired but in a moral sense never quite admirable. Sheilah embodied a diminished decade, the 30s. She was not dazzling the way Zelda had been but as a worker, an achiever, a caring nurse, she was admirable. Zelda and Sheilah were opposites, which the author held unreconciled in his mind.

I think that's absolute nonsense. The point is that both Zelda and I were glamorous women; we both had a glamorous relationship with Scott. In my case, he knew that men were often falling in love with me. But I had chosen to be the girl of this fascinating man who (except when drinking) was careful to show me the best side of himself, to keep intact my image of him as a strong, mature man.

There *were* differences between Zelda and me, an essential one being that I was never so dependent on him as she was. For all her fearlessness, Zelda lacked a streak of independence. She would take the rows and the drinking on and on, whereas I wouldn't. He knew that I would leave him if his miserable behavior kept up, and then I did leave. Twice I gave him up when I could no longer stand it. So he knew that he could no longer continue to abuse me. I told him that it was enough, that I would not take it anymore. And I went. Zelda never went. And he didn't, either, from her. She didn't condemn him or judge him. She wistfully wished that he wouldn't drink anymore. "Oh Dodo, please don't drink so much . . . the doctors say it's so bad for you." But she never put her foot down and said, "You will never see me again unless you stop drinking."

It's strange, given her reputation, to realize that Zelda was not really a fighter. She wanted many things but bowed to circumstances, especially in the years of her illness. In the last year, committed to the Asheville sanitarium, she wanted to leave and live with her mother. To persuade Scott to her plan, she even got Scottie to beg for her in addition to her mother and sister, Rosalind. Scott thought they conspired against him to set her free and that they blamed him for keeping her in the sanitarium. He was very depressed, I remember, in Encino (early 1940) after a letter from Rosalind accusing him of putting Zelda away for his own reasons. In actual fact, he was following the doctors' advice in keeping her in the hospital, even though it was costing him more money than he could afford.

Zelda humbly acquiesced to Scott's viewpoint, though three weeks before Scott's death she did finally win this particular argument. At her bequest the young, good-looking Dr. James

Rennie of the Phipps Clinic in Baltimore, came to Hollywood to convince Scott, who had just had his first heart attack, that she was well enough to live with her mother. Rennie, Scott, and I attended a film preview at M-G-M, and I was concerned when I realized we would have to walk up a fairly long flight of steps to reach the projection room. I pretended to have hurt my ankle and walked up in front of the two men at the slowest pace I could. Rennie's mission was successful, and Zelda was with her mother when the news came of Scott's death. She wanted to attend his funeral in Baltimore, but at the last minute her doctors decided it would be too much for her.

Zelda, I believe, never knew of my existence. Scott was convinced that he only need intimate the slightest interest in some other woman to bring on her insanity again. He felt he could make her psychotic in fifteen minutes if he wanted to. Zelda's sisters suspected there might be another woman, but they were as careful as Scott to keep this fact from Zelda. During 1926 she had tried to kill herself, falling down a long flight of stone steps at St. Paul de Vence on the Riviera while he was admiring the famed dancer, Isadora Duncan. Scott told me of the incident with some relish mixed with the anguish. Isadora, dining in the same restaurant as the Fitzgeralds and the Murphys, sent for Scott to come to her table. He was delighted to comply and knelt in homage at her feet while she rumpled his hair and called him her centurion. But after a few minutes Scott was distracted by shouts from his own table —Zelda had rushed out and deliberately flung herself down the stone steps. Fortunately they had a door at the bottom or she would have been hurled to the foot of a cliff.

A few years ago, Martin Poll, the film producer, gave a dinner party for me at this restaurant. The guests included Charles Boyer, Glenn Ford, and Hope Lange. I saw the stone steps and shuddered, visualizing the scene. Of course Zelda was not in her right mind, and it is incredible that neither Scott nor the Murphys realized this. Her behavior went beyond the limits of jealousy. If she felt in danger of being eclipsed, she could be suicidal. Another frightening story was her response to Scott's flirtation in 1927 with Lois Moran, the young Hollywood actress whom Scott admired as a worker. In revenge, Scott told me, Zelda set fire to all the furniture in the Ambassador Hotel suite.

In the years that I knew Scott, Zelda was less defiant and destructive, perhaps made more considerate of her husband by her own terrible suffering. But he felt that she would surely do away with herself if she knew that he was in love, really in love with another woman.

I dreaded the times when Scott visited Zelda—her doctors had written that it would help to take her out of the sanitarium to live with him for a week or so, supposedly as a normal couple. It was not that I was jealous. With unwarranted complacency, I believed that a man who was in love with me wouldn't want to have sex with another woman. It wasn't that he might sleep with her that worried me. It was the strain of these visits on Scott. As long as Zelda and he were apart he could love her. With contact he hated her for what she had done to his life. And there were always misadventures.

When he made his first trip East in 1937 to see her, I had only known him for a few months. Scott had been on the wagon and miraculously he did not drink in the time they were together. But this was the only such occasion.

The second visit to Zelda came toward Christmas. This time I thought it was rather sad that I was to be left alone over the holiday. Somehow Christmas—at least before I had my children—was always a bad time for me. Something always went wrong which intensified my sense of loneliness. The worst time would be when Scott died four days before Christmas, 1940. But already by 1937, I had spent one Christmas in a nursing home, recuperating from an operation, and another recovering from an unhappy love affair. King Vidor, the first man I thought I might marry when I was in Hollywood, went back to the other woman just at Christmas and spent the holiday with her. So when Scott went off, I thought, this is going to be the pattern of my life.

I was still feeling low when Scott telephoned me a few days after Christmas from the L.A. airport and said, "Zelda and I are getting a divorce . . . You and I are going to be married." I was delighted. While waiting for him, I spent the interim writing out my name—my new name—Sheilah Fitzgerald —doing it at first very carefully, then very fast. I was in the golden haze of happiness that I've sometimes had in my life.

Then Scott arrived. When I saw him, his face flushed, I realized he had been drinking. My happiness disappeared. I said no more about his proposal because I judged it was part of his binge. Perhaps, though, he meant it, or wished he could mean it. He had had a terrible time with Zelda. I believe this was the visit when he was so drunk and behaving so badly that Zelda tried to have him committed to a mental institution. He was supposed to be taking care of the mad woman, and the mad woman was taking care of him.

I do not think that Scott completely gave up on the idea of ever living with Zelda as his wife until the last year of his life. He had seen her in the spring of 1939 after our struggle for his gun. I had taken it from an open drawer during a drinking time. He had then gone to Zelda and taken her to Cuba where Scott was beaten up trying to rescue two cocks in a cockfight, while Zelda was praying for his salvation as the boys worked him over. Because he disliked me then, he invited Zelda to come to Hollywood, something she wanted to do throughout the 1937-1940 years. He believed he and I had parted for good. It was only when we got together again that he reneged on the offer to Zelda. And as it turned out, he never saw her again.

Perhaps when we quarreled and I left him, his life was less complicated. He could then give all his thoughts to Zelda and Scottie. But for a man of forty to forty-four, there was still a large gap in his life that the invalided Zelda could not fill. He needed to love and be loved and to have a steady companion. Once we were together, the urgency to be with Zelda dimmed.

In the year before Scott died, when he was sober and happily working on *The Last Tycoon,* he accepted that it would be destructive to return to Zelda, even for a visit, and he thought seriously of divorcing her to marry me. At the beginning I had wanted to be his wife. I lost this desire when I saw what happened to him drinking. But in that last year of serenity, I thought it might be possible, unless the severance from Zelda would start him drinking again.

Scott felt that our marrying could take place either if Zelda recovered sufficiently to live for the rest of her life with her mother or if she went so permanently mad that she lost all contact with the real world about her. Scott explained to me, "She is not unhappy when she goes insane and is moderately happy in the sane periods. It's when she's in that indeterminate stage that she suffers so terribly." Were Zelda's condition to stabilize one way or another, Scott hoped he could divorce her. Then he would have a normal life with me.

In late 1940, Zelda's health was improving and there seemed real hope that she could withstand a divorce. Scott wrote to his friends, Nora and Lefty Flynn, asking what they thought of the idea. Nora replied encouragingly. Scott showed me her letter: "I feel that Sheilah is right for you." She had met me a few years previously at a lunch in London with Viscount Castlerosse, who was writing the gossip column on page two for Lord Beaverbrook's *Sunday Express*. Castlerosse had thought that we would like each other, but in fact I was rather intimidated by her being one of the trio of beautiful Langhorne girls. I remember she gave me advice on how to dress my hair so as to balance my high cheekbones. And now here she was advising Scott to make me his wife—she had forgotten our first meeting. Perhaps it would have happened if he had lived.

When Scott died, Zelda told Harold Ober that while they had not been close in the past year, Scott was the best friend a person could have been to her. He had continued writing her once a week, and their late letters are full of mutual tenderness and consideration. After all the quarreling and recriminations, perhaps they found greater friendship with less passion.

5.

THE FATHER

SCOTTIE WAS ANGRY as she came out of the telephone booth. There were tears in her eyes. She had gone gaily inside to call her father after our visit to the Errol Flynn set. Her friend, Peaches Finney, was with us, and the anger might have been partly for its effect on her sixteen-year-old friend from Baltimore. Scottie had been quite happy and thrilled to have her photograph taken with the swaggering star, but now her face was clouded, and the afternoon seemed spoiled.

I listened while she explained to Peaches, "Daddy was making fun of Errol. He's always trying to ruin things." It wasn't true, but looking back to the summer of 1938, I have to admit that as the father of an adolescent girl, Scott Fitzgerald was a bust. He simply did not know how to deal with a girl of sixteen, seventeen, and eighteen. They had been friends when she was very young, and with Zelda's illness and her father's complete take-over of her life, they were even closer together. But now, emerging into adulthood, she was rebellious against parental authority as so many spirited teenagers are. Scott, himself, had said, "A good son usually kills his father" —metaphorically of course. It was worse with Scott and his daughter because he made every mistake in the book in his determined effort to control her. "I must save her from the pitfalls that destroyed her mother."

He was more like a stern headmaster than a father who loved his only child, and he really did love her. But he was emphatic that Scottie should not be like her mother, and he did not want her to be like him either, except in standards of principles and hard work. At one time he cautioned her that if he ever heard of her drinking hard liquor, he would go on such a binge that the world would know of it and censure poor Scottie as the cause.

Scott's exhortations to his daughter were mainly delivered by letter. Except for her few trips to Hollywood, Scottie was back East—first at the Ethel Walker School and then at Vassar—during the 1937-1940 years. Scott wrote her every week, and the collection of most of these letters reveals not only his hopes and fears for Scottie but also the ideals and obsessions that shaped his own experience. As Scottie remarked in a recent interview:

> When the letters first came, I was just interested in the enclosed checks. But much later, when I wanted to learn exactly what made my parents tick, I went back to those letters. They've since made a big impression on me . . .

Rereading Scott's letters to Scottie from Hollywood, I am aware of his harping on certain themes: that life is exhaustible and therefore ought to be conserved—sensibly allocated to the future—while one is young; that youth is the most important time of life—the time of greatest intensity and also the time when one establishes either sound or destructive patterns of behavior. "Everything you are and do from fifteen to eighteen is what you are and will do through life," he propounds in a letter of 1938, which continues still more ominously: "Two years are *gone* and half the indicators already *point down*—two years are left and you've got to pursue desperately the ones that point up."

Scottie's behavior that prompted this dire warning was really quite innocuous—she was perhaps more interested in her social life than in her studies. But Scott looked back to what he now considered his own squandered youth, reinterpreting it all—his consuming interest in the Triangle Club at Princeton, his romances, his and Zelda's pranks—in terms of his "tragic sense of life." He could then write puritanically to Scottie:

> For premature adventure one pays an atrocious price. As I told you once, every boy I know who drank at eighteen or nineteen is now safe in his grave. The girls who were what we called "speeds" (in our stone age slang) at sixteen were reduced to anything they could get at marrying time. It's the logic of life that no young person ever gets away with anything. . . . It was in the cards that . . . your mother should wear out young. I think that despite a tendency to self-indulgence, you and I have some essential seriousness that will manage to preserve us.

This from a man who had plunged so rashly into all extravagant experience, trying to save his daughter from similar waste. A letter of January 1940 begins:

> Communications having apparently ceased from your end, I conclude that you're in love. Remember—there's an awful disease that overtakes popular girls at 19 or 20 called emotional bankruptcy. Hope you are not preparing the way for it.

Emotional bankruptcy—this is the exact phrase that Scott used so often to describe his own "crack-up." Behind it is the notion that one's store of emotion, like one's money in the bank, can be thriftlessly consumed. With so little faith in self-regeneration of emotion, it is not surprising that he dreaded his own aging (though, paradoxically, it was his maturity that attracted me to him). For him, youth was the epoch of life to cherish and remember, the time of unspent idealism and energy. "What proms and games? Let me at least renew my youth!" he implores Scottie in one letter, when for a change he is not berating her for attending such proms and games. He wanted, however, to renew his youth with a difference. Like himself he felt Scottie had "a real dream of your own." But she must "wed it to something solid before [it] is too late." He envisions her as "useful and proud," "among the best of your race."

I doubt whether any young girl could live up to such high-minded ideals. It was only occasionally that Scott could relax about her sufficiently to be pleased with her actual accomplishments. Although he did not particularly want Scottie to be a writer, with its agonizing delving into the mind, he was excited when she sold an article to the prestigious *New Yorker*—they had written his profile on April 17, 1926. When she wrote to tell him about the acceptance of her piece, he called all his friends to tell them the good news.

I had a subscription to *The New Yorker*, and on the date given us by Scottie, he came over earlier than usual. I had scanned the magazine from beginning to end, and there was no article signed by Frances Scott, the name she was using as an authoress so as not to conflict with her father's. There had been a nasty scene in the Hollywood Brown Derby when Scottie had told him she was planning to be a writer. "You are not to trade on my name," he admonished sternly. I was amazed. Why not make it easier for Scottie by allowing her to use Fitzgerald? But that was the point. Scott wanted her to struggle, to know that nothing came easily, that life was a succession of obstacles that required enormous effort to be overcome.

Scottie had written us the page her story would be on. I handed Scott the magazine silently, hoping that he could find what I couldn't. I watched his face—so eager and smiling as he turned the pages rapidly, then the surprise at not finding it where it should have been, then his going through the rest of the magazine and starting from the beginning again. We were both disturbed. Had Scottie imagined the whole thing, and if so, what could this portend? We never quite finished the surmise.

There was no need to have worried. In those years, *The New Yorker* sometimes had two editions, one for the East, one for the West. Scottie's article was in the Eastern, and she sent her father a copy after he wrote asking for an explanation.

I do not know whether Scott can be credited that Scottie emerged into the well-organized, completely charming person she became. The charm, certainly, can be linked with him. She has all that her father had—the ready smile, the sympathy, the ability to make the person whom she is with feel intelligent and at the center of what is happening. She also has an air of serenity that sets her markedly apart from her parents.

"I had a happy childhood," Scottie insists. People, she complained to me, are always commiserating with her, saying what an awful time she must have had as a child. She knew that her parents loved her, and she seems not to have minded the constant upheaval of their lives as the Fitzgerald family drifted back and forth between America and Europe. Scottie, in fact, paints a picture of what heaven it was living in Paris, skiing in Switzerland, swimming in the Mediterranean, and making friends of her own age in Baltimore. Perhaps she was screened from the disorder, the desperation of these moves. A series of affectionate nannies took care of her, she attended elite schools, and she lived in her own sunny world.

Also I can understand how both her parents could have delighted her. After Zelda became ill, they were not close—by then, Scottie reports, her mother "loved to talk about the past and about flowers. There was little else." But before her collapse, Zelda would sometimes exercise her sharp imagination in enhancing Scottie's world. There were wonderful birthday surprises—though often they were too adult for Scottie to appreciate—like the exquisite doll house with paper cut-outs of children climbing all over it, and marvelous dolls, too beautiful for her to drag around.

Scott also gave his best effort to amuse his "dearest pie." On a trip to Quebec which he and Zelda took at the invitation of a Canadian travel bureau, he sent to her at Ellerslie a series of enchanting picture postcards, all featuring cartoon drawings of himself, "Mummy," and "the man with three noses." In the South of France he played for hours with his collection of toy soldiers for Scottie and the Murphy children. And his tricks with cards always amazed them.

Given all the drinking Scott was doing, it is hard to believe that Scottie's childhood was not sometimes darker. The photographs of the Fitzgeralds—Scott, Zelda, and Scottie—posing and laughing together on the Riviera beach cannot set its whole tone. But Scott, too, in the stories he had to tell me of early years with his daughter, dwelt on the bright and cheerful. One Christmas, he remembered, Scottie gifted her parents with a garbage bin, a discreet hint perhaps for careless Zelda. Then, he laughed, "Every morning she tiptoed to the bin to see if there was any garbage in it."

The first crack in their good relationship occurred in Baltimore when Scottie was twelve. Scott told me he had been drinking. Scottie's independence was beginning to show. She was dressed for a party and was wearing a red dress of which he disapproved. In a sudden rage, Scott said, he tore the dress from shoulder to hem. When he told me this story, remembering how I was at the beginning of my adolescence, I told him somberly, "She'll never forget it or really forgive you." He did not reply but I knew he wished he had not humiliated his daughter like that. Her subsequent rebellion from authority could have started then. (Actually, Scottie told me she has long since forgiven and forgotten.)

While I liked Scottie, I began to dread her letters to Scott, which often upset him, and even more to dread her visits to Hollywood. Father and daughter tried to refrain from antagonizing each other, but they always did. Only Scottie's first visit, at the end of July 1937, could be called a success. Scott was strictly on the wagon. He took Scottie to the homes of Norma Shearer and Joan Crawford for tea. Scottie was amused when Joan, trying to entertain her young guest, showed her a large album full of her own photographs, all beautifully posed, not a bad angle among them. Afterwards, Scottie asked me, "Wouldn't you think she was tired of seeing her own face?" "Actresses never tire of that," I assured her. We were a foursome for dinner with Jimmy Stewart. He was amusing and nice to her. Scott had invited him because of their Princeton heritage. But Scottie's other few visits were almost total failures.

I had rented a house for Scott at Malibu, believing that the sun and the sea would make him stronger and less likely to resort to alcohol, though, of course, I didn't tell him this. But away from the scrutiny and gossip of Hollywood, he drank much more, and he rarely went into the sun or the sea. He was the palest man in that tanned beach resort. In between drinks, we played ping pong. That, with an occasional visit to the local store where there was a bowling alley, was the only exercise he took in those last years of his life. *I* swam, *I* played tennis—he had done both with Zelda—while *he* remained indoors.

I was pleased when he told me that Scottie and Peaches were coming west to spend a few weeks with him at the beach. But I was dreadfully hurt when he asked me to collect my things and move out. (I had only been coming for weekends and had hired a good housekeeper-cook to look after him —how I loved her cookies!)

I understood why he had asked me to leave. The girls were sixteen years old, and in 1938 it was considered very improper for a married man to have a pretty young lady friend sleeping in his house even though we had separate bedrooms, as we always did.

But now I was to clear out as though I were a casual woman in his life. I could come down for the day, but I was to leave before night. I am sure that this was done more for Peaches and the report she would give her family than for Scottie, who knew that I was close to her father and had written me many letters thanking me for this or that. I sometimes saw her looking at me with her father's eyes, wondering how I could possibly be in love with such an old ogre of a man.

I was shattered, and it came home to me painfully that I was involved in an irregular situation. Zelda had been a remote shadow far away in her sanitarium, but now she came closer. She was Scott's wife and the mother of his daughter. I was merely his girl, who could be turned out as circumstances decreed. It was all right for me to take Scottie and her friend to the studios. It was fine for me to get tickets to the premieres for all of us, but I must not seem to be an integral part of his life.

In the week preceding the visit, I punished him with brooding silences. Perhaps, I thought defiantly, he will believe that I, too, am mad. Serves him right. What am I doing wasting my life like this? Perhaps I really was off balance. But mostly I understood. I have always been able to see both sides of a situation. Unfortunately.

After the girls left, I brought back my beach clothes, and I soon forgot my feeling that I had been abandoned in the name of respectability. There had been some stormy scenes between Scottie and her father, but life did not now become as peaceful as I had hoped. Scott was drinking like a thirsty man in the desert who sees water for the first time in weeks. This was his habitual reaction after and during Scottie's visits to him and his to Zelda. Scott simply could not cope as a husband or a father. Soon after his death I wrote Scottie this letter:

> 1443 North Hayworth Avenue
> Hollywood, California
> May 27, 1941

Scottie:

Something has been bothering me. I think I'm partly responsible for the existing idea that Scott drank more and chiefly when he saw you. Yes, he drank the last few times he saw you—but not because he saw you. It was merely that the tension of his life would be strained when anything new or unusual came into it. The tension was caused by past grief and present exasperation inflicted by studios on sensitive writers. You, personally, were not the cause of any drinking bout with perhaps that one exception—poor old Dorothy Burns. (I feel like a traitor to Scott when I write "poor old".) But even this had its roots outside of the incident. It goes back to nerves that had been worn out with repeated battering during a period (and after) when it was the thing to be more spectacular than your neighbor. And Scott with his good looks, charm, enthusiasm, gaiety, and tenderness was a natural leader. So don't ever think that you *caused* him to drink.

He was pleased that you had opinions of your own. Not for anything would he have exchanged you—if he could—for a supine, sweet thing whose "yes" and "no" followed the crowd. Of course, when your opinions clashed with his own, he liked them less—don't we all? When we think we are right, we are sure the other person is wrong. But he watched the unfolding of your mind like an ardent horticulturist with a cherished flower.

I'm not quite sure why I've gone on like this, but I was wakeful in the plane coming back here thinking about you and Scott, and how if you'd only had more time together, what a lot you'd have had from each other.

It was sweet to get your letter. I'm delighted about the possibility of working for "Time." Max Perkins told me about it and was sure that if you saw them the job was practically yours. I do hope so. The people there seem "alive, alert, allergic"—to gooey gush —not good—but I've just come from a studio where I've been trying to get something above a one syllable speech from Rita Hayworth. She's making a picture now with Fred Astaire, who has practically no hair left.

The Clipper leaves for Lisbon (if it hasn't been invaded by that time) July 15th. And I'll be in New York for about six days before that, and I'll call you at the Obers.

All my love,

Even when Scottie was not present to exacerbate him, he could work himself into a frenzy over her supposed misconduct. There was the time she and a friend thumbed a ride from the Ethel Walker School to New Haven. Scottie had graduated but was staying on to take her entrance exams for Vassar. It was boring with most of the students gone; the two girls had some friends at Yale, and they decided to pay them a surprise visit. Scott was frantic when he was informed of the escapade. He wrote his sternest letter to date, informing Scottie that she was rushing down the path to hell. His over-reaction was because he feared she would not now be accepted at Vassar.

Scottie was only sixteen years old, and when I mentioned this, trying to soften him toward her, he fumed, "That makes it worse. They'll think she is too immature for college."

He wrote her a very nasty letter. You have not read it in the various collections because I made him change the letter. I was aghast when he read it to me. "What are you trying to do?" I demanded. "Alienate her forever, or help her in these very difficult years?" He rewrote the letter and commanded Scottie to read it twice because he had written it twice. The letter is dated July 7, 1938. This preceded her visit with Peaches.

> Dearest Scottie,
>
> I don't think I'll be writing letters many more years, and I wish you would read this letter twice—bitter as it may seem. When I'm talking to you and you think of me as an older person, an "authority" and when I speak of my own youth what I say becomes unreal to you—for the young can't believe in the youth of their fathers. But perhaps this little bit will be understandable if I put it in writing . . .

Scott goes on to explain how Zelda had ruined both herself and his "dream" by her idleness and bad habits. Then, drenching Scottie in the moral of this fall, he continues:

> . . . For a long time I hated *her* mother for giving her nothing in the line of good habits—nothing but "getting by" and conceit. I never wanted to see again in this world women who were brought up as idlers. And one of my chief desires in life was to keep you from being that kind of person, one who brings ruin to themselves and others. When you began to show disturbing signs at about fourteen, I comforted myself with the idea that you were too precocious socially and a strict school would fix things. But sometimes I think that idlers seem to be a special class for whom nothing can be planned, plead as one will with them—their only contribution to the human family is to warm a seat at the common table.

My reforming days are over, and if you are that way I don't want to change you. But I don't want to be upset by idlers inside my family or out. I want my energy and my earnings for people who talk my language.

I have begun to fear that you don't. You don't realize that what I am doing here is the last tired effort of a man who once did something finer and better. There is not enough energy, or call it money, to carry anyone who is dead weight and I am angry and resentful in my soul when I feel that I am doing this. People like———and your mother must be carried because their illness makes them useless. But it is a different story that *you* have spent two years doing no useful work at all, improving neither your body nor your mind, but only writing reams and reams of dreary letters to dreary people, with no possible object except obtaining invitations which you could not accept. Those letters go on, even in your sleep, so that I know your whole trip is one long waiting for the post. It is like an old gossip who cannot still her tongue.

You have reached the age when one is of interest to an adult only insofar as one seems to have a future. . . .

and on and on.

It was a gloomy letter for a young girl to receive but much better than the original epistle. This was more in sorrow than in anger, but its effect was about the same. Poor Scottie and poor Scott.

She was accepted at Vassar, to Scott's relief. He was always measuring her behavior and progress against Zelda's, even though these were the late 30s when young people did not behave as their parents had in the 20s. Children of a severe depression, they were sober, reacting against the preceding decade. Still, Scottie was lively and full of her father's gaiety when he was young and life was so full of promise. At Vassar she was voted the most popular girl of her class. She wrote a musical performed by the drama club and started the Oh My

God It's Monday Club. This was enough for Scott to warn sternly of what had happened to himself at Princeton when he had been so involved with the Triangle Club. He was the most anxious father I have ever known, but I sympathized with him in his desire for Scottie to avoid the dangers of his and Zelda's recklessness. And perhaps his sternness is why Scottie has developed into the responsible person that she is.

It was even worse when Scottie took off for a weekend in Baltimore without asking his permission or letting him know. Talk about the Oh My God It's Monday Club! This was Oh My God, It's Daddy's Saturday and Sunday Anguish. Scott, who always seemed to know when Scottie was doing something he did not approve of, had telephoned her at Vassar and learned she had gone away for the weekend. He tracked her down late on the Sunday. Her allowance was halved for the next three months. I felt sorry for Scottie but apprehensive that her father would start drinking again, which of course he did. In time the flouting of his authority was forgiven but never forgotten. From now on they were wary of each other, Scottie trying not to provoke her father, Scott stern and hoping vainly they could resume the relationship of their earlier years.

When Scott complained in October that the beach was too cold for him—it seemed he was always cold, wearing woollen sweaters and his old raincoat even when the weather was warm—I found him a house in Encino in the valley where it was ten to twenty degrees warmer than in Malibu. It was a large house on the Edward Everett Horton estate, one of three homes there in addition to the main residence. Mr. Horton, famous for his "double take" in his films, called his property "Belly Acres," a name which the fastidious Fitzgerald loathed. "You're not to tell anyone," he cautioned. There was an empty swimming pool which Scott paid to have filled up for me, a tennis court where I played for hours on the weekend with Mr. Horton's brothers. In the house there were two enormous bedrooms upstairs and a smaller room which Scott used for his study with a large adjoining balcony. If I awakened at night, I could hear him pacing up and down, up and down. At three or four in the morning, he took several sleeping pills and the pacing stopped. There was quiet until nine or ten in the morning, then pills to pep him up to work.

Scottie came to visit in the summer of 1939 and slept in the extra bed in my room. A boy she knew from the East telephoned, and he brought a whole group of his Pasadena friends to stay. The girls slept on the floor in my bedroom, and I liked that. I felt like everyone's mother. The boys slept downstairs in the large living room. There were jokes and much laughter and confident youth. Scott managed to control his drinking. But he had some fierce undertone arguments with Scottie, correcting her, worrying over her, telling her how to behave with boys.

One of his suggestions, however, delighted her. He asked her to take a series of driving lessons. "I want you to know how to drive," he said, "in case you are ever in a car with a drunk, and then you can take over. I don't want you coming home with a broken back." At Princeton Scott had seen a man killed in a car accident and he could not forget the horror. Of course Scottie was never to take the wheel from *him*. And it wasn't necessary. Sober, Scott rarely drove more than twenty miles an hour. And drunk he had the good sense to drive alone—usually to the nearest liquor store.

Scottie was to see her father one more time when we came East the following spring for the Army-Navy game in Philadelphia. We were in high spirits—not alcoholic, because Scott was totally on the wagon. Scottie was eighteen, she had slimmed down and was angelically pretty. It was a beautiful day and I can still see Scottie raising her arms to the sky and exclaiming, "I wish I could be eighteen forever." Scott smiled at me over her head, remembering his own passion for youth. He was now forty-three. We went to the station with Scottie, who was returning to what she called her "intellectual Turkish bath," and that was the very last they would see of each other.

Scott wisely did not attend his daughter's "coming out" in Baltimore—he could not cope with such self-conscious occasions and usually ended up disrupting them. Also he had emphasized so often that he wanted Scottie to be a worker, to have a career, that the social event seemed at odds with his aims for her. She was to be presented to society at the Baltimore Cotillion with her friend Peaches. His cash was low, and without telling him I sent Scottie the money for her dress. I teased him about it: "I'm surprised that you want her to be a debutante—I thought that now you didn't believe in that sort of thing." "It's just in case," he hedged. I didn't ask him what the "in case" meant. I suppose it was just in case she preferred to be social, to have an entrée to the best society.

Around this time, however, Scottie's subsequent great interest in politics was burgeoning. In one of her letters to her father, she expressed strong opinions about government and social reform. "You see," he almost shouted with excitement. "She's growing up. She's maturing. She's thinking about things outside herself."

Scott's letters to Scottie were now in a softer vein, and one time he telephoned her to explain why he had been so strict with her. "It's because I want you to be different from your mother." "Well," flipped Scottie, "Why doesn't *she* change?"

Scott's last letter to his daughter, on December 21, 1940—he died an hour after writing it—was signed by me, but the words are his. I was sending her some of my clothes and didn't want her to think I was patronizing her by sending cast-off stuff. "Will you tell me what to write?" I asked him. He was delighted to do so:

Dear Scottie, [he dictated]

I bought this dress to go to Dallas for "The Westerner." The winter is slipping away and because of my natural unpopularity I find no reason to use it. So there it sat in my closet, losing style week after week. I mentioned this to your father and he told me you burned up dresses at the rate of one a month and suggested that instead of selling it down the river I contribute it to the conflagration. The coat also seems to have been waiting in my closet for the victory celebration and I don't think now we will win before 1943. By that time it will be unusual for English people to wear furs. . . .

I added a request for her to send her father a recent photograph, wished her a happy Christmas and New Year, and, happily, "Your father has not been well but he's getting better now. He hasn't had a drink for over a year."

The coat referred to in my letter was the fox fur jacket that Scott had given me for my September birthday in 1937, the same coat he had written into his script for Joan Crawford, and stolen in our last quarrel in 1939, sent to Scottie, and then had to ask it back from her. Now of my own choice I was sending it to Scottie once again. Scott's own letter, written earlier, concerned the receipt of this present:

> There has reached you by this time I hope, a little coat. It was an almost never worn coat of Sheilah's that she wanted to send you. Frances Kroll's father is a furrier and he remade it *without charge!* So you must at once please write the following letters: i) to Sheilah, not stressing Mr. Kroll's contribution, ii) to Frances, praising the style, iii) to me (in the course of things) in such a way that I can show the letter to Sheilah who will certainly ask if you liked the coat . . . A giver gets no pleasure in a letter acknowledging a gift three weeks late even though it crawls with apologies. . . .
>
> Ecclesiastes Fitzgerald

I went to New York soon after Scott died and spent many hours with Scottie, who came down frequently from Vassar to see me. She wanted to know more about her father and asked me many questions. Why had he been so strict with her? What made him drink so much? Did I think he would be remembered as a writer? We were both angry about him not living long enough to finish *The Last Tycoon,* and both glad that Scribners was planning to publish the book in its half-finished state with Edmund Wilson to edit and put it together. As for trying to explain his anxieties as a father, I gave her diplomatic replies, not of course stressing his fears that Scottie would be a disorganized idler like her mother.

While Scott was alive, I had liked Scottie really more for her father's sake than for her own. It is true that I had acted as her champion and go-between with Scott, but this was to prevent him from being upset. I had found her a pleasant girl, but I had also thought she was a bit snooty with me. Once when she was spending the night at my home in Hollywood, she asked me for something to read. I was at this time well into the "Education" and, proud of my mastery of Proust, I offered her the first volume of *Remembrance of Things Past*. "Oh," she said, "I'd rather read it in French." So would I, I realized much later, if my French had been as good as hers.

After her father died, Scottie became the remnant of Scott for me, which I clung to. She also became someone I enjoyed for herself. And we have been friends ever since. I am pleased that she likes me because I consider her an honest, intelligent person with high standards of conduct. Also I think my satisfaction in the friendship goes back to my wanting to be respected. For Scott's daughter to believe that I'm a good person means that I'm being accepted by a member of the respected classes. Scottie is respected both as her father's daughter and as an enterprising, charming woman in her own right.

I kept in touch with Scottie during her last year at Vassar. As far as I could see, I was trying to carry on for Scott, trying to make sure his daughter was not unhappy and not in need of money, helping her to buy what she might need. From Vassar after Easter 1941, she wrote me:

Dearest Sheilah:

Please forgive me for not writing before. I feel doubly guilty since the reason I have not written has been largely the result of your magnificent present. I was just wondering whether to give up the idea of going to Florida when your check came. So, a couple of days later, I was on the train bound for Fort Lauderdale, the most beautiful place that looks like the French Riviera, with cabanas and colored umbrellas and boardwalks. It was without a doubt the most wonderful vacation I have ever spent, and I feel all happy and healthy again after a perfectly dismal

winter. In Baltimore on the way back I had to see Mr.
Coe about all the stuff in storage, and he told me he
had talked to you on the phone in California and that
you had been sick. Sheilah, I'm sorry to hear that,
and I hope that you aren't lonely and unhappy. These
months must have been terrible for you. When are
you coming East? Soon, I hope. Thank you again for
my present. If you knew how brown I was and how
healthy and what fun it was down South, you'd feel
like the angel Gabriel.

> Much love, Scottie

Almost to the day of the first anniversary of Scott's death,
unable to cope with the unexpected terrifying memory, I married Trevor Westbrook in Arlington, Virginia. It was shortly
after the "infamous" December 7, 1941—Trevor was in Washington with Churchill, Lord Beaverbrook, and all the arma-
ment experts. I had met him when I went to England in July
1941 as a war correspondent. Not long after our marriage, he
returned to London, and I found out I was pregnant. Scottie
immediately announced that she would be the baby's god-
mother. A letter from Vassar, sent to me shortly before her
graduation in 1942, reads:

> Really I'm so happy about the baby and I know it
> will be adorable. I have got my knitting needles out of
> mothballs and am madly making tiny garments. Only
> two more weeks of classes now, and it will all be over.
> Life is so very easy and so very removed from Hit-
> lerian agitation up here that it makes me sad to leave.
> Then I am coming to consult you. You probably hate
> playing Dorothy Dix, but I sure admire the way
> you've ordered your life, and I'd like to get some
> psychological tidbits from you. . . .

Six weeks before the end of my pregnancy, Scottie and I
spent a weekend with the Gerald Murphys at their attractive
home in East Hampton, Long Island. It was the very late
summer of 1942, and I was quite large. My dear Dr. Rubin tried

to restrain me from overeating, but I'm afraid that in having a
baby I had found a wonderful excuse to eat whatever I desired.
The Murphys had lost their two teen-aged sons, Baoth and
Patrick—I had visited their graves and sat on the stone bench
for visitors in the cemetery at East Hampton. Which reminds
me of a discovery I recently made at the Princeton Library,
something which has been overlooked previously by all the
professors and biographers. They assumed that Scott was
referring to himself when he wrote:

For BAOTH 2nd stanza poem

There was a flutter from the wings of God
And you lay dead
Your books were in your desk
I guess and some unfinished
Chaos in your head
Was dumped to nothing
By the great janitress
Of destinies.

How could they all have missed the dedication to Baoth? But,
coming back—Scottie and I returned to New York by train,
and some college boys, seeing my obvious condition, whistled
a popular song of the time, something about spurs that jingle
and I'm glad to be single. We laughed, but I was a bit embarrassed.

When my daugher Wendy was born, Scottie sent her one of
those snug baby cover-alls, sewn at the bottom to keep the feet
warm and with a hood for the baby's head. When she had the
first of her children, we exchanged toys. I remember the tiny
painted chair that Scottie brought to my house after she had
visited New Mexico.

Soon after Wendy's birth, I returned with her to California
and to my Hollywood job, while Scottie went to work in New
York for *Time*. We continued to write, keeping up closely with
one another's lives. I shall quote from a few of Scottie's letters
as I think they not only communicate what we both were doing
at the time but also convey the feeling of our friendship. From
her office at *Time*, she wrote:

Dearest Sheilah,

I just loved the picture of Wendy and was glad to hear from you as I had come to the conclusion that Errol Flynn had got you and you were done for—no more leaving his motor on while he saw you to the door.

(Errol had called on me after I interviewed him on the set at Warners. Luckily I was all dressed to go out when I answered the bell and soon got rid of him. It was John O'Hara who kept the engine running while he saw me to the door. He was suffering with a social disease at the time, but I remember saying to myself, "Does he think I'm going to rape him or something?")

Your description of Hollywood is marvellous . . . and your address is very glamorous—if South Palm Drive is where I think it is, it is a pseudo tropical fairyland and I envy you the tennis.

(Actually the small stucco Spanish-style house was on the wrong side of the tracks. I didn't make the right side until 1945 when I had a radio show as well as my column.)

But how on earth do you get from studio to studio? I picture you on a motor cycle with Wendy strapped to your back like a papoose, drifting from M-G-M to Paramount.

Things back East are much the same with fashionable refugees in every hotel lobby. I don't hear from Jack any more . . .

(Scottie had become engaged to Samuel [Jack] Lanahan, III. He was exactly the man Scott would have chosen for his son-in-law—a Princetonian, from a well-to-do, good, Baltimore family and very handsome.)

. . . and conclude he is in the Solomons. The job is *marvellous*, I really am ecstatic. . . . Sheilah I miss our long analyses of all phases of existence. Was going through Daddy's folder in the *Time* library the other day and came across a note by one of the reporters: "Contacted Sheilah Graham—she is very beautiful and charming." There is a folder about me which I think might amuse you—one clip says "Born Frances Scott etc. etc." then a yellow slip of paper saying, "As yet shows no artistic leanings"—and that's all! That's a hell of a classification is all I can say.

> Much love to you and
> Wendy . . .

Here is another letter with the March of Time letterhead:

> . . . I *loved* my Christmas present and couldn't believe my eyes! Nor my legs when I got them on. It was the first time I had a pair of nylons in six months
> . . .

(It was hard to get them in the war.)

> . . . Saw your friend the other day in the elevator of *Time* and he looks very sad without you. I suspect he has joined the bread line of broken hearts waiting for the crumbs of interest you have in anything but Wendy (block that metaphor) . . . I say this nastily as I am jealous of all these admirers you have. It is preposterous that a woman should all her life have the equivalent stag line at her feet as a girl of seventeen! . . .

Before long I was hearing from her on notepaper with her new initials, F.S.L.:

Dearest Sheilah,

The enclosed clipping tells most of the hard facts. What it doesn't describe is the frenzied activity the week before the wedding from Monday night when I saw Jack for the first time in seven months and the big decision was made, to Saturday afternoon when we finally got our licence after a series of adventures that would make your hair stand on end. To begin at the beginning, Jack is on, I think I told you, an aircraft carrier. They must have gotten bored with the Pacific or something, anyhow they suddenly up and sailed through the Panama Canal and put in at the Brooklyn Navy Yard to have some new guns put on, a stroke of unparalleled good fortune. I'm so damned glad I married him as he was undoubtedly the destined spouse. . . . The wedding was I think very nice. We had about a hundred people and Sheilah I do so wish you'd been there. I really missed you and silently drank your health. The Perkins, Judge Biggs, the Murphys, the Myers and Edmund Wilsons, the John O'Haras, the Finneys, Laws and Mrs. Turnbull came up from Baltimore. We had a Catholic wedding thanks to cousin Tom who did some tall winking as I don't think for a moment he was fooled as to my theological views. Pictures will describe it better than I can. The Mama situation was a little touchy but she couldn't get reservations . . .

(We had thought Zelda was attending which is why I couldn't.)

. . . so it was very neatly settled . . . Sheilah, I loved my wedding dress and you were *wonderful* to buy it for me . . .

(Nancy Milford, in her book *Zelda*, erroneously stated that Mrs. Ober had bought the wedding gown. I asked her to correct this in future editions, but so far as I know, she didn't.)

. . . My dress was sort of lavenderish dusky pink, very pale and beautifully floaty, and came from Milgrims. It was $55 . . .

(I had sent her a check for $100.)

. . . so I return the surplus with many thanks . . .

(I sent it back for her to buy some luggage—you could do so much more with less money in 1943.)

> . . . I really do wish so you'd been here, after all our discussions about men, marriage and life! I wish Wendy had been a boy so if I could have had a daughter in the next couple of years they could have gotten married. Perhaps your son, who I maintain will be born before very long, will still have the jump on little Cecelia as *my* daughter will be called . . . Very much love and thanks again many times for my beautiful wedding dress . . .

I shall quote from just one more of her letters, although I have many others. I always keep letters I like.

> Dearest Sheilah,
>
> I've been waiting for pictures of the wedding, so I could send one along with a letter. Apparently they are never coming . . .

(I can't remember receiving one but I must have eventually.)

> . . . I want to thank you again for your superb wedding present. All this and the wedding dress too. And of course I used the charming little suitcase on what I shall laughingly call my honeymoon (two days). Anyway your fine present is neatly tucked away in The Bowery Savings Bank—of all unromantic sounding places, and will buy much fine glass and china after the war. Lately I've been doing much thinking about Daddy because I've had to go through reams and reams of correspondence before turning the impersonal part over to the Princeton Library. It has been absorbing but has left me so confused I doubt whether I shall ever completely know him. I can't figure out whether he was wise or foolish, rational or irrational, etc. etc. and would very much like to talk to you some more very soon. The further away from me it gets, the more curious I become to really

understand him as a person, not as a father I didn't get along with. I long to see you Sheilah—please come East soon. At least write me a long letter *please.*

Love to Wendy

Rereading Scottie's letters to me, I seem to be boasting about my generosity to her. This is not my intention. I am generous only for the pleasure that I get—so there's no merit in that. It gratified me to be of help to Scottie, especially since she received no immediate legacy from her father. When Scott died he left $706 in cash, of which $613.25 went for burial expenses, $13 in a drawer in his desk "For emergencies," and an insurance policy for $250,000 that had dwindled to $30,000 through much borrowing against it and nonpayment of premiums —barely enough to keep Zelda in the sanitarium. It was only because some of Scott's friends—the Murphys, Judge Biggs, and Perkins—paid for Scottie's tuition at Vassar that she was able to finish her college education. She herself wanted to quit school and get a job. But I—eager to see Scott's wishes adhered to—impressed upon her and upon Judge Biggs, Scott's over-riding concern that his daughter have her graduation.

Scottie reaps the advantages of being Scott's daughter, while I suffer some of the disadvantages of not having been married to him. This is a fact, but it has never clouded our friendship. I was so pleased with her letter to *Weekly Variety,* late in 1958, after the paper intimated that *Beloved Infidel* had annoyed her: "Not only did I love the book," she wrote, "but there is nothing that Sheilah Graham could ever do that could make me angry with her." She must have told something of this to her children, because they have always treated me with affection.

I wish Scott had been alive to know Scottie's children. I am sure he would have been far less strict with them than he was with her. But he would have taken them over as he did everyone else he loved.

I know, too, that he would have been delighted with Scottie as she is today. She is a good human being, relaxed and popular. Also, she is a great organizer and gracious hostess in Washington society. She and her husband "Jack" Lanahan gave a party for Adlai Stevenson the night of the 1956 presidential election. They had hoped he would win—Scottie worked hard for his campaign. When he lost the party continued.

The only adverse effect of her parents that I can see on Scottie is a vagueness about dates and such. For instance, when I came to Washington in 1959 to talk to the Women's Press Club about *Beloved Infidel*, Scottie wanted to meet me. I gave her the time of arrival, but she went to the station two days before and was sure I had given that date. Perhaps the vagueness was necessary to put a sheet of lead between herself and her adolescence.

That first time in Washington, Scottie had wanted me to stay with her, but I was jittery and preferred to be by myself in a hotel. I was nervous about the next day's talk because I knew those gals would be laying for me, and they were. A gossip-columnist mistress to write a book about her experiences with a famous author! But with Scottie sitting next to me at the head table on the dais, the worst question I was asked was, "Why did you have a collaborator?" It was because I wasn't sure I could do Scott Fitzgerald justice, and I wanted an expert to help me put the book together.

One Easter I brought my son and daughter to Washington to see the great capital. Scottie took us all in tow—to the Congress, Senate, subway, Lincoln Memorial, etc. Does anyone wonder why I like Scottie with all her affection, sweetness, and friendship.

6.

THE DRINKER

WHILE SCOTT WAS alive, I made little effort to understand his drinking. All I knew was that it transformed him from a man of quiet charm into a belligerent bully. In the early phase of a binge he was still charming—a sparkling wit and organizer of other people's amusement. And then suddenly, with the one drink too many, he was horrible—rude, boastful, wanting to fight everybody. I loved him without reservation when he was sober. When he was drunk, I had mixed feelings, sometimes wanting desperately to get away from him. But as to why he drank, I gave this little consideration. I just accepted that he did.

In the years since Scott's death, I have thought seriously about his drinking, wondering and trying to analyze when the kind Dr. Jekyll became the monstrous Mr. Hyde. It all started, I think, because of his desire to be popular and daring, to keep up with the times—the permissiveness of the new motorcar society, then Prohibition and the recklessness of the "lost generation" after the world war. Also he had to cope with the excitement and pressure of his young success. Scott wanted to be the best, but he was always unsure whether he was entitled to sit with the people he admired. He drank when he was successful because the world seemed too dazzling to be seized without some support. To keep his energy flowing and maintain his position as the madcap of the intelligentsia, he had to keep on drinking. Then, when he was considered a failure, the support—liquor—was even more necessary for this man who bloomed with acceptance and applause. His sense of diminished vitality now haunted him. He needed the liquor to give him the illusion of his old brilliance or to help him forget that he had lost it.

Sober, Scott could accept the reality of his maturity. But however I respected him for precisely this maturity—the sureness of his knowledge, the absence of any need to put on a show—to him it was a painful reality, a falling off from the glitter of his youth. And perhaps the discipline he exerted on himself when he was sober, to write and function at a good level, was building up tension that could only be relieved in the alcoholic release, where he would yield himself to the other, utterly undisciplined extreme of his personality. Drunk, he would explode the inner sores that had been festering.

It was shattering for me because the sober periods were long and productive, especially in the first eighteen months that I knew him. To hear this man who normally frowned if you said "damn it" use foul language and wear filthy clothes, reflecting the turbulence he felt inside him, horrified me. A man who was as mature as Scott had become was ridiculous when he drank. Watching him chase a bellboy around a hotel room or tear out a stairway railing, or listening to his account of the drunken escapades of his past, I felt I was seeing and hearing about someone who bore no relation to the man I loved.

Recounting to me the pranks of his legendary drinking days, Scott never explained or excused his behavior. He simply stated it as an historical fact. At the age of fifteen he had graduated from sweet sherry to hard liquor. He felt he was ahead of his group. Then, at Princeton, he gained a reputation as a heavy drinker. He passed out when he was elected to Cottage Club, and was later on suspended from the club for making a drunken fool of himself. "I only knew about the suspension," Scott told me, "when they threw me out the window."

Why, I wonder, should he have taken a sort of pride in such an incident? Was he already building up his legend, creating a personality which would make him the equal of the Anglo-Saxon Easterners he idealized? Scott spoke to me at length of his admiration for the football heroes, the top polo players such as Tommy Hitchcock, and intellectuals like John Peale Bishop and Edmund Wilson, who knew, it seemed to Scott, precisely who they were. He never felt quite up to these people. But drinking, he could make a spectacular stir, and forget his own insecurity.

Later on in Paris, it was the same with Hemingway or James Joyce—to prove his respect for Joyce, Scott threatened to throw himself out a window. After he had left—by the door —Joyce remarked, "That young man must be mad." Mrs. Edith Wharton, who was not only a famous writer but also the scion of a New York society family, provides an excellent example of Scott's unsureness. "When I was invited to visit her at her home outside Paris," said Scott, "I blurted out that an American couple I knew had spent three days in a Paris brothel, believing it to be a hotel." When he stopped from embarrassment, Mrs. Wharton demanded majestically, "But Mr. Fitzgerald, your story lacks data." No wonder she wrote "Horrible" after his name in her diary. Of course, he had been drinking, as he seems to have been doing all the time he was in France.

Zelda also was often drunk in the 20s. The Fitzgeralds were intoxicated—with gin and with their image—when Dorothy Parker espied them riding outside a New York taxi—Zelda on the hood and Scott on the top. They were in the same condition when they started to undress at the Follies and were hustled out. Drinking in New York City, drinking in Westport, drinking in Great Neck, Long Island, drinking in Paris, they played their scenes of restlessness and bravado. And when they behaved badly, Zelda wrote the apologies the next day. Scott rarely remembered what had happened. Unlike Scott,

Zelda drank mostly because it was the smart thing to do and she wanted to maintain her reputation for gaiety and irrepressible conduct. She had no problem stopping, with the first of her sanitariums or when she abandoned her flapper image to immerse herself in the ballet.

With Scott the drinking was more insidious—a reflection of a certain deficiency he felt in himself. He makes a revealing comment to Max Perkins in a letter of 1924:

> . . . I feel I have an enormous power in me now, more than I've ever had in a way, but it works so fitfully and with so many bogeys because I've talked so much and not lived enough within myself to develop the necessary self reliance. . . .

And six years later, writing to Zelda about their collapsed lives, he looks back on their frenetic activity, evaluating it as his attempt "to make up from without for being undernourished from within." Certainly his drinking, which, as he says, could give him back his self-esteem "for half an hour in the Ritz Bar," was part of this rather sad quest. I always considered Scott such a confident, secure person. What a different impression emerges from these letters.

Even more frightening than his confession to a sense of emptiness, and for me even more difficult to understand, was the allure for him of self-destruction. During his time with the advertising agency, before the publication of *This Side of Paradise*, he writes a shattering sentence in a 1919 letter to Edmund Wilson: "I tried to drink myself to death." I think this was partly, but not entirely, bravado.

Another letter of 1925 to Max Perkins reads:

> . . . You remember I used to say I wanted to die at thirty—well, I'm now twenty-nine and the prospect is still welcome. My work is the only thing that makes me happy—except to be a little tight—and for these two indulgences I pay a big price in mental and physical hangovers. . . .

His drinking and his work—both, he says, make him happy and both deplete him. I believe that some of the drinking was a conscious effort to create incidents for his fiction. Scott envied Joseph Conrad, with all his experience of the sea to draw on, who was forty years old when he began his career as a novelist in the English language. Scott, on the other hand, was a famous author before he had done much living. To fill his books, he had to create his life, to make it as fascinating as possible. The drinking heightened his experience—as Rimbaud did with drugs—and yielded material for fiction. It was then almost impossible for Scott to stop, even when he realized his health was being damaged. He found himself at forty looking back rather wistfully on used-up life and reflecting "that all prize fighters, actors, writers, who live by their personal performance ought to have managers in their best years."

Scott felt he had used himself up not only by living recklessly but also by the effort necessary to achieve "the sustained imagination of a sincere yet radiant world." He told me of the searching deep within himself to come up with something new, something that had not been said before. He drank, he said, to escape from the strain of this extraordinary effort and perhaps to give himself the courage to make it once again. When I heard that Kirsten Flagstad always drank a half bottle of gin before a performance because she would be giving herself so intensely, I thought of Scott. What a terrible price to pay for feeding the imagination of others.

Finally Scott reached a point where he drank because he felt there was nothing left to do but to court his own self-destruction. "The worst drinking time," he confessed to me, "was when I realized that Zelda could never be cured and that I was no longer in fashion as a writer. The eight years of working on *Tender Is the Night* had sapped all my energy. I was bankrupt emotionally, physically, and financially."

He shuddered, explaining what had almost finished him off in September 24, 1936, his fortieth birthday. Michel Mok, the reporter from the *New York Post*, asked for an interview at the Grove Park Inn in Asheville, North Carolina, where Scott was staying to be near Zelda's sanitarium. Mok had told him a sob story about how his job depended on fulfilling the assignment. Scott's shoulder and arm were in a plaster cast—he had injured himself (in mid-air, he told me) diving into a pool. The "Crack-Up" articles had recently appeared in *Esquire,* and Mok's editor thought an interview with "a cracked plate" would be titillating for his readers. The great god of youth was forty. Perhaps he was now ready to jump out of the window and end it all.

Scott, who could always press the button of charm, thought the interview had gone well. He was dismayed to the point of an at least pro forma suicide attempt when he read the newspaper article. Mok wrote of his trembling hands, the restless pacing to and fro, the frequent trips to a drawer in the chest to get the bottle, and the pleading with the nurse to let him pour "just one more" into the measuring glass by his bedside.

Discussing his generation with the reporter, Scott said, "Some became brokers and threw themselves out of windows. Others became bankers and shot themselves. Still others became newspaper reporters. And a few became successful authors . . . Oh my God, successful authors." The overdose of pills made him ill, and when the nurse cleared away the vomit, he knew he had fallen as low as it was possible to go. Shortly after this he caught hold of his thin thread of caution, and pulled himself together and in July 1937 came to Hollywood—with the determination to stay on the wagon that carried us through the early months of our acquaintance.

The first time I was aware that Scott was drinking was at the Los Angeles Airport in October 1937. It was in the period when we were still occasionally dating other people. A few days earlier I had dined with Arthur Kober, whose "Bella" stories in *The New Yorker* I enjoyed. Although Scott and I did not yet consider ourselves bound to each other, his jealousy was showing, and he told me he would phone at eleven that night to make sure I was safely at home. Throughout the date I kept looking at my watch, and I made sure that I arrived back at my house at the designated time. But Arthur started a long conversation after opening the door of his car for me. I could hear the phone ringing inside the house but didn't want to be rude to my escort, who had given me a good dinner and was obviously disappointed that I did not ask him in.

When I was able to call Scott, he punished me by saying that my tardiness had caused him to start drinking. (This was the same bout he also blamed on Ginevra King.) To me, however, he sounded quite sober. And never having seen him in his cups, I thought that he was joking. Scott, as far as I was concerned, was a totally abstemious person—I had even found myself wishing sometimes that he would take a social drink now and then like other people. As for the bender he had been on for a week, I was unaware of it until I heard him ask for a double gin at the airport lounge while we were waiting to board the plane for Chicago.

As I've previously mentioned in *Beloved Infidel*, Scott had decided to accompany me to Chicago to help me with my radio sponsors who loathed my British accent—very pronounced at that time. They didn't mind Cary Gra-ah-ant, but George Ra-ah-ft was too much. My five-minute cut-in from Hollywood was nationally broadcasted after seventy-five engineers on the route had each pulled a switch, one after the other. By the time I said, "This is Sheilah Graham from Hollywood," my voice was a breathy shriek and more British than ever. Perhaps if I came to Chicago and did my five minutes without the long pause, the sponsors would like me better. Perhaps, they grudgingly assented, but reiterated that they wanted my gossip, not my voice. Scott was determined they should have both. He appointed himself my knight errant.

I was startled but not upset when I realized that he was drinking gin, not water, as I had thought. But when I gently pushed the glass away, he grabbed my arm ferociously. I was stunned. He was normally a person of great gentleness. Now his face was angry, almost vicious.

Scott downed his double gin and ordered another. He was somewhat unsteady climbing the stairs onto the plane and totally unbalanced by the time we found our seats. I became increasingly anxious. It would be a difficult argument with my sponsors. I had been grateful when Scott offered to help me, but how could he in his present condition? My North American Newspaper Alliance Syndicate boss, John Wheeler, had always said, "He travels fastest who travels alone." And now I wanted to be alone.

Scott had a bottle of gin with him, and he swallowed the contents in large gulps on the way to Albuquerque where the plane was to stop for a refueling. In those days you came down four or five times for what Scott would describe in *The Last Tycoon* as "the sharp rip from coast to coast"—a journey of nineteen to twenty-one hours. From Los Angeles to Chicago was also an overnight trip, and the planes were equipped with two-deck berths for sleeping.

Scott had been talking to the other passengers, telling them who he was and what a great writer he was and what a great lay I was. I felt I simply had to get rid of him. "Okay, baby, okay," he slurred when I asked him to get off the plane. "You'll always be a lone wolf like me. I'll go. Good-bye."

I was lying in my lower berth, thinking about his "lone wolf" words and feeling sorry for myself because I thought they were true. I was sad, too, because I knew it was over with Scott and I was beginning to love him so much. Why had I made him leave? The plane was taxi-ing for the take off. My throat constricted, and I was crying softly when the curtains of my berth parted. There was Scott, flushed and grinning devilishly with a bottle of gin sticking out of his coat pocket. This is what he had got off to buy—he had had no intention of parting from me. I was delighted to have him back, drunk or not. I took him in my arms. He lay beside me and slept until I awakened him as the plane descended at the Chicago airport.

It was my first experience of drunkenness at close range, and I thought, well, it isn't *too* bad. But that was only the beginning. At the Ambassador East Hotel we had two bedrooms, opening into each other. Scott came into my room with his bottle of gin. There was no enjoying his liquor, just pouring it down his throat. When a small busboy brought him another bottle and waited for a tip, Scott ferociously chased him around the room and to the door where he escaped.

It was a nightmare I can never forget. When my sponsor

arrived, Scott demanded, "Well, does she or does she not go on the show tonight?" The man hesitated and then said, "Well . . . ," whereupon Scott punched him in the mouth. He agreed through bloodied lips that I could go on, and I hurried him through the door. When I closed it behind him, I promptly had hysterics, lying on the floor and kicking my legs as I have seen my tiny grandchildren do, and screaming at Scott, "You have ruined me! I hate you, I never want to see you again!" Scott left, but appeared at the rehearsal hall, conducting me with an imaginary baton, now mincingly soft, now blaringly crescendo.

In the film version of *Beloved Infidel,* Deborah Kerr pleaded "Scott, Scott." *I* cried, "For God's sake, someone get him out." Then there was the agony of trying to sober him up with the help of Arnold Gingrich, the editor of *Esquire* magazine (who advised me to keep him in a taxi until the next plane, which was five hours later). I had to get him back to Hollywood where he was due at M-G-M in the morning to work on the script of *Three Comrades.* He finally made it to Hollywood, but he wasn't able to work for several days. He sent a message to the director, Joe Mankiewicz, that he was sick. There was some consternation at the studio, where they were well aware of his drinking legend.

Scott realized this could be the end for him in Hollywood, and there was nowhere else to go. "I'm getting a nurse and I'll sober up," he told me. "You are not to phone me or visit me until I am all right again." He was worried that after his awful behavior in Chicago—oh, those four-letter words, every one you can think of—that his position with me was precarious. It was.

After getting him back to the Garden of Allah, I decided not to see him again. When I flew to Chicago the following weekend to do another show, I informed him, "I'm going alone." And in truth he was too weak to put up an argument. He saved that for when I called him from Chicago after my performance to say I was going to New York for a few days (where a man I had been in love with was eagerly awaiting my arrival). I had earlier told Scott about him. "I suppose you will see him," said

Scott. "I suppose so," I said cruelly. I had had it with him. I was not going to be tied to a drunk for whom I had given up being a respected Marchioness. He had called me a "cunt" to the film critic of the *Chicago Daily News*. Well, he wasn't going to have this one anymore to boast about.

Then in a quiet, serious voice, Scott said, "If you go to New York, I will not be here when you come back." I realized that he was capable of fulfilling such a threat though he needed the M-G-M salary for Zelda and Scottie. And if he was prepared to go to such lengths to have me return, he really loved me and I must go back to him. It was like someone saying, "I'll kill myself if you leave me." I did not go to New York.

As for the radio show, it was cancelled. After that second try in Chicago the sponsors were more emphatic than ever that they loathed my British accent. So after a total of five shows —three previously in Hollywood—they asked to pay off my six-month contract, hoping I would take a settlement to be free to do radio for someone else. I had no intention of doing that. I made them pay for every week of those six months. Radio had terrified me—on the air I somehow couldn't breathe. I was relieved the show was over, and it was lovely getting the $200 a week without working for it. This has been a rare event in my life.

Scott's drinking continued intermittently, usually beginning innocuously with a bottle of beer. He'd say apologetically, "I'm only having beer, that's all. No liquor, I promise." But this would build up to dozens of beers a day and no food at all and then inevitably to the hard liquor. Finally, when Scott felt he had punished himself, the world, and me enough, he would call for a doctor and a nurse and start the painful drying out process. One of the nurses revealed to me, "He can't hold any solid food down and this can last for several days. He is fed glucose intravenously until he can. He becomes terribly dehydrated and weak and depressed."

As soon as Scott was more or less normal, he would telephone me and we'd resume seeing each other. At his request I never saw him in the drying out periods. The claim of the *Crazy Sundays* author that I was Scott's nurse when he collapsed from the withdrawal from alcohol is completely erroneous. I have nursed my children when they were ill but never Scott Fitzgerald when his sickness was the result of drinking. As I have already asserted, our relationship was not that of nurse and patient. It was based on mutual respect. And fearful of losing mine, Scott kept me away until his agony was over. Once he described the DTs to me in full skin-crawling detail—how in 1935 he saw beetles and pink mice scurrying all over him and elephants dancing on the ceiling. But he recounted this in the same vein in which he joked he would like to walk on a heap of newborn babies and hear them squish. Scott sometimes had a macabre sense of humor.

All his caution to show me his strongest side and to spare me his degradation vanished, however, when he was actually drinking. Then his ambivalence toward me erupted with a vengeance. And his actions were calculated to shock and insult me.

The beach house at Malibu in the summer and early fall of 1938. If I had known what was going on in the locked room between Scott and Nunnally Johnson, I think I would have left him then. Scott would soon be leaving the beach for the warmer climate of Encino, and he had decided to give an afternoon party. The usual group was there—Eddie Mayer, Herman Mankiewicz, Dorothy Parker, Alan Campbell, Bill Warren, whom Scott had known in Baltimore and sent on his way to Hollywood—Bill was to produce the very successful "Gunsmoke" television series—Nat West and his wife, Joe Swerling, the writer who had the house next door, John O'Hara, and Nunnally.

Scott organized a ping pong tournament for the adults, another game of seeing who could get to the bar first, which he won, and card tricks for the group of children who had been looking wistfully from over the fence until he invited them over—I remember the Swerling boys and, I think, Loretta Young's small daughter among them. Some of the guests were in swim suits, though Scott wore his usual sweater over gray flannel pants. There was no chill, however, to his ebullience. He was having a merry time at the bar, as always very active in the early stages of drunkenness. Restless as though he must go somewhere, he reminded me in his movements of the way Groucho Marx sort of shrank and walked fast with his head forward. Seeing that he was getting more and more inebriated, I went into the house and took away his car keys. We had agreed that when he was "tight" I was to keep his money and his car keys. He usually scattered the money, and it was dangerous for him to drive.

With the sun going down, Nunnally, who was between marriages at the time, told Scott he had to leave. He was taking a girl to dinner in town. "Oh no, you don't," said Scott, leading him into his bedroom and locking the door. The rest of the story I heard later from Nunnally. Somewhat alarmed, he asked why he shouldn't leave. "Because," Scott shouted, "you'll never come back here. Never." "Of course I will, Scott," Nunnally tried to reassure him. "Oh no, you won't," roared Scott. "Because I'm living here with my paramour. That's why you won't."

It was a quaint expression even then—a married man's illicit lady. I suppose I was, but that was not how I regarded myself. When Scott was drunk he had called me worse names than a paramour, but I never believed that this was how he really felt about me, so completely did I separate the drunk from the sober man.

When the guests from the party had departed, Scott found the car keys in the drawer of my dressing table and drove at breakneck speed to the local liquor store. He could have been killed or been arrested, but, as Robert Benchley once said to me, "God takes care of drunks and little children." I had my own car but there was no use going after him. When he returned, he took a long swig from the bottle of gin and then, fully clothed in pants, shoes, sweater, and all, for the first time since we had been at the beach, plunged into the ocean—this man who never swam or played tennis or went into the sun because it was bad for his TB.

He was a funny sight, floundering in the waves, and it made me laugh. I admired him his abandon, I who was always so careful about the correctness of my public behavior. I was worried as well. If Scott had gone out too far, I could not have saved him because, while I love swimming, I'm not good at it. The weather in my native England is not conducive to swimming at the beach, and my orphanage did not have a swimming pool. Sometimes when I dreamed about the orphanage it had a pool, tennis courts, and all the luxuries that go with expensive private schools.

The drinking was somewhat better at the beginning of the year and a half Scott spent in Encino. He loved the big house with each room downstairs leading into the next, so that from the living room with all the doors open in between you could see into the dining room, the big kitchen, and the pantry that led to the large courtyard.

But after a few months the whole process started up again; beers by the dozen, then gin or whisky—anything that contained alcohol. It always took me a while to catch on when he switched from the beer. Reversing the usual pattern, Scott seemed to drink more as he got older. In Encino he remained considerate and charming until one day I found eleven empty gin bottles in a drawer and stupidly confronted him with them. In defiance he became more sozzled. After a hellish week he collapsed and called in the doctor and the nurse, while I returned to my apartment in Hollywood until he sobered up and sent for me.

One night he called me at five in the morning. It seemed the nurse had gone out for a while. Would I, he asked, come to Encino and sit with him until she returned? I drove over Laurel Canyon, pleased that he must be over the drying out, and raced upstairs to his room where he was in bed, looking flushed and impish, but seemingly sober. He was not, and had the grace to say, "You'd better go home. The nurse will soon be here."

Leaving the room, I saw the gun in an open drawer, grabbed it quickly, and was on my way when Scott tackled me with a thirty-yard leap, or so it seemed. Realizing the gun was slipping through my fingers, I flung it away and slapped his face as hard as I could. (He returned the slap in spades on his final binge.) The next day when I had cooled down, I telephoned his house only to learn from the beautiful black housekeeper that he had left to visit his wife, and would not be back for at least two weeks. At first I pretended I didn't care, but as the days followed, I longed to have him back. But after that slap, would he have me?

I was frantic, and called again and again. I wanted to apologize. How could I have humiliated him so much? When he returned, the housekeeper told him of my calls, and after some delay he did get in touch with me, though his voice sounded very cold. "Yes," he said distantly, I could come over for dinner.

He was sober, having spent two weeks in a New York hospital after taking Zelda to Cuba and behaving by far as the more insane of the two. As soon as he was hospitalized, Zelda returned to her sanitarium.

When Scott began to thaw, he soon melted altogether. He told me of the cockfight, of being beaten up when he tried to rescue the cock, and of going to New York with Zelda where he had threatened to throw a waiter down the elevator shaft at the Algonquin Hotel.

A few months of heavenly sobriety. It was now mid-1939. He and I began the two-year education course he had mapped out for me. Then, late in the same year, the last and terrifying time of The Great Binge. I had found him giving two hoboes he had picked up on Ventura Boulevard all of his good clothes, and his money. I ordered them to leave or I would call the police. After they had gone, with Scott protesting, "They're my frenshs—you go," I set about preparing him some tomato soup. Frustrated, he picked up the plate and flung it and its contents against the wall. I thought, it is dripping like blood. Scott then slapped me hard on my right cheek. I stepped back when I saw he was winding up to hit me on the left. "I'm going to kill you," he shouted, following me into the kitchen where I would escape to my car in the courtyard.

I walked slowly, realizing that in his present state he could be dangerous. He ran ahead of me and stood with his back to the kitchen door. "You're not leaving here alive," he hissed dramatically. I sat on top of a low group of cupboards and swung my legs, nonchalantly I thought at the time. As my daughter once told me, I am usually cool in times of real crisis.

Scott left the door and came to the telephone which was next to where I sat. He called Frances Kroll, his secretary, and said he needed to know where his gun was as he thought he heard some prowlers. Frances and I had hidden the gun when he started drinking. It was in a top cupboard, an arm-stretch from where we were. Luckily for us both, she said she didn't know. Scott returned to the door. I then called the police and without giving any names informed them I was being held against my will at the address, 5521 Amestoy Avenue. They would be right over. And then Scott let me go. Sad, frustrated man, wanting to destroy everything and everyone who loved him so he could die in his own way. But the resilience of his nature always vied with his self-pity and self-destructiveness. A week later I received a typewritten letter from Scott's secretary.

Dear Miss Graham,

Mr. Fitzgerald is himself again, after six days in bed, and everything he did seems perfectly abominable to him. He wants to know if there is any material way in which he can partially atone for the damage. He will, of course, replace anything, and more particularly he wants to know if it will be any help if he leaves Hollywood for good . . .

(I doubted whether he would leave Hollywood. But the ploy had been successful once, so, he reasoned, why not try it again?)

. . . He has no idea where you are [of course he knew where I was] nor has he any intention of trying to see you. He merely wants to remove as much of the unhappiness as is possible from what he did to you.

Sincerely,
Frances Kroll

I knew that Scott had dictated the letter, and when Frances called, I told her not to bother me. But after vowing I would not see him ever again, I of course went back to him.

Normally when Scott sobered up, we did not discuss his drunk behavior. But after the excesses of this terrible time, he talked to me about his misguided reliance on liquor, particularly to help him write. Several of the Pat Hobby stories, which he agreed with me were hack work, had been dashed off under the influence. But liquor, he realized, no longer helped him to write anything good. He assured me he would never drink again. I didn't quite believe him but I loved him. He was sober up to the day he died, a year and a month later, during which time he worked on *The Last Tycoon*, my education, and a couple of jobs in the studios. But why didn't "whatever gods may be" allow him another few months to finish the book?

Perhaps it was simply not in the cards for Scott to be an old man. Perhaps he was right that a person can use himself up—physically, if not emotionally. The excesses of his twenties and thirties were too much for his forties, and that's what killed him. Few young people who go in for riotous living survive beyond middle age—"are in the grave," as Scott had written his daughter.

When I think now of the abuse that Scott inflicted on himself, it's a miracle that he lived as long as he did. Aside from his drinking there was, drunk or sober, the incessant smoking and also the reliance, when not drinking, on coffee and dozens and dozens of bottles a day of Coca-Cola. He would line up the Cokes all around the walls of his office at M-G-M and announce, "I'll drink these up, and when they're gone I'll go back to beer." Dr. Richard Hoffman, who had examined him in New York, told my *Beloved Infidel* collaborator, Gerold Frank, that Scott drank—both the liquor and the Cokes—because he had the reverse of diabetes, an insufficiency of sugar in the blood. Is this true for all who drink unwisely?

Scott's heart had always been strong, but with such abuse—the liquor, the Cokes, the cigarettes, the sleeping pills at night, the pep pills to get him started in the morning—and so much digitalis—it's not strange that the heart, the only organ "that can repair itself," weakened. He took as many as six Nembutals a night—after his death, two would knock me out for days. When I first saw him take this quantity, I called his doctor because I was worried. But the doctor said, "Oh no, it won't upset him. He could take ten." This doctor also prescribed the great amount of digitalis for him. I always thought it was excessive.

It has seemed a sad irony to me that Scott should die after staying sober for more than a year. But perhaps with so much past strain on his system, his heart could not handle the withdrawal of the liquor that had acted as a stimulant for a quarter of a century.

Had Scott lived to finish and see the publication of *The Last Tycoon*, I wonder if he would have gone back to drinking. I did not think so, provided the novel was a success. But, now, I don't really know. If it had been a failure, then I think he would have committed suicide. But if it was a success—coming after "The Crack-Up," when he felt he was absolutely finished both in personal relationships and in working, to be accepted by the world again as a great author might, I hoped, put him on the right track for the rest of his life.

Recently, I voiced this opinion to a friend of mine who is a psychiatrist, and he disagreed with me. "I think," he told me, "that life would never offer perfect rewards for a person like Fitzgerald. What he wanted was the recapture of his marvelous youth, and that was gone forever." My friend also judged that without the help of psychoanalysis to understand his condition, Scott inevitably would have felt new stress, whether from success or failure, which he would have been unable to cope with.

I can imagine Scott's response to this prognosis. He believed in psychiatry for Zelda, but not for himself, or for that matter, for me, to whom he said, "Your impulses are all near the surface. Therefore, you would never need analysis." I was pleased then; now, I believe he was wrong. Of all people I know, I have needed it most—or why do I still carry the scars of my childhood? As for Scott, he felt that he knew far more than the psychiatrists about human behavior, a point he set out to illustrate when I got him together with Dr. Hoffman in New York.

I had met Scott at the Weylin Hotel in New York, after his disastrous trip with Budd Schulberg to Dartmouth in March 1939, to work on Walter Wanger's *Winter Carnival*. He was drunk and ill, and not quite knowing what to do, I contacted the psychiatrist to come to the hotel and talk with him. I left them together in my room, and when I came back, it was Scott who was psychoanalyzing and obviously charming the doctor.

Scott resisted my idea for him to get outside help for his problems. After one bad drinking period, I suggested that he join Alcoholics Anonymous. "I was never a joiner," he replied contemptuously. "AA can only help weak people because their ego is strengthened by the group. The group offers them the strength they lack on their own." Scott would never acknowledge that in the area of his drinking he was a weak man. He had been treated like a god and loved by a goddess—Zelda. It was unthinkable to him that he would sit around with a bunch of boozers and ask for help. If he wanted to stop drinking, he felt he could. But until the last year, he wasn't convinced of the need to stop. When Zelda's doctors suggested to him that it would help his wife if he gave up liquor entirely, he had protested that his drinking was his own business with no bearing on her condition.

Understanding someone else's compulsion is a difficult task. I see now that it was simple enough for me to come up with AA or psychiatry as a solution to Scott's drinking. But I don't have any notion, really, of what it's like to be an alcoholic. One whisky sour makes me a little giddy, and as I know that another will make me ill, I never order it.

The closest I can come to understanding his craving for liquor is in my own mania to overeat. My life in the orphanage with its dearth of good meals and affection created insecurities in me that I quench, not with alcohol, but with food. A hunger for food has always been with me, and I alternate between the comfort of stuffing myself and the stringent effort of dieting because I am depressed at being fat—and since the 1950s I have been more often fat than thin.

I can therefore understand something about giving in to a compulsion which one knows is self-destructive. Aside from not helping my health, my overeating destroys my self-confidence, making me withdrawn and insecure. At those times I prefer to stay at home, wearing an old dressing gown, as Scott did when drinking. But falling off the food wagon has never been like Scott's liquor, a matter of life and death, and it has never reached the insane proportions of his histrionic intake.

When Scott was on the drink, he seemed just as mad as Zelda. You could never anticipate what he was going to do. And while this could be exciting, it became unnerving when he erupted, as he so often did, into violence or cruelty. There was the time in the summer of 1939 when he started breaking up the stairway at Belly Acres. Edward Everett Horton, who was very proud of having a once-famous author as a tenant, decided to please some guests by bringing them over for an introduction. As they entered the house, they saw Scott, sitting on the stairs, maniacally tearing out the wooden railings and hurling them down. Horton and his friends beat a hasty retreat.

When I think about this incident, I wonder if there is much difference between drunken and mad behavior. Perhaps one feels that the drunk is indulging himself whereas the insane person has no choice. And therefore one holds the drunk more blameworthy. It seems to me that Scott's drunkenness gave him the excuse to unleash his hostility on the world, to say and do terrible things to people that were part of his response to them but that he wouldn't dream of expressing when he was sober. It was Robert Benchley who, early in my time with Scott, told me about his behavior in the South of France, sending the tray of sweetmeats of an old woman vendor sky-high with a football kick. "That was awful," I told Scott when I asked him if this were true. "Yes, but I paid her," he replied. Somehow this made it worse.

Recently at the party Scottie gave for the opening of Paramount's remake of *The Great Gatsby*, one of the Fitzgerald second cousins told me of meeting Scott at a railway station in Asheville, North Carolina, and he'd really had a few, to put it mildly. A big man came swinging through a door onto the platform. Scott staggered up to him and said, "Sir, you have a big belly." The man clutched his stomach and shrank away.

Perhaps a better analogy than insanity to Scott's drinking would be the rage of a spoiled child. Life frustrated him, and when the sweets were taken away, he kicked and screamed and tried to hurt everyone. I think his friends understood this about him, though I didn't at the time. Dorothy Parker and Marc Connelly, for example, accepted the drinking and treated him as a fine writer and a beautiful person with the charm of an endearing baby that you want to love and cuddle and give things to and satisfy, but can't.

I was less tolerant of the drinking because the demands it made on me were greater than those on his friends. Scott, I think, craved infinite succor from the world, especially from the women he loved. But I was not an inexhaustible goddess. No one is. And when I failed to satisfy him, he turned on me and even wanted to kill me in his terrible frustration. When he was drinking he tried to see how far he could punish me. But there were limits to what I could take. And that I think, in the end, was my great value for him. Even though he went away to Zelda when I cried, "Enough," he always came back to me because I was teaching him, without realizing it, to accept responsibilities and limits. Looking at our time together in terms of what I might have done for him, I think this was my chief contribution to his life.

7.

THE LOVER

FOR ME, SCOTT FITZGERALD was the ideal lover. He was intelligent, sensitive, and he loved women. When I say this, however, I am thinking of when he was not drinking. One time I added up the total of his alcoholism. It came to about nine months of our three and a half years together. So it is more correct to say that Scott was the ideal lover most of the time, but with some terrible lapses.

At the beginning of my contact with the drinking, before I knew how dreadful it could be, I found it somewhat sexually stimulating. The smell of alcohol excited me—it was not a bland smell but a promise of something wild. It both frightened and enticed me, like my recurring dream of a man with an unseen face, whom I passed in the dark of a narrow street with high wet walls on each side. The man would be coming toward me, wearing a black cape and a black, broad-brimmed Spanish hat. We'd be getting closer and closer, and I would have given anything to turn back, but I couldn't. At the end, I'd meet his cavern-like eyes, the world would explode, and I'd wake up.

Scott's drinking at first reminded me of those dreams, and in its early phases we made energetic love. (With the liquor in full flow, I'd be too apprehensive, and I doubt in any case if he could have functioned.) The stimulation, however, wore off after the first few binges. By then I knew what to expect—the eventual breakdown and collapse, with a nurse around the clock. I dreaded seeing him starting on the beer.

The lover I remember, then, is not the sometimes exciting, sometimes beyond-the-pale drinker, but the sober man of amazing understanding, a man who could make any woman he was interested in feel admirable and beautiful. "Where did that gorgeous face come from?" he would ask, his head on one side, his loving eyes taking in every feature and expressing the wonder that he had been so lucky as to find me.

According to the author of a recent book, Scott boasted to him in 1935 of having had "hundreds of affairs with women." This sounds to me like Zelda having kissed "thousands of men." I doubt that it is true, not only because of Scott's shock when I numbered my lovers at eight, or because of what he told me about his past—he had been faithful to Zelda, he said, until her breakdown in 1930—but also because of his whole attitude toward women and toward love. Scott was remarkable for the wholeheartedness and fidelity of his devotion. He made one woman of absolute importance to him, lavishing on her all his charm, energy, and time. His approach to women, moreover, both in life and in his fiction, was on a spiritual rather than sexual plane. This is not the outlook of the casual philanderer.

As for another allegation in the same book—I am deliberately not mentioning the title—I am adamant in my disbelief that Scott could have had a prolonged affair with a prostitute during his 1935 stay at the Grove Park Inn in Asheville. Were there any truth in this, I'm sure he would have written about her. After all, he never wasted any material.

The only important extramarital affair which Scott described to me occurred during that 1935 summer. The woman was a married belle from Memphis. Scott told me that he had been in love with her. Certainly he needed someone in the lonely times of living in cheap rooms in small hotels, and I'm sure that he dazzled her with all his charm. But he was also wary of the involvement, making it clear to her from the beginning that they could never marry while Zelda needed him. When the infatuated woman pressed to make the liaison permanent, Scott wrote her what I consider a fairly cruel letter, enclosing a message he had received from Zelda, to underscore his wife's helplessness and dependence on him. Part of the letter, dated September 1935, reads:

> . . . Your charm and the heightened womanliness that makes you attractive to men depends on what Ernest Hemingway once called . . . "grace under pressure." The luxuriance of your emotions under the strict discipline which you habitually impose on them, makes that tensity in you that is the secret of all charm—when you let that balance become disturbed, don't you become just another victim of self-indulgence?—breaking down the solid things around you and, moreover, making *yourself* terribly vulnerable—imagine having had to call in Doctor Cole in this matter! The *indignity!* I have plenty [of] cause to be cynical about women's nervous resistance, but frankly I am concerned with my misjudgment in thinking you were one of the strong—and I can't believe I was mistaken.
> . . . You once said that "Zelda is your *love!*" (only you said "lu-uv"). And I gave her all the youth and freshness that was in me. And it's a sort of investment that is as tangible as my talent, my child, my money.
> The harshness of this letter will have served its purpose if on reading it over you see that I have an existence outside you—and in doing so remind you that you have an existence outside of me. I don't belittle your fine intelligence by supposing that anything written here *need* be said, but I thought maybe the manner of saying it might emphasize those dull old truths by which we live. We can't just let our worlds crash around us like a lot of dropped trays . . . If you are not *good*, if you don't preserve a sense of comparative values . . . your love is a mess and your courage is a slaughter.

"She finally understood," said Scott, "what I had told her at the start." But what woman ever believes what is said at the beginning?

Perhaps because I was a more independent type of person, Scott never felt the need with me to bring up his obligation to Zelda as a restraint to our involvement. He probably did not at first contemplate marrying me. I wonder if he shared Stahr's worry in *The Last Tycoon*, that Kathleen's background and exterior did not fit into his own idea of grandeur? But I never pressed Scott. And then, almost imperceptibly, we grew so deeply enmeshed with one another that in our last year together he would have liked very much to be free to marry me.

I doubt if Scott retained any reservations about us in our last year, though I remember his shock when I suggested we have a child. I thought he was going to faint. He was terribly disturbed, mostly, I think, at the idea of any further responsibilities. What a pity, though, that we didn't have a child, someone who might have looked like Scott. That I who am so careful to observe propriety could have contemplated such a flaunting of it, shows how unreservedly I loved him. This was the most fulfilling relationship—for mind, heart, and body combined—that I have ever experienced with a man and lover in my life.

So what makes a man a good lover? The ideal is not necessarily a bull in the bedroom, a label, it strikes me, that would fit a certain famous writer. In my opinion this man would be the antithesis of a satisfactory lover. To judge from his contemptuous attitude toward women, the net results of his love-making might satisfy a physical need, but the mind, where sex is born, would be a barren territory. The act by itself is important only for pleasure or if it goes wrong—fails to bring the climax. But it seems that most men can perform this duty one way or another.

I have often had the thought that Scott's nature was more spiritual than my own, which I always considered earthy. (It is interesting that Zelda drew a similar comparison; she claimed that she was more sensual than Scott.) Certainly he was an aesthetic, finely tuned man. But this did not preclude a healthy sexual appetite. As a lover, in terms of giving physical pleasure, he was very satisfactory.

Zelda had tried to emasculate Scott by telling him that he was too small in the vital area to give a woman satisfaction. I never thought of the size, as there was no doubt about the satisfaction, either during intercourse or afterward when we would lie close together, suffused with great tenderness for one another. This, I think, is what a woman cherishes and remembers even more than the exciting frenzy of sex itself.

I don't believe we ever saw one another completely naked. Because I have suffered life-long embarrassment concerning the largeness of my breasts, I always kept on my bra. As for Scott, I retain the image of him walking about the bedroom in his boxer shorts and sleeveless undershirt. But if we both had a sense of physical modesty, there was no emotional reserve between us. Our love, I have thought, was like being in a warm bath—totally suffusing and delightful and relaxing.

I know that Scott was very fond of me sexually, as I was of him. But it was what he did, how he behaved when we were *not* making love that bound me to him "with hoops of steel." The little pillow placed under my head in the bath is just one illustration of his extraordinary ability to make a woman feel loved and desirable. Knowing my shyness about my body he took care to look only at my head!

I remember the delight in his face when he greeted me, wherever it was—in the street, in his home or mine—as though his life was now fulfilled and he was happy. I can't believe this was a calculated exercise of charm. In any case, it certainly worked. My whole being melted into his.

His telephone calls to me many times a day also gave the impression that he was thinking about me constantly. "What are you doing?" he would gently inquire. "What are you thinking?" "What are you wearing?" He would tell me what he was doing at the studio, whether his work was going well, whether he was having trouble with his collaborator. And during the time I had my radio show, he would leave M-G-M for a nearby garage to hear it, then phone me afterward to say I had been good, although I hadn't been. I broadcasted too much breathing and obvious fright—you could hear me gasping from coast to coast. Perhaps this was part of my appeal to Scott. I was an unfinished product which he could mold, whereas he could do nothing like this with Zelda.

Scott also took great interest in my tour across America in 1939, delivering the lecture on Hollywood that he had written for me. This led to his famous nonduel with Billy Wilkerson of the *Hollywood Reporter*, whose reporter had filed a nasty untrue review of my lecture in Kansas City. I honestly believe Scott's outrage was not that the lecture he had written had been attacked, but that I was crying when I called to tell him about it. I had been complimentary to Hollywood in a most intelligent way and I had expected to be praised by the Hollywood reviewers. Scott, who had been drinking, called John O'Hara to act as his second in the duel; which didn't, however, progress beyond the planning stage. It was the last time he spoke to Scott. O'Hara writes about this incident in his introduction to *The Portable Fitzgerald.*

Even more than Scott's knight-errantry on my behalf, I appreciated the telegrams from him while I was on my lecture tour, sent to encourage me and let me know how much he missed me. He was always, in fact, making me feel at the center of his life. When I was in Hollywood and seeing him every day, I would receive flowers with a humorous message attached, at least twice a week.

He later told me, after I filled his Malibu house with cut flowers, that he hated them, but all during my time on North King's Road, off the Sunset Strip, he sent me sometimes a little flowering plant, but most often cut flowers in long boxes or a Victorian posy of simple flowers. There were never orchids, which he disliked, but often roses or lilies of the valley, daffodils, tulips, lovely pink blossoms on branches, and mimosa with its heavy scent. I treasured the little notes, which are now at Princeton. It interested me recently to read the letters of H. G. Wells to Rebecca West, full of his little drawings and their own private baby talk. All this was fresh to me in Scott's notes, and I would look at them constantly and smile and love him.

I once said to him, "We are on a small bridge, you at one

end, me at the other, and there's nothing in between as we come closer and closer together." Scott agreed with the feeling of this image, and he also rather jealously guarded our exclusiveness. I remember his resentment of John Boles, the singer, who flirted with me. One of Scott's cards to accompany the flowers was signed "From *Mister* Boles to you." He disliked Errol Flynn because I told him of Errol trying to date me, and Randolph Scott for calling on me at four in the morning to return my swim suit which I had left at the Santa Monica beach house he shared with Cary Grant. Also Scott was jealous —as well as intensely amused—when he heard my story about the producer and narrator of travel shorts who had moused around me on board the Aquitania, in June 1933, en route from England to New York, then crashed into my cabin begging for "quick relief," which I did not give. The idea! Scott wrote this incident down, and I think it would have appeared somewhere in a short story or novel had he lived.

I did not mind Scott's jealousy, though sometimes it could be inconveniencing. He loathed my good woman friend from New York, Margaret Brainard, and did everything he could to kill my friendship with her. When Margaret arrived in Los Angeles to begin a job as manageress for the Saks Fifth Avenue beauty parlor there, Scott insisted on taking me away for the weekend to Santa Barbara. I knew I was letting her down terribly by not being around to greet her. But my whole attitude at the time was to reassure Scott that I was his forever, no matter what. Also, I was afraid he would drink again to punish me.

There was his dread of a former friend of mine who was coming from the East for a two-day visit to California. In order to reassure Scott that he had nothing to worry about, I chose those two days to be in the hospital for a minor operation. It was something that had to be done, but nothing pressing. I remember feeling ill when I came out of the ether, and found a note from Scott saying it had been a trying day for us both. Then he came to sit with me until I dozed off, leaving another note, "Rest well, my darling." Well, I'd only gone into the damn hospital to reassure him that I would be unable to see the former friend. I don't think I would do that today. But you can do things when you're young which you wouldn't consider when you're older. Yet if he could come back today I'd be more understanding of him and glad because it was such a lovely relationship—drink and all. It was completely round. There were few holes in it.

I remember another part of Scott's note left by my hospital bedside: "Loving you is a luxury like everything else about knowing you, dear face, dear heart, dear, dear Sheilah." The jealousy looms less petulant and childish when I remember his concentrated love for me.

I always had the feeling that Scott was absorbing me and appreciating everything about me. I have never met anyone who was such a great listener. (And isn't intense listening the secret of charm?) I had made Robert Benchley laugh in my conversations, but Bob laughed all the time. Scott didn't, and this made his laughter when I said something funny all the more valuable to me. It was intimate, almost conspiratorial —sort of a choking sound as though it had difficulty coming out of his throat.

Scott not only charmed me, he also won my confidence. I told him absolutely everything about myself. And what a relief it was after all the lies I had told to get my own way or to protect myself. I had never been quite honest with anyone else. With my family I always had a life they did not know about—the dreaming on top of the bus taking me to the West End, my longing to be someone, my unconscious but relentless pursuit toward that end. With Johnny, my first husband, my Mr. Micawber, his continual business chatter about the fortune he was going to make bored me. I would shut my mind to the talk and never tell him about what I was doing when I went to supper with other men. I didn't want to distress him, and I knew he didn't want to know.

I also pretended that I knew a great deal about books and poetry—I could make a show of knowledge because my orphanage had had a decent English course—or just nod wisely when others discussed subjects I knew nothing about, such as painting and ancient Greece. But with Scott, when he said something I did not understand, I would admit my ignorance, and it gave him great pleasure to instruct me.

Scott knew every thought I had and every dishonesty of my past. I didn't have to pretend with him, nor for that matter did he with me. When he first met me, he may have softened or exaggerated some of what he had done in the 20s. But I had the sense that he spoke openly and honestly, without guilt or apology, although some of his stories shocked me as, perhaps, mine did him. We did not criticize or nag one another. We made no demands on each other to be different—except for his drinking. And I cannot remember any quarrels, except when he or I became exasperated during the drinking bouts.

Otherwise, our most intense disputes were our friendly "quarrels over England and America," which Scott refers to in one of his letters to me. He tended to downgrade the British, insisting that Americans were better, but I was then too fresh from England to take his criticism without contradiction. Of course he was mainly teasing me, but I staunchly defended my native land without either of us becoming bitter. And after Dunkirk, he had to agree with me that the British would not be beaten, that they would win the last battle, though of course with American help.

Accepting one another so wholeheartedly and joyfully, we seemed to need only each other to have the sense of absolute well-being. I can still hear the promising toot toot of Scott's car as he drove around the bend of the steep hill to the back of my rented house on North Kings Road. Sometimes he would spend the night, and a nosy neighbor opposite would remark to my maid Christine on his visits—she thought the situation was shocking and was on the point of calling in the chief of public morals. Fairly unperturbed by her prurience, Scott and I would stand on the balcony off my bedroom, which overlooked all of Hollywood, taking in the view and breathing in the then unpolluted air. We were so comfortable with one another. For the first time in my adult life, I could be completely natural and know that what I was, pleased this man I loved. Looking down on Hollywood and Los Angeles, Scott said to a friend, Corey Ford, was like contemplating the Hanging Gardens of Babylon.

I would have liked to live more openly with Scott, but there were Zelda and Scottie to consider and also my reputation in Hollywood. A gossip columnist must only write about other people on these matters. She must not live them. Her life must be completely bland—without scandal. Louella Parsons had been in love with a married man, but that was before she came to Hollywood. And Hedda Hopper, the stern judge of Hollywood morals and politics, wouldn't dream of being involved in anything that could be whispered about. When *Beloved Infidel* was published, the people I had seen every day in the studios were amazed. Hair designer Sydney Guillerof said to me, "To think you are a femme fatale!" It simply did not go with my sensible, sober, sometimes bitchy, but always correct, image.

"The ideal for us," Scott said, "is to find two houses side by side, with," he grinned, "a secret passage connecting them." In our last year together we did the next best thing, living in the next street to each other and sharing the same cook-house-keeper.

But throughout our time, whether we were in his home or mine, we settled into our wonderfully warm intimacy. We could laugh over so many small things—our shadow boxing, our dancing to records on the phonograph, the ping pong games where Scott would cross his eyes and do a fast pirouette before hitting the ball, the searching for *The New Yorker* which he insisted I had hidden.

We also both loved to read, though at first when we started doing this together, I found it somewhat difficult to sit still. Soon, though, the habit took hold, and our greatest interest in the last eighteen months was the education Scott prepared for me, which I will discuss in a later chapter. It was another way of him showing his love for me—a project to share together and evidence that he cared enough about me to want to make me more comfortable with his intellectual friends.

We were on the same wave length—today, we would say we

Sheilah—before her time with Scott.

F. Scott Fitzgerald, as he looked shortly before
Sheilah met him in Hollywood in 1937.
(Carl Van Vechten)

<u>Some interrupted Lines & Sheilah</u>

Once you were so far away
    Nothing was so far
On the edge of space you lay
    Like an outer star
Even your most tender word
    On that week we met
Was a station dimly heard
    On a short-wave set
Was a lost imperilled boat
    Sending far alarms
Oh, so infinitely remote
    Even in my arms

Now you are so near, so near
    That no furth'rest wing
Takes you where you cannot hear
    Your faint whispering
Hear the clamor of your hands
    Thunder of your eyes
Your most far-sent wish commands
    Me to Paradise —
— There! you've phoned — ten minutes late
    Driving me insane.
Why'd you make a down-town date?
    I've stood up again!

S.

A poem Scott wrote for Sheilah, here reproduced
for the first time in his own handwriting.

The Garden of Allah—Scott's home when he first went to Hollywood.

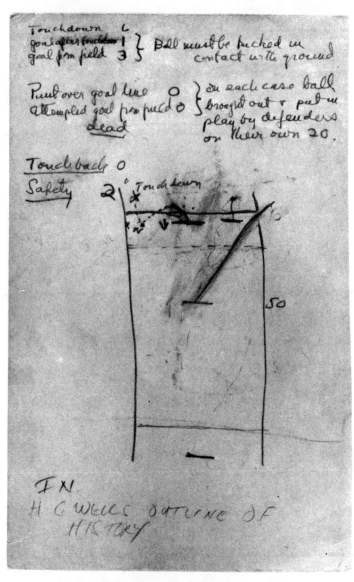

Football play Scott drew in Sheilah's copy of
H. G. Wells's *The Outline of History.*

Drawing of Sheilah done at 1939 San Francisco
World's Fair—the words *glamor girl* were written
by Scott.

Sheilah, just before her 1939 lecture tour.

Last photograph taken of Scott—Encino, 1939.

December
2
1939

Dear Sheilah:

I went berserk in your presence and hurt you and Jean Steffan. That's done.

But I said things too--awful things and they can to some extent be unsaid. They come from the merest fraction of my mind, as you must know--they represent nothing in my consciousness and very little in my subconscious. About as important and significant as the quarrels we used to have about England and America.

I don't think we're getting anywhere. I'm glad you no longer can think of me with either respect or affection. People are either good for each other or not, and obviously I am horrible for you. I loved with everything I had, but something was terribly wrong. You don't have to look far for the reason--I was it. Not fit for any human relation. I just loved you -- you brought me everything. And it was very fine and chivalrous-and you.

I want to die, Sheilah, and in my own way. I used to have my daughter and my poor lost Zelda. Now for over two years your image is everywhere. Let me remember you up to the end which is very close. You are the finest. You are something all by yourself. You are too much something for a tubercular neurotic who can only be jealous and mean and perverse. I will have my last time with you, though you won't be here. It's not long now. I wish I could have left you more of myself. You can have the first chapter of the novel and the plan. I have no money but it might be worth something. Ask Hayward. I love you utterly and completely.

I meant to send this longhand but I don't think it would be intelligible.

                              Scott

Letter from Scott to Sheilah—December 2 1939.

When I finally came to myself last
Tuesday I found this, which seems
to be yours.

It is very quiet out here now. I went in
your room this afternoon and lay
on your bed awhile, trying to see
if you had left anything of yourself.
There were some pencils and the
electric pad that didn't work and
the antenna out the window that
wont ever be the same. Then I
wrote down a lot of expressions
of your face but one I cant
bear to read, of the little girl who
trusted me so and whom I loved
more than anything in the world—
and to whom I gave grief when I
wanted to give joy. Some things
should have told you I was extemporizing
wildly— that anyone, including Scottie,
(over)

Letter of apology to Sheilah from Scott —
approximately January 1940.

should ever dare criticize you to me. It
was all fever and liquor and sedatives
—what nurses hear in any bad drunk case.

I'm glad you're rid of me. I hope
you're happy and the last awful
depression is fading a little till
someday you'll say "he can't have been
that black."

Goodbye, Sheilo, I wont bother you
any more.

Scott

Dearest Scottie:

There has reached you by this time I
hope, a little coat. It was an almost never
worn coat of Sheilah's that she wanted
to send you. It seemed very nice to
me — it may fill out your rather
thin wardrobe. Frances Kroll's father
is a furrier and he remade it without
charge!

So you must at once please
write the following letters:
(1.) To Sheilah, not stressing Mr.
Kroll's contribution
(2) To Frances praising the
style.
(3) To me (in the course of things) in
such a way that I can show the letter
to Sheilah who will certainly ask me
if you liked the coat.

You make things easier for me if
you write these letters promptly. A
giver gets no pleasure in a letter
acknowledging a gift three weeks late
even though it crawls with apologies — you
will have stolen pleasure from one who

Last letter from Scott to his daughter, Scottie.
Written in December 1940 within a week of his

has tried to give it to you. (Ecclesiastes–Fitzgerald)

Easily drum up some story for Alabama that you bought the coat from some ~~girl~~. Don't say it came through me.

For the rest I am still in bed — this time the result of twenty-five years of cigarettes. You have got two beautiful bad examples for parents. Just do everything we didn't do and you will be perfectly safe. But be sweet to your mother at Xmas despite her early Chaldean rune-worship which she will undoubtedly inflict on you at Xmas. Her letters are tragically brilliant on all matters except those of central importance. How strange to have failed as a social creature — even criminals do not fail that way — they are the law's "Loyal Opposition", so to speak. But the insane are always more guests on earth, eternal strangers around carrying x broken decalogues that they cannot read.

death and here reproduced, for the first time, in his own handwriting.

(3)

I am still not through Tom's world's novels
can't finally report it but the story of
the fire is magnificent. Only I'm afraid
that after all the grand character planting
nothing is going to come of it all. The
picture of "Amy Carleton" (Emily Davies
Vanderbilt who used to come to our
appartment in Paris — do you remember?)
with the cracked grey eyes and the
exactly reproduced speech, is just
simply perfect. ~~~~~~~~~~ ~~~~~~~~~~ ~~~~ She tried hard
to make Tom — sans success — and
finally ended ~~it~~ by her own hand
in Montana in 1934 in a lonely
ranch house. ~~~~~~~~~~~~~~~~~~~~~~~~~~~~~~
~~~~~~~~~~~~~~~~~~~~~~~~~~~~~~ I believe her
~~~~~~~~~~~~~~~~~~~~~~~~~~~~~~ absolutely.
~~~~~~~~~~~~~~

With Dearest love
Daddy

P.S. With name of Somerset Maughan, the _letter_ !

Sheilah Graham and Deborah Kerr—who played
Sheilah in the movie version of *Beloved Infidel*.
Here they are reviewing the script during the
making of the movie in 1959.

Sheilah Graham today.

had the same vibes. We could take up conversations that had started hours before as though there were no interruption. I shared his enthusiasm when he was given a new assignment, and he was always ready to listen to anything I had to say about my work. There was normally no time for gossip, though whenever anything outrageous happened at the studio, Scott would tell me about it with great relish. Or if I were upset by a star or producer or publicity man, I would tell him, usually in tears, and he became my advisor and champion, ready to take on my battles. He spent literally hours thinking up a suitable revenge against Connie Bennett who had snubbed me on the studio set, and whom Scott had known from long-ago Princeton proms. After dismissing an idea about Mickey Mouse, he produced an item which he considered suitably malicious and which I printed in my column: "Poor Connie—faded flapper of 1919, and now symbolically cast as a ghost in her last production!" (She was playing the ghost wife in a Topper picture.)

Scott and I also attended all the new films, and he was delighted to accompany me because he was learning about writing for the screen. On such occasions, however, he was extremely diffident about being noticed. He would almost hide behind me, and in the photographs taken by the studio publicity people to make me feel I was important, you would see behind me a half of Scott's hat—me, a purveyor of Hollywood gossip, and Scott, the great writer. It was ridiculous. But when he wasn't drinking, Scott, in public, tended to be very subdued. It was, for instance, a shy, almost dim man who went with me to a dinner Gladys Swarthout and her husband Frank Chapman gave for John McCormack, the Irish singer. While the other guests swirled around, Scott remained awkwardly standing alone, not talking to anyone. But he was annoyed when I patted the chair next to mine, indicating that he should come over and sit with me. This was early on in our relationship, and it taught me that I should never patronize him.

Scott was comfortable with our select friends, such as Dorothy Parker, Eddie Mayer, Nunnally Johnson, Marc Connelly, Ogden Nash, and Donald Ogden Stewart. Charades were a favorite pastime with this group. I recall how proud I was when I acted out Picasso's *Blue Period,* and it was guessed by Dorothy Parker. But most of all we enjoyed doing things with just one another. In addition to the films, we went to all the plays that came to town. I was so excited by Maurice Evans' performance as Hamlet that for once it was as hard for me to sleep as it always was for Scott. We went to concerts at the Hollywood Bowl and to art exhibitions, especially during the education period. There were the Saturday football games in the Los Angeles Coliseum and in summer our Saturday lunches at the elegant Vendome Restaurant in Hollywood, at the Brown Derby in Hollywood or in Beverly Hills, and our dancing in the evenings, particularly in the first year, at the Trocadero. Scott danced the collegiate style of the time—heads close together, rears at a thirty-three-degree angle.

Looking back, I marvel at what a full, active life we had. We also went away together for weekends, especially in the first two years before Scott was so hard up—to Santa Barbara, La Jolla, Del Monte, Monterey, over the south U.S. border into Mexico, and to the San Francisco Fair. I loved those long drives with Scott, even though he drove at twenty to twenty-five miles an hour. He would never willingly let me take the wheel, and if of necessity I was driving my own car he would be in an obvious state of acute anxiety, stiffened up and half standing in his seat with an agonized expression on his face. Why did this make me love him more and inherit his phobia after he died? I remember our singing as, with Scott at the wheel, we slowly zipped along. He taught me all the songs he had liked in the 20s. There was one especially, "Lulu," that always made us laugh. I forget most of it now except for the refrain ". . . but don't bring Lulu," which we sang with such gusto.

My attractive secretary, Pat Duff, told me she would never marry until she found a love as complete as ours. After I decided for the second time to leave Hollywood (this was after Scott's death), I gave her an introduction to the Warner Brothers. As I told them, I was doing them a favor. She was speedily promoted but gave it all up when she found the right man and married him.

Our love was complete—at least this was my sense of it. I

loved Scott with every fiber of my being. And he loved me with all that was left of his capacity to love. Since reading the biographies of him and his published letters, I have realized and accepted that his loss of health, the gaiety of his youth, and his disbelief now that life was something he could easily conquer, must have somewhat constricted the joy of his time with me. But he still retained some of what Nick Carraway describes in *The Great Gatsby*—"some heightened sensitivity to the promises of life," "an extraordinary gift for hope, a romantic readiness such as I have never found in any other person and which it is not likely I shall ever find again."

When Scott died, it seemed that he took everything we had together with him, and this made me angry. But with the passing of time, just the pleasure of the love remains and not the desolation of the loss. I have a few things around me that are my physical reminder of him—a silver jug, a heavy encyclopedia—it was my present for Christmas, 1939. I gave all my Fitzgerald books and papers to Princeton.

The antique silver jug was for my birthday in 1940. From much packing and traveling it has two small dents in one side. But when I fill it with flowers—the flowers that Scott used to send me—it seems to me, to use the word Scott chose to describe Cecelia's emotion toward Stahr in *The Last Tycoon*, that Scott blooms again.

THE WRITER

WHENEVER I SAID something which Scott thought inane, he put me down as severely as an impatient professor would a stupid student. We were at Encino and there was a glorious sunset—a yellow and green and black and "hectic red" sky that I can still remember. Scott and I were standing outside his house taking it all in when I remarked, "Oh, isn't the sky lovely." He silenced me sharply. "Don't ever tell me what the sky is like." Perhaps he had been composing a description of that sky for his notebooks and I had interrupted his thoughts with my commonplace remark. I apologized but now I find his reproof somewhat harsh and my submission to it too compliant. But I was then—as now—in awe of his talent. I have always respected talent of any kind—a good secretary, a fine dancer, composer, artist, actor, cook, and above all an excellent writer.

I had not been much impressed with *This Side of Paradise*, which I read after Scott went to enormous trouble to find a second-hand copy for me because this, his first novel, was out of print—as were all the others. "Well," I said, while he waited eagerly for my opinion, "it isn't Dickens." He was naturally annoyed. How could I have been so tactless? And even though he told me in later years that he was embarrassed by his first novel, he had hoped I would find it interesting. At that time I knew nothing of American college life and, in addition, had no idea that he had based most of the characters in the book on real-life Princeton people—Bunny Wilson, John Peale Bishop, and his first love, Ginevra King.

Nor was I more enthusiastic about his second novel, *The Beautiful and Damned*. The people seemed very silly to me, especially Anthony Patch and the girl modeled on Zelda. But I instantly loved *The Great Gatsby*, and I found some of the prose in *Tender Is the Night* as stirring as the poetry of Keats and Shelley. I was interested in what he read to me every night of *The Last Tycoon*, just a few pages each time. He worked slowly and dug deep into his gut, he told me, to make this novel about Hollywood's powerful film executives as compressed and cohesive as *The Great Gatsby*. I admired greatly some of the prose which I thought was as good as anything he had written, but I was reserving final opinion on the book—which was only half finished at the time of Scott's death.

I loved the short stories he picked out from the vast number he had written—about two hundred. My favorites were "Absolution," which *he* preferred to all the others, "Babylon Revisited," and "The Diamond as Big as the Ritz," which we saw performed in the upstairs rehearsal hall of the Pasadena Playhouse. Also "The Baby Party," based on a party given for the very young Scottie.

Some years after Scott's death, when I reread everything he had written, I realized that I had not done him full justice as a writer while he was alive. Except for a few short stories which he himself considered "trash"—especially some of the "Pat Hobbys," I now admired all his work, including the copious notes for past, present, and future use and the first two novels, which I could now appreciate for their humor and knowing who the characters were. I decided Scott was right to place himself in the ranks of Henry James, Joyce, and Conrad, and I agreed with his estimation of the particular nature of his talent. "If I had lived in another age," he had told me, "I would have been a poet. But there's no money in poetry now." In the eighteenth and nineteenth centuries poets were fashionable and well paid; in our day they got very little. "But I try to make my prose into a sort of poetry and still be paid as a prose writer." Like Shakespeare and Samuel Butler, Scott was always aware of his financial worth to the public. Dr. Johnson said that a man was a fool if he did not write for money. Scott was not a fool, and he always needed money. He studied his market and wrote prose—remarkable for its poetic quality.

My love of poetry was emotional rather than analytic. Today, some of the sentences and paragraphs from Scott's work stir me as deeply as Keats' "The hare limped trembling through the frozen grass," or Shakespeare's "Hid in death's dateless night"—two lines that Scott would repeat over and over again. And the last lines from *The Great Gatsby*: "So we beat on, boats against the current, borne back ceaselessly into the past." In such a sentence, it seems to me, Scott had realized the artistic ideal that he describes in a letter to Scottie:

> If you have anything to say, anything you feel nobody has said before you, you have got to feel it so desperately that you will find some way to say it that nobody has ever found before, so that the thing you have to say and the way of saying it blend together as one matter—as indissolubly as if they were conceived together.

I think that the whole of *The Great Gatsby* comes together in such a way. Singling out just a few of the passages that resound for me with such wholeness and with Keats' beauty and truth, I can quote: "The lights grow brighter as the earth lurches away from the sun." "In his blue gardens, men and girls went and came like moths among the whisperings and the champagne and the stars." "I saw the skins of tigers flaming in his palace on the Grand Canal." "Daisy and Jordan lay upon an enormous couch like silver dolls weighing down their own white dresses against the singing breeze of the fans." If this isn't poetry, I don't know what is.

There is also the last paragraph from "Absolution":

> The collapsed man lay there quite still, filling his

room, filling it with voices and faces until it was crowded with echolalia and rang aloud with a steady shrill note of laughter . . . Outside the window the blue sirocco trembled over the wheat, and girls with yellow hair walked sensuously along roads that bounded the field, calling innocent, exciting things to the young men who were working in the lines between the grain. Legs were shaped under starchless gingham, and rims of the necks of dresses were warm and damp. For five hours now, hot fertile life had burned in the afternoon. It would be night in three hours, and all along the land there would be these blonde Northern girls and the tall young men from the farms lying out beside the wheat, under the moon.

For me *Tender Is the Night* is sheer poetry all through, though the story is not so tightly knit as *Gatsby*. *The Last Tycoon* Scott planned as a "constructed," "dramatic" novel like *Gatsby*, and it is also full of his poetically powerful writing. I have recently reread it, and so many of the descriptions beat in my mind:

Across the four feet of moonlight, the eyes he knew looked back at him, a curl blew a little on a familiar forehead . . . An awful fear went over him and he wanted to cry aloud. Back from the still sour room, the muffled glide of the limousine hearse, the falling concealing flowers, from out there in the dark—here now warm and glowing. The river passed him in a rush, the great spotlights swooped and blinked.

And, to quote just one more passage:

The curtains blew suddenly into the room, the papers whispered on his desk, and his heart cringed faintly at the intense reality of the day outside his window . . . What would happen if he saw her again—the starry veiled expression, the mouth strongly formed for poor brave human laughter.

I could go on, but you must reread the books and short

stories, and you'll find over and over again Fitzgerald's poetic felicity, his success in the creation of "a sincere yet radiant world" because what he has to say and his way of saying it blend together indissolubly as one matter.

"In a small way I was an original," Scott wrote to Max Perkins in the late 30s, wistful at the eclipse of his reputation. It depressed him "to die so completely after having given so much." No one today would dispute his claim to originality, except perhaps to argue that there were not enough books. But interestingly, the writers who disliked Scott, such as Robert Benchley, attacked him on the grounds of his unoriginality. It was Bob's complaint that Scott went about stealing other people's remarks. And certainly there was a modicum of truth in this. Scott was never without his little notebook, and whenever he heard a good observation, he would write it down. A number of my remarks appear in *The Last Tycoon*, as did Zelda's in *The Great Gatsby* and *Tender Is the Night*. Also Scott would make use of other people's experiences—Zelda's, the Gerald Murphys', Ring Lardner's, mine. Or if he heard a story from a casual acquaintance that he thought he might use he would pay for it—"about $30 for each anecdote," he revealed to me.

Scott, nonetheless, *was* an original. His originality lay not in where his material came from but in how he fused it into his own vision and gave it his particular stamp of genius. It is indisputable that he made use of other people's lives, other people's words, and also for that matter of his own—more than from any other source he stole from his own behavior, creating himself into a character, then writing about this character's experiences. But his fiction was not just a matter of compiled anecdotes and observations. He was an extraordinarily conscientious writer, in league, he liked to think himself, with Flaubert in writing a taut story, making the right "imaginative leaps," cutting unnecessary words, polishing until his mind was exhausted.

To gain some understanding of Scott's response to Hollywood as an author, one must appreciate the great respect he had for his own talent. He regarded it as Elizabeth Taylor would regard a jewel—it was precious, and when he hurt his talent, he was angry with himself and with anybody else who helped him to hurt it, such as Hollywood producers and collaborators. However, because of his undauntable faith in his ability, he was always excited over a new script project, sure that this time he would succeed and was able to dismiss from his mind all previous frustration and failure.

I think that if Scott could have worked alone on his scripts, as he wanted to do, and if his health and the system had permitted him to direct them, he would have been completely happy in Hollywood. As it was, he did not dislike the place as much as his despairing letters to friends might indicate. Scott's letters, addressed to posterity as much as to the recipient, always struck a dramatic note. Also, it was hard not to fall in with the stock attitude of his friends, who were always complaining how they hated working on film scripts and in the studios. Metro-Goldwyn-Merde—I believe the description was Dorothy Parker's. Scott, however, never shared Dottie's cynicism. He was a natural enthusiast, always eager to make the best of any new opportunity and, less fortunately, always vulnerable to the sting of new disappointment.

When Scott was first told that he would be writing *Three Comrades* in tandem with Ted Paramore, Jr., he was fairly pleased, having known Ted in the East and respecting him as a good writer. But Scott's ideas for the script and Ted's were completely different. He expelled his frustration when he saw me. "Paramore's a hack. They've taken away his originality and talent."

Three Comrades was important to Scott. He needed the precious screen credit for his option to be taken up, when his salary would jump for another year to $1,250 a week. And, of course, he wanted the script to be good. Determined to keep the project under his and not his collaborator's control, he wrote Paramore a long letter, part of which I reproduce. It is dated October 24, 1937. They had been working together for just a few weeks:

Dear Ted,

I'd intended to go into this Friday but time was too short. Also hating controversy, I've decided after all to write it.

First let me say that in the main I agree with your present angle, as opposed to your first "war" angle on the script, and I think you have cleared up a lot in the short time we've been working. Also I know we can work together even if we occasionally hurl about charges of pedantry and prudery.

But on the other hand I totally disagree with you as to the terms of our collaboration. We got off to a bad start and I think you are under certain misapprehensions founded more on my state of mind and body last Friday [he was still weak from the big binge in Chicago (Oct 1937)] than upon the real situation. My script is in a general way approved of. [The director, Joe Mankiewicz, told Scott it was the best script he had ever read, sending Scott to heights of joy, but when it was turned in, Joe rewrote three-quarters of it, sending Scott to the depths of misery and a new drinking spree.] There was not any question of taking it out of my hands . . . The question was who I wanted to work with me on it and for how long. *That was the entire question* and it was not materially changed because I was temporarily off balance.

At what point you decided you wanted to take the whole course of things in hand—whether because of that day—or because when you read my script you liked it much less than did Joe or the people in his office—where that point was I don't know. But it was apparent Saturday that you had and it is with my faculties quite clear and alert that I tell you I *prefer to keep* the responsibility for the script as a whole . . . This letter is sharp but a discussion might become more heated and less logical. Your job is to help me, not hinder me. . . .

And so on.

Mankiewicz, not Paramore, proved the real spoke in the

wheel. But in spite of the director's rewrite, the credits for *Three Comrades* read, in smallish print, "Screenplay by F. Scott Fitzgerald and Edward Paramore, Jr." It was at least half a credit, and the only one for Scott in those three and a half Hollywood years. (Nor were there any from his previous times in Hollywood in 1927 and 1931.) How he would have enjoyed seeing his name alone in big letters on the big screen in the recent remake of *The Great Gatsby*. It made me sad at the New York premiere that this had not happened for Scott when he was alive. Today, most of the studios where he worked are digging into their vaults to resurrect some of the scripts he wrote. Arthur Knight, the film critic for *The Saturday Review*, discussed with me at a private showing of a film that we should find all of Scott's film scripts and put them into a book.

If Scott had little success in putting his ideas across to directors and producers, at least he could laugh at Hollywood's absurdity. One day he came home full of amusement at something he had learned that day—a stock bit the writers used in their scripts called "The Pratfall." He demonstrated it to me several times, laughing as he did so. It was what in *The Last Tycoon* he describes as "a double wing." This meant flapping both arms out, slapping the thighs, sort of crowing like a rooster, then falling down.

Another funny incident occurred in a story conference with George Cukor, then directing the much-directed *Gone With the Wind*. Cukor had asked Scott to make visual Aunt Pitty bustling quaintly across the room. "How," he asked me, "do you bustle quaintly across the room?" I gave him a demonstration with my rear end swinging from side to side, but it only made him laugh more. "They won't change a word of the book," he complained. "They think Margaret Mitchell is Shakespeare."

He would have been the first to insist on changing some of the phrases, beautiful as they were in print, in the last *Gatsby* movie. In a film you cannot block the action with literary description even if it is by Shakespeare—or Fitzgerald. Scott was never asked to write the script for the first version of *Gatsby*—a silent in 1926 with Warner Baxter. There was a second in 1949 with Alan Ladd. It was awful.

Except for working on the script of his own story, "Babylon Revisited," I think he was happiest writing the film for *Madame Curie*. She was in line with his new type of heroine—a worker, not too beautiful, and "endowed with a little misfortune." Hunt Stromberg was a producer he admired—he had done some polishing for him on *Marie Antoinette*. Scott was cheerful when he came to see me in the evenings after work. He was sure of a credit this time. He discussed Madame Curie's noble character with me. It made me yearn to be as fine as she was and to discover something as beneficial for humanity as radium. But after a few weeks, the inevitable happened. Someone else took over the script, although Scott continued to be paid for the rest of the three-month contract. I went to the preview and a few of his touches had been left in. But other writers had the screen accolade.

Strangely, the producers would be fascinated when he told them of his plans. But when it came to the writing, he would sometimes change what had impressed them—for the better, I thought—and they would dislike the new ideas. I especially remember the case of one of his last jobs in 1940—the scripting of *The Light of Heart*, from the play by Emlyn Williams.

The hero, to be played by John Barrymore, was a lush—the reason perhaps why Zanuck chose Scott for the job. But Scott refused to approach this sadly. He infused humor into the pathetic story of a drunk who had dropped his daughter, portrayed by Ida Lupino, when she was a baby, crippling her for life. He made his alcoholic amusing, having him in one scene dressed as Santa Claus, in line to meet a sitting Santa. That might have been kept in, but I don't think so. What I remember is Scott's gloom when they took him off the script and gave it to Nunnally Johnson, whom he had advised to leave Hollywood before it corrupted him. I have seen Nunnally quoted as saying Scott's script was unscreenable. I didn't think so then, nor do I now—although I haven't read it for some time.

Scott's most enjoyable work in Hollywood was also the worst paid. He had broken with Harold Ober as his agent (Harold could not lend him any more money and Scott took this to mean that his agent had lost faith in him) before he made a ridiculous deal with Lester Cowan, a former prize fighter turned producer. Harold had been generous, lending Scott money in many previous years, but finally he had to say, "No more." He had a wife and family to look after, and no one was sure at this time that Scott was capable of sustained writing. No one except Max Perkins, his secretary, and me, that is. We knew how painfully he was dredging up the prose-poetry in *The Last Tycoon* from the depths of his being. Scott angrily crossed off Harold's name as one of the executors of his will, a change which could have made the will invalid. It was decided that Judge Biggs would be the sole executor.

Scott made the deal himself with Mr. Cowan for "Babylon Revisited." One thousand dollars for every conceivable film right and $400 a week for ten weeks of work. Scott thereby earned a not-so-grand total of $5,000, less the writer's sweat and blood. But the money was a godsend for him, as at this time he had almost no cash at all. The $1,000 plus the salary enabled him to pay his rent and to look after Zelda and Scottie.

At first, Scott and Lester got on very well. The author admired the producer for his tough background. He was grateful for the assignment and determined to make the project a success. It was his own work, and, as he wrote to Zelda on May 11, 1940:

> I think I've written a really brilliant continuity. It had better be for it seems to be a last life line that Hollywood has thrown me. It is a strong life line—to write as I please upon a piece of my own, and if I can make a reputation out here (one of those brilliant Hollywood reputations which endure all of two months sometimes) now will be the crucial time. . . .

But with Lester's daily phone calls that went on for hours and hours, Scott became exhausted. He dreaded the ring of the telephone which he must answer.

The film was planned for Shirley Temple to play the little girl, Honoria (named for the Murphys' daughter but based actually on Scottie), and for Cary Grant to play her father, Charles Wales (Scott). "Baby, can't you see me as the gorgeous

Cary Grant?" Scott strutted, mimicking the star's British accent. (Scott's attempt at a British accent was atrocious, but because I loved him I found it amusing.) He had met Shirley at the home of her parents and was impressed with her brightness. She was eleven or twelve at the time but looked younger and could pass for the eight-year-old in the story. "She reads *Time* magazine," Scott told me. "She's intelligent and will be very good."

But Mr. Cowan caught the prevailing disbelief in Scott and hired the Epstein brothers to rewrite his script. The film was not made during or after Scott's lifetime. So exit even a partial credit. Some years after Scott's death, Lester sold the Epsteins' script to M-G-M for $100,000. They retitled it *The Last Time I Saw Paris*. And, instead of Shirley and Cary, it starred Elizabeth Taylor and Van Johnson! Mr. Cowan still has Scott's original script and has announced that he will finally put it into production. But I am not holding my breath, as Lester hasn't made a movie for about 20 years.

For his three and a half years in Hollywood, with Scott receiving just the one-half screen credit for *Three Comrades*, he came to detest the studios' handling of writers—the system of throwing them together and playing them off against one another. It was not that he disliked the notion of a helping hand. Quite the opposite, Scott always cherished a strong sense of comradeship with other writers. He was ready to help anyone he thought had talent. And in his keenness to encourage new writers, he sometimes allowed unknowns to work on his manuscripts, as Leonardo da Vinci or Michelangelo might allow a pupil to paint in a leaf or a fingernail. I heard after Scott's death that Gary Moore had worked with him a bit on *Tender Is the Night*. And he allowed Bill Warren to make a film script of *Tender* although it was not sold to the movies until 1947 when David Selznick paid $27,500 for the book as a vehicle for his wife, Jennifer Jones. By the time it was filmed, Miss Jones was too old for the role, and Jason Robards with his gloomy, hound-dog face was totally wrong for the hero based on Gerald Murphy-Fitzgerald. It was a typical example of Hollywood miscasting.

What Scott loathed about his position in Hollywood was

being at the mercy of ignorant producers and untalented colleagues. He felt particular disdain for the writers who had turned out just one successful book, then rushed to Hollywood where they failed to produce anything further of importance. They remained for the money, their enthusiasm clipped by the system of team writing, one set of collaborators taking over from the team up front, sometimes even before the preceding group had finished their work. Irving Thalberg had initiated this system of piggy back writing. Sometimes the writers would endeavor to inject a little of what they believed into the scripts. But they were a small part of a big machine. The director could change everything on the set, and the producer could fire the writer at any point. Most of them had more or less given up and were satisfied to do as little as they could.

Ted Paramore, Jr, was such a man, and Scott came to despise him. What he saw of Ted and of similar types at M-G-M and the other studios gave birth to Pat Hobby, the hack who spends his time conning producers. Pat was a shallow, rather despicable man who had no business to call himself a writer. He has been long ago found out by the producers who treat him with contempt. So, as he has to make money somehow, he cringes before them and serves as a butt for their jokes.

Scott wrote the bulk of the seventeen "Pat Hobby" stories—*Esquire* paying him $200 a piece for them—while he was at Encino during the summer and fall of 1939. It was a bad time for him—he was desperately hard up, and the studio people were not rushing to his door. It was known generally that he was drinking and most were afraid to take a chance on him. Nonetheless, Pat Hobby was definitely not based on Scott. Some people have imputed this. Such a suggestion would have made Scott furious. He always knew that he was a superior writer. Even when he felt discouraged with his chances of success within the system, he still meticulously did his best on each new assignment. His only hack work in this period, rather ironically, was some of the Pat Hobby stories which he wrote when he was drinking.

A few days after Scott's death, I wrote to Arnold Gingrich

about four of these stories which the editor had in hand but
had not yet published:

> 1443 North Hayworth Avenue
> Hollywood, California
> December 24, 1940

<u>PRIVATE:</u>

Dear Mr. Gingrich:

You know how much Scott meant to me three years
ago when I called for your help in Chicago. What he
meant to me has multiplied by three more years with
him. He died alone with me.

I want to tell you something about the "Pat Hobby" stories that I am almost sure Scott would have
wanted me to. In the first place, it was a life-saver
financially to have you buy them all, promptly and
without question. And this includes the time of his
row with you, I think last year. When he came to
himself, I know he appreciated having the "Esquire"
market. Now you know, and he knew, and I know
that some of these were very good, some fair, and
some confused and not good. Most of the good ones
at his request were published first. I don't know
which were the two in the two last editions. He
wouldn't let me see them and was quite embarrassed
when I asked him to show them to me. He said they
were terrible. So I let it go. All of the previously
published Pat Hobbies he had wanted me to read. I'd
already read them in manuscript form.

Before talking about the Pat Hobbies you still have,
I don't know whether you knew he was writing a
novel? He was three-fourths of the way through the
first draft. It had brilliant passages, but, of course, he
had intended to polish. But I know the finished result
would have been as brilliant as anything he ever
published. It might have been more brilliant. We'll
never know. I tell you this because I hope you will do
something that I know Scott would want. I think you
have four Pat Hobbies left. Against two of

them—"Two Old Timers" and "Mighter Than the Sword"—on the copies of these he had written Poor". As for "College Days"—this was written during a drinking period, and he did not read it to me so I don't know whether it was as good as the best Pat Hobby or as bad as the worst. I think you still have "Fun In An Artist's Studio" to publish. This one he liked very much. Would it be asking an awful lot of you to refrain from publishing the two Pat Hobbies he had marked "Poor"? And, if you think "College Days" not good, to refrain from publishing that one as well? It breaks my heart to have people, young people who didn't know how good a writer Scott could be, to read those bad ones and say, "Oh, so that was the sort of thing he wrote. I wonder why they made all that fuss about him?"

About a week ago I read the "Great Gatsby" again, and he was a great, great writer. I told him at the time that if he never wrote another line again, his place in literature was fixed for all time on "Gatsby". And, of course, there were passages in "Tender Is the Night" that are the best I've ever read, and I've done a lot of reading.

I'll tell you the story he liked best of all the recent stories he sent you—"Between Planes", which I believe you were going to publish under another name. Of course, there's no need to hide the identity now. I know he would appreciate it if you could publish that one next, because the next story by him that appears will naturally have a wider interest, and I think this one is the best of those you have. I think he quite liked "A Woman from 21", and I've forgotten how he felt about "On An Ocean Wave".

Yours sincerely,

Sheilah Graham

December 27, 1940

Dear Miss Graham:

I appreciate your letter very much and I may write

you again about these remaining Pat Hobby stories
after I have had a chance to re-read them.
Meanwhile, however, my instinct is to publish them
for, as I remember them, I feel that they are all better
than average. Scott was such a perfectionist that he
was sometimes prone to exaggerate both minor
excellencies and minor defects out of their
proportionate importance to the readers. This is not
to say that I feel that the Pat Hobby stories were of
anywhere nearly uniform excellence, and I was guilty
of winking at a couple of them because I felt that Scott
needed the money more than the customers needed
their money's worth, but I feel that we have already
published the weakest ones, and my feeling on the
matter now is that I would like to keep his banner
waving as long as possible.

Scott meant much more to me for all of twenty years
than I could ever possibly hope, at any time, to mean
to him. It was with a true sense of personal pain and
loss that I read of his death. Probably you will feel
that I don't know you well enough to talk about this,
but I can't refrain from thinking out loud to the extent
of telling you that if he had had your influence ten
years sooner he might have lived 20 or 30 years
longer.

You are quite right, of course, about *The Great Gatsby*.
It is one of the best books of our time. The fact that it
was barely mentioned in most of the obituaries was
infuriating. *Tender Is the Night* was a magnificent
failure. It tried to combine two books that were like oil
and water to each other. And yet, even as it stands,
there are great hunks of it that are as hauntingly
beautiful prose, as prose, as any ever written. Scott
drew the finest tone from the English language (as a
violinist draws a tone from his instrument) of any
writer this country ever had. That's why it burns you
up to see his passing commented upon in the papers
as if he were a verbal equivalent of John Held, Jr.
That, of course, is something that neither you nor I
can set right but that time will finally rectify, because
The Great Gatsby will be read and studied a century

hence when *Gone With the Wind* has long lived up to its title.

Well, let's call this an acknowledgment rather than an answer to your letter. I will read the scripts at my earliest opportunity. Meanwhile, thanks very much for your interest.

Cordially,

Arnold Gingrich,
Editor

Every one of the Pat Hobbys not only appeared in *Esquire,* but inevitably they were published as a collection, introduced by Mr. Gingrich. Some were very good, some very bad. But I know that all were interesting to admirers of Fitzgerald. Perhaps I was wrong in my initial desire to suppress the poorer ones. Some of them, though, really made me wince, as they did Scott.

Scott would have been more surprised than anyone that the Hobbys merited their own volume, for he never regarded *any* of them as his best writing. Still, it amused him to put everything he disliked about the studio writers onto Pat's back. It relieved some of his own frustration against "the practiced mediocrity." He could stand away from himself and look at the others with a tolerant smile.

Sometimes in his dealings with other writers, I thought Scott was a bit hypocritical—or perhaps he just wanted to be encouraging. The time he had criticized Thomas Wolfe, suggesting that he adopt a less verbose style, Wolfe wrote back citing Shakespeare and other wordy models and saying in effect, "What do you know? One can be too brief as well." This interchange dissuaded Scott from trying to offer further helpful criticism. Ernest Hemingway sent him an early copy of *For Whom the Bell Tolls.* This was well after the allusion to "Poor Scott" in "The Snows of Kilimanjaro" but still at a point that Scott believed he and Hemingway could never again be close. As he had written to Max Perkins in a letter of 1935:

I always think of my friendship with him as being one of the high spots of life. But I . . . believe that such things have a mortality, perhaps in relation to their excessive life, and that we will never see very much of each other.

Scott was disappointed with the new novel. "Ernest wrote it for the movies," he commented to me with a mixture of disdain and a small bit of envy. But he sent Hemingway a warm letter of appreciation, pronouncing *For Whom the Bell Tolls* "a fine novel, better than anyone else writing could do."

Likewise, Scott expressed varying opinions to me and to the author after reading Budd Schulberg's book *What Makes Sammy Run*. Never underestimating the competition, he had been somewhat apprehensive when Budd said he was writing the story of an unlikeable opportunist who becomes a Hollywood producer. Scott received a copy of the manuscript, read it carefully, then with relief said to me, "The book about Hollywood still has to be written." But he wrote Budd a letter of praise to be used as a quote on the book cover.

Scott knew his superiority to a writer such as Schulberg, but this never made him smug or ungenerous. It was his instinct to encourage and to see the best in others. His letters show this very well. They vaunt his own achievement but alongside that of his contemporaries. To Max Perkins, for example, he writes in 1925, "Together with 'the enormous room' and I think 'Gatsby,' it [Boyd's *Through the Wheat*] is much the best thing that has come out of American fiction since the war." And another letter to Perkins, this one written in 1934, deliberates:

This morning before breakfast I read Tom Wolfe's story in Scribners [*The House of the Far and Lost*]. I thought it was perfectly beautiful and it had a subtlety often absent from his work, an intense poetry rather akin to Ernest . . . What family resemblance there is between we three as writers is the attempt that crops up in our fiction from time to time to recapture the exact feel of a moment in time and space, exemplified by people rather than by

things—that is, an attempt at what Wordsworth was
trying to do rather than what Keats did with such
magnificent ease, an attempt at "a mature memory of
a deep experience."

(I could write the same for this book.)

Scott believed that certain writers of his generation such as
Hemingway, Wolfe, and himself were the equals of the great
masters. Other writers, such as Zelda and myself, he
encouraged just as avidly, but also somewhat patronizingly,
never losing sight of the distinction between our achievement
and his own. Zelda disliked the patronage and resented the
use of only his name on stories they had written together or
that she had written with Scott just editing. I didn't mind at all,
thankful for his interest in my writing and for the
improvements he made.

Scott never involved himself with my column—except to
help me in my fight in early 1940 with Connie Bennett. But
under his aegis I wrote several short stories which he then
edited. My first short story, which I titled "Beloved Infidel,"
written in 1939, concerned a woman who marries a compulsive
gambler. The night after the wedding he goes off to gamble
and is mortally stabbed in a brawl. Scott made many
corrections, including changing the husband's name from
John O'Brien to Carter O'Brien, and slightly altering the
story's ending. My last paragraph was as follows:

He was dead before the hospital was reached. Mara
remembered saying to the surprised porter, "I'm
going to faint." She did not know how much she had
lost until three weeks later and the doctor told her she
was all right now.

Scott changed the last line to:

. . . and the doctor told her she was sure to be all
right. He was quite sure that she would be alright.

It emphasized that she would not be all right.

Determined to make me into a first-class writer, Scott

decided that under his guidance I should set to work on my autobiography. He bought me a big, lined ledger and marked the pages with months and years for me to remember all the details. The first page had me at three months. But as I grew up, more pages were allotted to each section. I stopped my story when Scott died and instead wrote what I remembered of him—it's easy to forget and I didn't want to forget Scott Fitzgerald. The notes on my time with him and on my own earlier story—about 100,000 words in all—were useful when I started to write *Beloved Infidel*. So in a way I did, with Mr. Frank's help, finish the task that Scott had set me.

An equally ambitious project was our play, *Dame Rumor* (included in the Appendix). Scott thought I had a good ear for dialogue and for sharp dramatic remarks. I was to do the first draft and he would undertake the revisions. Also, he wanted me to taste some of the success he had enjoyed in the 20s, and he judged that the fastest way for me to make a reputation and money was to write a successful play.

I learned recently that Scott had asked Mr. Ober to make out a contract between us. It was never signed, but it gave each of us 50 percent and stipulated that all decisions about everything were to be made by him. I am still wondering why Scott concealed this from me. At the time I would have signed it readily. Today, I'm not as sure—oh, of course I would still sign it.

Our first task was to settle on a subject. What did I know most about? As I was always in hot water for my sharp remarks in the column, we both thought the play should be about a Hollywood columnist who gets into trouble through knowing and publicizing too much about the stars. He loved the name Judy (which I used in *Not in the Script*—see Appendix) and that was the name for the girl. His title was *Institutional Humanitarianism*, but after some discussion with me it was changed to *Dame Rumor*.

As I knew absolutely nothing about writing plays, Scott bought me Baker's *Dramatic Technique*—I believe that Baker had taught drama at Yale. I read it carefully and painfully, absorbed some of it, then set to work. Scott was to have done more of the writing, but he was tied up all day at a studio—this was about a year after we met, while he was still under contract to M-G-M—and he was too tired in the evenings to look too closely at what I had written. I had hoped that he would write a great deal of it because I had infinite faith that with his writing and some of mine the play would be a success. But after his massive correction of the prologue he simply did not have the time to do much to the rest (see Appendix).

We were on a weekend in La Jolla, I remember, when he read the prologue, made many changes, and encouraged me to continue. Thus I floundered on, trying to recall what Baker had instructed. There had to be a strong curtain for the end of each act, and at the beginning of the first act, the characters had to explain who they were, what they were doing and where. But it must not be laid on with a trowel.

I enjoyed writing the play. Visions of fame and money filled me with delight. But it was more daydreaming than anything else. And after correcting the prologue and the two acts I had finished, Scott decided the project should be abandoned. It would be impossible for him to do more than correct what I had written, and the material, he deemed, wasn't really good enough.

I had forgotten all about the play until I received a letter in 1965 from Professor Dan Piper, a Fitzgerald biographer. Going through the papers at Princeton, he had found the play. Rereading *Dame Rumor* recently, I thought it wasn't bad, especially the prologue, here reproduced.

There were to be three acts for *Dame Rumor*. Two were completed plus a prologue and the outline for the third act which consisted of 16 scenes! Herewith the prologue. (Act I, Scenes I and II are reproduced in the Appendix.)

PROLOGUE

The drab exit of a big studio, where everybody goes in and out except the carriage trade and the clock-punching proletariat. Door to the studio in the rear—door to the street at left. On the right behind a cage (open toward the audience) sit two young clerks on high stools. Between the two doors a man and two women occupy chairs against the left wall.

As the curtain rises, a small female urchin has just come in, autograph book in hand and is defying them.

FIRST CLERK
—You get out of here.

URCHIN
(Waving the book)
—Yah-yah. I got Dick Powell in his automobile.

FIRST CLERK
—Get out.

URCHIN
—I got more than any kid at school.

FIRST CLERK
—You can't come on studio property.

(Urchin looks out the door)

URCHIN
—Whew! Whose limousine?

(Exit)

FIRST CLERK
—Learn something today?

SECOND CLERK
—I can't memorize a thousand faces in a day.

FIRST CLERK
—Nobody gets in without a card or a slip—except there's a guy named H. G. Wells you got to let by.

SECOND CLERK
—Is he a star?

FIRST CLERK
—No, he's a writer. I think he was on those Tarzan series.

SECOND CLERK
—Suppose I kept out a star?

(Tom Ritchie, a rather handsome, futile man of thirty, rises from his seat against the wall and goes to desk)

RITCHIE
—Surely it wouldn't matter if I walked to my wife's stage. You don't believe who I am?

FIRST CLERK
—Sure I do, Mr.—

RITCHIE
—Ritchie.

FIRST CLERK
—But how do I know she wants to see you. Once I let a husband by like that and it turns out he was the wrong husband. There were two others between him and now. Did I get it?

RITCHIE
—I am Miss Ritchie's first and only husband.

FIRST CLERK
(Carelessly)
—Congratulations.

(Ritchie sits down)

(Gabriel Weatherby—description—enters from studio and stops at desk)

GABRIELLE
—Will you pass me tomorrow? I'm a journalist.

FIRST CLERK
(Shakes his head)
—If we get a slip from Publicity.

GABRIELLE
—I represent twenty French and British papers.

FIRST CLERK
(Insolent)
—Do they have talkies over there yet?

SECOND CLERK
(To First Clerk)
—Will they fire me if I kept out a star?

(A woman enters from the studio wearing dark glasses four inches in diameter. She goes slowly, almost blindly, toward exit. During her passage, First Clerk has turned to answer Second Clerk's question)

FIRST CLERK
—The stars mostly drive in by the gate. I've been here two years and I never seen Solita San Martin.

(The outer door clicks shut after the woman. Gabrielle, who has been staring at her, turns to First Clerk)

GABRIELLE
—You'd have seen her then if you'd been minding your business.

(He exits upon their consternation)

(Major Crandall, a dignified man of fifty, comes through)

RITCHIE
—Hello, Major.

CRANDALL
—Hello, Mr. Ritchie. I'm dining with you tonight.

RITCHIE
—We're looking forward to it.

(Crandall nods and goes out)

SECOND CLERK
—Who's he?

FIRST CLERK
—Major Crandall from the Hayes Office. Big shot.

(Ritchie rises again)

RITCHIE
—Can I at least phone my wife?

FIRST CLERK
—All right.

(Urchin's head appears at the door)

URCHIN
—Hey! Ain't there anybody worth looking at?

(A portly Jewish producer comes in in a hurry)

PRODUCER
—Send my car to the drugstore across the street.

FIRST CLERK
—Yes, sir.

URCHIN
—Ain't there anybody more coming?

(She blocks the entrance)

PRODUCER
—Excuse me.

(She lets him by)

FIRST CLERK
(Fiercely to urchin)
—That's Mr. Bortz. He only owns half the studio.

URCHIN
(Unimpressed)
—Oh, say, listen, I got to go home now. Ain't there anybody—
(First Clerk opens door and makes a rush for her)

RITCHIE
(On phone at extreme right of stage)
—Oh, hello, dear—I'm right here in the office. They won't let me in . . . Never mind if you're coming right over . . . Were you in good voice? . . . Ah, fine, fine.

(Hap Hapsburg comes in from studio. He is an insignificant body with a rather noble and incredible head and a haughty manner)

HAPSBURG
> (To First Clerk)
—Have I any mail?

FIRST CLERK
> (Shortly)
—This isn't the mail desk. Say, you're not employed here, are you?

HAPSBURG
> (Smug)
—Scarcely.

FIRST CLERK
—What's your name?

HAPSBURG
—Baron Hapsburg.

FIRST CLERK
> (Looking at book)
—I haven't any record of you and I don't know how you keep getting in. But you slip by again and I'll put the police on you.

HAPSBURG
—If they should dare to touch me there'd be an international episode.

> (As he exits, little Joy Terry and her mother come in. Joy is about 12 years old—rather thin, but with masses of golden curls. She wears an organdie party dress. The mother is like a freshly painted doll, her round eyes move like a doll's; what she says has a doll's range and mechanical sound. The clerks and the people waiting stare.)

MRS. TERRY
> (To Clerk)
—I want a 1938 card, please.

FIRST CLERK
—I'll have it for you tomorrow, Mrs. Terry.
> (During this, the urchin has put her head in and is staring at little Joy)

URCHIN
—Joy Terry. Whoops! Write it.

FIRST CLERK
—You get out—

JOY
—I don't mind.
>(She writes in book. Urchin wets her finger and touches her, staring)

>(Two women, waiting, begin ad libbing, "Isn't she cute, isn't she the sweetest thing?" "Oh, she's adorable, adorable." Joy smiles all around and exits with her mother and urchin)

SECOND CLERK
—No stars, eh—just the biggest one of all.
>(Robert Acton comes in. Description)

FIRST CLERK
>(To Second Clerk)
—And here's another.

>(Ritchie has been at phone with back turned, now he hangs up—sees Acton)

ACTON
>(Surprised)
—Hello, Tom.

RITCHIE
—Hello, Bob.

ACTON
—How's Josie?

RITCHIE
—I'm waiting for her. You're coming to dinner tonight, aren't you?

ACTON
—Yes—yes.

(Josie Ritchie comes in. She is spectacularly attractive—her red hair is a startling frame for her pale handsome face; her lipstick is the same shade as her hair)

ACTON
—Hello, Josie.

JOSIE
—Hello, Bob. Hello, Tom.

ACTON
—You have a devoted husband.

JOSIE
—You're coming to dinner tonight?

ACTON
—Yes, I've got to make Malibu and back.
    (He exits)

JOSIE
—I've got to wait for my maid.

RITCHIE
—I couldn't help coming. I was playing the piano. The aria from Rigoletto—do you remember—and thinking how happy we were—once—
    (She gives an anxious look around and walks down center)

JOSIE
—Oh, Tom—please—you promised.

RITCHIE
—I know—your glorious voice comes first. But there should be a little left for me.

JOSIE
—Tom, don't—I can't stand this sort of thing. When the season is over, we'll go away somewhere. Tom, you mustn't forget it was you who taught me that music comes first. Remember Martha Sorel.

RITCHIE

—That's different. She had a hundred affairs before she was 21. She didn't have time to sing. But Constinelli—certainly didn't live like a monk.

(Looks at her and breaks off)

—Oh, I'm sorry, darling. I know it upsets you when I talk about him.

JOSIE

(Primly)

—Constinelli was a tenor—that's different.

FIRST CLERK

(Hanging up phone)

—Your maid is waiting in the car, Mrs. Ritchie.

JOSIE

—Thanks.

(The Ritchies go out)

FIRST CLERK

(To the two women waiting)

—We're closing. Only the big gate's open now.

(The women rise and go out. The curtain begins to go down.)

SECOND CLERK

—What are you doing tonight? I feel like a change.

FIRST CLERK

—So do I. Let's take in a picture.

(As they begin to turn out the lights—)

(*The Curtain is down.*)

9.

THE LAST TYCOON

THE MOST IMPORTANT writing project for Scott during the time that I knew him was, of course, *The Last Tycoon*. He had conceived his novel about the most famous of all the Hollywood producers, Irving Thalberg, and the questionable, yet fascinating, grind of studio wheels before he met me—back in 1931 when Thalberg brought him to Hollywood. But it was not until eight years later that his return and prolonged residence there, combined with his lack of steady work at the studios, finally started him on this project.

Thalberg died in 1936—a year before Scott's new contract with M-G-M. His few impressions of the producer were culled from the earlier visits. They had encountered one another both at work and socially. But as Scott spent much of his 1927 and 1931 time in Hollywood drinking, his views of the place and its people were fragmentary. To give his novel an authentic Thalberg dimension, he put the time back to 1935.

Norma Shearer, the superstar of the 30s, had liked Scott, and he had been invited to a party at the Thalberg-Shearer beach house at Santa Monica. He made a fool of himself, taking over the piano and singing an awful ditty about a dog to a response of deafening silence. Scott used this incident in his short story, "Crazy Sunday," in which the actress wife is

173

based in part on Miss Shearer. But in explaining to me the identity of the husband, Miles Calman ("the only American-born director with both an interesting temperament and an artistic conscience"), Scott never told me it was Thalberg he had written about, but rather King Vidor, the then popular director.

I still find this somewhat mystifying. Perhaps Scott wanted me to have no preconceptions of Thalberg, whom—by 1937, when we had this discussion about "Crazy Sunday"—he was definitely planning to deal with in his next novel, temporarily titled *The Last Tycoon*. I assume he did not want me to link the exalted Monroe Stahr with the talented but personally weak and neurotic Miles Calman. As to why he brought in Mr. Vidor, I had told him about my fling with the director, his asking me to marry him, and about his having me okay the plans for his new house, to be built high up in Beverly Hills.

Perhaps, Scott told me, Vidor was the man who is almost cuckolded in "Crazy Sunday" in order to punish him or me for his being in love with me. But conceivably Vidor was at least a partial model for the husband. Scott had told me of a conversation in 1931 at the height of the Depression, in which the money-careful King said that if there was a revolution by the working classes, he would take to the mountains and pretend to be a laborer. "But they'll look at your hands," Scott told him, "They are not the hands of a working man." This, said Scott, had worried Mr. Vidor. Scott used this incident in *The Last Tycoon*. Most likely, Miles Calman was a compound of several of the Hollywood magnates, Thalberg among them, since Scott rarely used a single real-life prototype in his stories. It was his custom to blend the characteristics of several people, his own included, to make one character.

But Thalberg, however, was the inspiration for Stahr in *The Last Tycoon*. Hollywood's boy genius struck Scott as exactly right for the hero of the book he wanted to write. Always the enthusiast, Scott told me he wanted his story about the movie world not only to reveal its faults, its falseness—as Nathanael West was doing in *The Day of the Locust*—but also to extol its virtues and capture its glamour.

Scott was always appreciative of glamour—even when he

could see through it—and Hollywood in the era of the early 30s to the late 40s certainly had this quality. Its films influenced the whole world in manners, mores, fashion, and beauty. The big stars of the time included Carole Lombard, Claudette Colbert, Ginger Rogers, William Powell, Myrna Loy, Fred Astaire, Garbo, Gable, Robert Taylor, Margaret Sullavan, Charles Laughton, Bette Davis, Merle Oberon, Leslie Howard, Ronald Colman, Gary Cooper, all the Barrymores—John, Lionel, and Ethel—also Mickey Rooney, Judy Garland, Deanna Durbin, Joel McCrea, and Norma Shearer. And not only actors, but shortly before World War II started—September 1939—in Europe, the most famous people in all areas of the arts flocked to Hollywood to work—Artur Rubinstein, Thomas Mann, Aldous Huxley, Stravinsky, André Malraux, etc.

Hollywood was then an exciting place to be, "lavish and romantic," as Scott observed in a letter to Max Perkins, with great intrigues, great disasters, and great triumphs—not so different from the Jazz Age which had been Scott's earlier subject. And to incarnate such a place, this legend at its most scintillating and complex, Irving Thalberg—with his personal drive and power, respect for excellence, astute commercialism, and doomed life—seemed the perfect choice.

I remember Scott asking me early in our relationship whether I had ever met Thalberg. I told him that shortly before the producer's death, I had interviewed him in his office at M-G-M. He had given me his complete attention and answered all my questions very seriously. I have now forgotten what these questions were exactly, though one might have been, "Why don't you put your name on the films you produce as others do?" But Thalberg was more than a producer. He was the boy genius with complete authority over every aspect of his films—the writing, casting, directing, editing, producing, just as Stahr has in *The Last Tycoon*. So powerful a figure didn't need the credit. "When you are in a position to give credit to yourself, you don't need it," he had said. I told Scott that Thalberg was a gentle, sympathetic man of great charm, but that he looked frail, and it was hard to believe he was carrying so much of the studio responsibility on his shoulders.

Some people—mostly the writers—accused Thalberg of paternalism—the same charge that is levelled against Stahr. Scott explained to me about the feudal lords of medieval England who committed themselves to the welfare of their peasants, and took good, personal care of them, yet kept themselves quite removed from these lower orders. In the same way, Stahr cares for and stands apart from all those beneath him at the studio. He cannot join them on their level as his consciousness elevates him so high above them.

I think that Stahr is Scott's most glorified hero. The writer made this character everything he would have liked to be himself. As the narrator, Cecilia, observes in the first chapter, Stahr is like a bird who flies up very high to see "and when he is up there, he had looked on all the kingdoms with the kind of eyes that can stare straight into the sun." Then he settles to earth but with the memory of what he has seen. Actually, Thalberg had told Scott (in 1927), as Scott has Stahr confiding to the Communist Brimmer, very often no one really knows the way but someone has to make the decisions, to be the leader—something Scott himself never really was. Though I thought of him then as one, I now realize that except as an author, he was a follower who tried, but failed, to join the game.

Also, unlike Scott, Thalberg had complete control over himself. Though he took chances with new ideas, he used his own self cautiously. When Scott has Stahr in Chapter VI breaking down under the pressures of his job and personal life, this is not in keeping with Thalberg's history and personality. After Norma Shearer read *The Last Tycoon* she said to me, "But it's not a bit like Irving." She was annoyed that everyone assumed Stahr to be her husband.

It seems to me that Scott developed Stahr rather as he had Dick Diver in *Tender Is the Night*. He establishes him as a stable, commanding character, then has him disintegrate, getting drunk and challenging Brimmer. But is it plausible that a man like Thalberg/Stahr would get drunk? I personally do not find the change convincing, just as I failed to believe that Dick Diver, who also starts off strong, based on Scott's ideal of

Gerald Murphy, falls to pieces. (Diver goes even further than Stahr since he is denied Stahr's grace of dying.) But a Gerald Murphy could never have gone to live in small towns, each smaller than the other. *He* would rather have died. I think that in both *Tender Is the Night* and *The Last Tycoon*, Scott was also writing about himself, believing he had once been strong before life beat him down and he became a drunkard. But was Scott ever a strong character?

Scott freely acknowledged how much he inevitably drew on himself in creating his protagonists. And if Stahr the producer was meant to be Thalberg, Stahr the lover was always Scott. The love story in *The Last Tycoon* was an afterthought to his initial concept of a novel about Hollywood. I don't know who would have been the heroine if he had not met me. Undoubtedly he would have found someone, as there had to be a girl in his life. But I like to think that my story, our story, made an invaluable contribution to the book. My background was different from that of any other woman Scott had met. I was his new type of heroine, not an ornament, although I was quite pretty then, not an heiress, but a worker, a woman "dower(ed) . . . with 'a little misfortune.' "

"What can I do to make it [the love story] honest and different?" Scott queries in his notes. This sense of its difference made it so important to him that at one time he was calling the book, *The Love of the Last Tycoon* (with the subtitle, *A Western*). This was despite the fact that the Stahr-Kathleen romance was only to comprise 16,500 words, a third of the planned 50,000-word book. It was much longer in the actual writing, but the book was also longer. Scott became more and more intrigued with his characters, and as the novel progressed, it doubled in length. Though he planned to cut about 10,000 words from the 60,000 he had written, the finished book would have been 90,000 to 100,000 words long.

Scott was secretive about his work on *The Last Tycoon*, not wanting people to know what he was up to. He began by very quietly gathering all the material he could about Thalberg whose rivalry at M-G-M with Louis B. Mayer was well known. It was Mayer, I told Scott, who once tearfully implored the studio's top writers to take a cut in salary so that he would not have to reduce the pay of the stenographers. When they agreed, he went ahead and cut the stenographers' pay anyway. Pat Brady, in the novel, is based on Mayer with some characteristics of Eddie Mannix, a beefy Irishman, thrown in. The Hollywood tycoons and their executives were mostly Jewish and sometimes Irish.

The reason Scott was secretive in gathering his information was because he believed that authors are often thieves. "We have all stolen," he said to me once, "from Shakespeare on down. It's how the story is written that makes the difference." Actually Scott had "stolen," according to his critics, from Compton Mackenzie, Willa Cather, and Joseph Conrad. Taking no chances of being stolen from, he was zealous to keep his project unpublicized. A letter to Max Perkins of May 1939 frets that the publisher—Scribners— "seemed under the full conviction that the novel was about Hollywood and I am in terror that this misinformation may have been disseminated to the literary columns." Scott then denies that his book had to do with Hollywood, though, of course it did. Also, before hiring Frances Kroll he was careful to make sure of her loyalty and discretion. "How do I know I can trust you?" he asked sternly. He informed her that he was writing a book about Hollywood, that it was a great secret, and that she must not divulge the theme to anyone. He then asked her to get his address book from a drawer where there were also several bottles of gin. When Frances did not remark about the liquor, she had passed his test. He couldn't have had a better secretary. Frances was absolutely devoted to Scott and would never have breathed a word of anything he wanted kept secret.

Even to me Scott was fairly reticent about the project—not that he didn't trust me—he didn't want to dissipate the freshness of his ideas. It was his policy never to discuss any of his intentions for the story or the characters. "If you do some of the freshness is lost." As a result I was surprised when I read some of the notes for the novel's second half. Scott had told me, for example, of a newspaper account of some adults coming across a crashed plane near the mountains and rifling through the pockets of the dead passengers. But he did not tell me that Stahr would die in a plane crash (just as Miles Calman had) or that children would find the plane and rob the dead passengers.

From the material that Wilson put into his editing of *The Last Tycoon* in 1941 and "The Crack Up" and other stories in 1945 by the New Directions Publishing Corporation, I realized that Scott would have continued to fictionalize many of our experiences in the rest of *The Last Tycoon*.

Still, if Scott never divulged what he was going to write, he was always eager to show me what he had written. Almost every night he would read aloud to me that day's work. And this is how I discovered that he was writing about us and that I was Kathleen, the heroine of *The Last Tycoon*.

There are, of course, differences between Kathleen and me. Scott makes her Irish, which I was not—I was British—though she shares my years of living in London. More importantly, he makes her more secure in herself than I ever was and gives her a middle-class rather than lower-class childhood. But otherwise we are alike: he endows her with my complexion, my blue hat with flowers, my experiences, my observations. And like me, she is quintessentially an outsider. At the end of the novel Kathleen was to be seen outside the studio gate and, with Stahr dead, she knows that she will never be asked inside. Similarly, I never really felt a part of Hollywood or for that matter of any group with which I may have been associated. As Scott read to me, I very fully recognized myself in Kathleen.

It was particularly gratifying to me when he would incorporate phrases that I could remember as mine. At one point Kathleen ventures her impression of the California rain ". . . so loud, like horses weeing." This was my description that Scott had laughed at and recorded in his notebook. "It's exactly right," he enthused.

He also gave my remark, "I have nice teeth for an English girl," to Kathleen. And my observation that the Ping-Pong balls on the dark grass at Encino looked like stars, he put in a line of description in the scene of Stahr's fight with Brimmer.

I think, though, that an important contribution to the novel—aside from Scott's use of my past and of our romance—was providing him with a stable, quiet life, conducive to writing. Edmund Wilson observed in his review of *Beloved Infidel* that I had given Scott "a base from which to work . . . Undoubtedly we would not have had *The Last Tycoon* but for Sheilah."

It's agreeable to look back on myself and realize that I was of help while he worked on this excellent novel. But if for the most part I stayed quietly and virtuously in the background, I also felt free to make a few suggestions when he read me his material. Scott Fitzgerald was never a man to underrate a suggestion if it was good. The heroine's name was initially Thalia. But he changed it to Kathleen when I told him about a C. B. Cochran chorus girl I had known in England called Thalia. She burned to death when her long blonde hair caught fire. Scott did not like the association. So he changed the heroine's name. In his notes for the book, the girl is sometimes called Thalia.

Also I contributed to the seduction scene at Malibu. In Scott's original version, when Stahr starts to tremble and relaxes his hold on Kathleen, this was the end of the love-making. He had Stahr being very gentle with her, but there was no continuation of sex at this time.

"No, no," I said emphatically, "that's not how she would react." A girl like Kathleen who wanted sex and was in love with the man would be provocative and helpful to get satisfaction for them both. She would be sufficiently experienced to know how to arouse him. I knew too well from my first marriage how to deal with sudden impotence, the result of worry and/or nervousness. "The only way to make the man perform is for the girl to be obviously inferior to him," I told Scott. "She would become coarse so that Stahr would at once feel superior and lose the tenseness. The blood would come down from his head to the proper area." I found this suggestion in his notebooks and he changed the scene to include my suggestion. Many years later I was pleased when an editor said to me, "It's the best seduction scene I've ever read." "I wrote it," I responded, a boast which was not exactly true.

In Scott's use of my past experiences and of our time together, what always impressed me was his ability to heighten the interest and glamour. For example, Scott's first glimpse of me, was transformed into Stahr's first sight of Kathleen and his subsequent search for a girl with a silver belt with stars cut out of it. This was Scott's mistake as well. When Robert Benchley asked him to return to that first party, Scott cautiously asked, "Who is still there?" and particularly if there was a girl wearing a belt with stars cut out of it. Scott went back, expecting to find me. But it was not me and it was not Kathleen. The mix-up is put into the novel just as it happened, as is Scott's impression of my resemblance to his wife. But by shifting the encounter from a smokey, crowded party to the moonlit studio back lot during an earthquake—Scott had been at M-G-M during a California earthquake in 1931—he gives it an added magic.

Similarly, the fictional setting for the seduction scene adds so much. Stahr and Kathleen arrive at the door of her house, just as Scott and I came to mine after our dinner with Scottie. Like us, the characters are ready to part; then suddenly they are drawn together. But rather than have them go right inside the girl's modest home as we did, they drive back to Stahr's half-finished beach house at Malibu with its fake grass. Scott and I never made love in such a setting. But the scene in the book is so vivid that I have half come to believe it really happened.

Scott also made some good changes in our meeting at the Screenwriters' Ball. In actual fact, the Writers Guild had held their banquet at the Biltmore Hotel. This was where I was at Marc Connelly's table for ten and Scott was at the adjoining table in Dorothy Parker's party of ten. At one moment near the end of the evening, I was alone at my table, "the high priestess," as Scott puts it in the novel, and he was alone facing me at Dorothy's. This was when we first talked to one another, and I asked Scott if he would like to dance. But the party broke up before we had the chance. Our dancing together was not until a few days later at the Clover Club.

Taking these occurrences, Scott altered the hotel to the Ambassador, because he knew it better—it was where he and Zelda had stayed on their visit to Hollywood in 1927. And he had Stahr and Kathleen dance together there and also at the Screenwriters' party, thus combining into one dramatic scene what for us was two encounters.

Another combination—this one of different people—helped to make up the character of Kathleen's exlover. Scott pooled the characteristics of three men I had known—Johnny, my first husband, Donegall, and himself—to create the exking. The man has Donegall's nobility, Johnny's poverty (it was a true story that one day Johnny and I had just "a shilling between us," or more precisely it was a sixpence, with which we were going to buy bananas but Johnny dropped it down a crack on top of a bus and we went hungry.), and Scott's drinking problem and zeal to educate me—the real-life education was also geared to my reading Spengler but like Kathleen I never got that far. Kathleen left her man and Scott died before the reading of Spengler.

An impoverished, royal-blooded devotee of Spengler, who drinks, makes a colorful figure. Knowing how to bring such strands together was an important part of Scott's talent. He knew how to make the best fictional use of the people he met or knew of and of the stories he was told. How he dealt, for instance, with my account of a London caterpillar plague in 1932. I had told him about a day when I was horseback riding with Johnny in Rotten Row in the midst of this plague. The furry horrors were all over me, wriggling down my back, crawling on my face. Scott takes the incident and turns it into a simile as Kathleen talks on the phone to Stahr. " 'Do you know how you make me feel?' she demanded. 'Like a day in London during a caterpillar plague when a hot furry thing dropped into my mouth.' "

Another story I had told Scott is used to establish the character of Wylie White. Eddie Mayer had confided to me and I then related to Scott, that he had once had an affair with

Norma Talmadge, a top star and the wife of Joseph Shenck, the biggest share holder at 20th Century-Fox. As they were lying in bed one afternoon, Norma turned to Eddie and said, "If you ever tell anyone about this, I'll have you thrown out of Hollywood." And, to Eddie's look of surprise, "My husband's a much more important man than you are." Scott gives this experience to Wylie, the hack writer, and his telling it to Cecilia (the female character based on a composite of Scottie and Budd Schulberg, the producer's son) underscores his slightly ingratiating familiarity.

There is so much in the novel that I recognized from our experiences, yet marveled at Scott's transformation—a drunk at the airport behaving just like Scott before our flight to Chicago; the soles of the lovers' shoes touching, just as our bare feet did when we sat facing one another on a sofa; the night Stahr and Kathleen join the grunion run at Malibu Beach—we went grunioning too though we didn't meet a Rosicrucian Negro as Scott has it in *The Last Tycoon;* Stahr's conversation with the writer, George Boxley, about picture-making, conveying the same feeling and many of the same ideas as the lecture on Hollywood that Scott wrote for me; and Kathleen's presentation at court—just like mine, only Scott gives her a stepmother, whereas I was presented by a Birmingham acquaintance of Johnny's.

Nor was Scott above caricaturing my friend, Margaret Brainard. He puts her into the story as Edna, the overly friendly, questionable friend. Margaret may have been a bit sweet in her friendliness, but she was a very admirable person.

Also in Scott's copious notes for the second, unfinished half of the novel, I recognized much that we had talked about and experienced together. There were nine episodes in his plan for the whole book, numbered A to I. He had completed the first draft to the start of F, so for the rest of the story there are just his outline and the notes. One note in the F section says simply, "The Cummerbund." I had told him of my decision not to marry a man who was wearing a red cummerbund when he met me at the airport. It had embarrassed me. This amused Scott and he wrote it down. I wonder how he would have transformed it. Maybe Smith, "the American," the man Kathleen was to have married, would wear a red cummerbund.

In the G section, Scott includes "Last fling with Kathleen, Old stars in heat wave at Encino." There had been one unbearably hot day when I came to see him at Belly Acres. It was so hot that you could touch the heat in the air. Arriving at Scott's house, I looked down the long vista of his ground floor and saw everyone in the briefest attire—Scott in shorts and no top, Frances in a swim suit typing in the dining room, the maid in the kitchen "wearing only a towel," as Scott informed me. We were all sweating profusely, and I made a hasty dash to the swimming pool where I stayed until the sun eased down in the sky.

Scott was obviously planning to use this hot day as a background for a party to be given by Stahr for some of the old stars—to whom Thalberg gave employment whenever it was feasible. I wonder if this heat wave scene would have excelled the marvelous one in *The Great Gatsby* where the characters drive into sizzling New York and their lives unravel.

Finally, in Section I there is the note, "Johnny Swanson at funeral." Like Gatsby, Stahr was to have died violently, and the novel was to culminate in a funeral. But there the resemblance between the endings stops. Stahr's funeral was to be completely different from Gatsby's—or rather it was to be pathetic in a totally different way. The only mourners at Gatsby's were Nick Carraway and Owl Eyes, but for Mr. Stahr everyone in Hollywood was to be on display, vying for prominence. I had told Scott that at Irving Thalberg's funeral, Harry Carey, an old-time Western star, was invited by mistake for Carey Wilson. He unexpectedly found himself a pallbearer, and because of this everyone thought he must be important, and his career revived. And the note about the "blind" cameraman. This was a rumor only but it had ruined his career.

Scott wanted to finish the first draft of the novel by January 1941. But when he died a month before his deadline, he was behind schedule. Not only had the scope of the project expanded, but he had only been able to work on it in spurts. Whenever he ran out of money, he had to find work on a script until there was enough in the bank for him to get back to his book. How he regretted wasting the fortune he had earned in the 20s. His letter of praise to Ernest Hemingway on the publication of *For Whom the Bell Tolls* ends rather plaintively:

> Congratulations to you on your new book's great success. I envy you like hell and there is no irony in this . . . I envy you the time it will give you to do what you want.

Scott was also impeded in his writing of the novel by his failing health. In the last year he could only work for a few hours at a stretch before having to lie down, exhausted by the effort. As he confided to Edmund Wilson, he had written the novel "with difficulty" but he thought it was good. He believed, in fact, that it was to be his best book and that it would give him back the readers he had lost or thought he had lost.

Scott had hoped that *The Last Tycoon* would be in the shops in the fall of 1941. It was, all 60,000 words, with the book a little more than half finished. Edmund Wilson did the editing, and this would have made Scott happy. Also Scribners coupled *The Last Tycoon* with *The Great Gatsby*, which Scott had been unhappy to see dropped from the Modern Library Series.

Max Perkins had comforted Scott when the first chapter of *The Last Tycoon* failed to bring the advance of $6,000 against the total $30,000 from *Collier's* magazine that the hard-up writer had hoped for. "They wanted to see more," he told me sadly, "they wanted to be sure that I was capable of finishing the novel." After Scott's death, Mr. Perkins wrote me a letter saying, "The first chapter alone is good enough to stand by itself. It breaks a man's heart to see what this book could have been." I was discussing this recently with Scottie and she said, "I'm sure that somewhere he knows."

10.

THE EDUCATOR

WHY DID SCOTT FITZGERALD decide to educate me? What did it mean to him, this man who was broken in health, neglected by his once enormous audience, and dreadfully short of cash? Had he been sorry for me or possibly ashamed of me, realizing how tense I was with his intellectual friends and how maladroit I felt in my desperate, rare attempts to join in their conversation? Was his motive that I should be socially acceptable among these well-educated people who made up our circle? Or that I should be a fit companion for himself, at least be as well read as the women he had known intimately in the past? Why did he care about me to the extent of spending so many hours and months during the last years of his short life to try to give me the same degree of education as the average university student?

Such questions arise only in retrospect. During the eighteen months that we were actually immersed in our College of One curriculum, I never stopped to ask myself, "Why is he doing this? What can he gain from it?" The project was such a joyful one for us both that it was its own justification. I also believe that Scott's love for me provides the best explanation of his zeal. Nevertheless, I have sometimes considered other

186

motives. And perhaps by my looking in a level-headed, unromantic way at our educational undertaking, I can answer some of the questions that cropped up in the reviews of *College of One*.

One review by Morley Callaghan in *The New York Times Book Review* ended with such a misleading suggestion that I countered it with my own letter to the paper. Mr. Callaghan wound up his piece with "a question about Fitzgerald, an old nagging one":

> . . . In those last years he was working on *The Last Tycoon*, the legend is that with all the drinking and the hack work, he couldn't find time to get on with the novel. Yet he planned and worked on these studies for Sheilah Graham. Even aside from the studies, as she says, he catalogued everything, simply everything. And as we know, he kept composing all those fine letters. All this means that he was spending long, serious reflective hours at his desk. Then why couldn't he get to the novel?

To appose my education in this way to the writing of the novel with the suggestion that Scott used our project and his other preoccupations, such as the letters to Scottie to evade his serious fiction, is totally erroneous. This simply wasn't the case, and my response to the *Times* read as follows:

> Mr. Callaghan asks why did he [Scott] find time to write those beautiful letters to his daughter and give so much time to my "education," instead of finishing his book, *The Last Tycoon*. A man cannot live by work alone. The project for my education gave Scott great pleasure and it was an experiment for a book he planned to write on the subject. Also it was a rest from his own writing. He was greatly devoted to his daughter and the letters to her with the advice for her reading were as important to him as the novel he was writing. And while he suspected that he would never be an old man, he did not expect to die before finishing his book which he expected would be some time in the following summer. I was to have

graduated in May from our college of one. So he thought there was time. When he died, I was angry with him for not having finished his book. If only we knew what was going to happen tomorrow, we would all behave differently, perhaps.

Yours sincerely,

Sheilah Graham

If Scott could have foreseen his imminent death, I wonder if he would have chosen to spend more time on the novel and less on the education and the letters. In even approaching, let alone answering such a question, one must understand how much the notion of education meant to him. His creation of the College of One, his pedagogical letters to Scottie, his suggestions even to Zelda in the hospital that she broaden her literary horizons, all underscore the importance that he placed on knowing and profiting from good reading. In one letter to Zelda, he urges her to read some books: "You know, those things that look like blocks but come apart on one side—I mean loads of books and not just early Hebrew metaphysics." This description might have amused Scott, if not Zelda in her phase of humorless religious zeal. But Scott saw Zelda's lack of interest in reading as one cause of her inability to deal with experience. In a letter to Scottie, he explains:

> Your mother's utterly endless mulling and brooding over insolubles paved the way to her ruin. She had no education—not from lack of opportunity because she could have learned with me—but from some inner stubbornness. She was a great original in her way, with perhaps a more intense flame at its highest than I ever had but she tried and is still trying to solve all ethical and moral problems on her own, without benefit of the thousands dead.

Scott may not have finished his formal schooling at Princeton, but he considered himself an educated man with great respect and enthusiasm for what could be learned from "the thousands dead." They not only taught him much of his literary craft but also helped him to form his moralistic outlook, his larger vision of life. If Zelda muddled through all moral and ethical problems on her own, Scott was determined to do the opposite. "A moralist at heart," as he called himself, wanting "to preach at people in some acceptable form," he was eager to blend his own originality with the wisdom of past generations. Then, too, because he was a moralist, a man who liked to preach to others, he happily—but seriously as well—undertook to extend the benefits of education to me, his willing pupil.

It is this seriousness of purpose on Scott's part that I think many of the critics overlooked in their estimations of our College of One. I recall one reviewer who saw the education as a kind of dream world, saying of Scott and me that "each was eager to assure the other that the joint dream world in which they existed for two years was, which it wasn't, a real one." But I insist that however Scott may have been a romantic, who glamourized beautiful women and loved Keats' "Ode to a Nightingale" more than any other poem, he was also a realist, keen to understand life in exact, uncompromising terms. And his interest in my education was as much, if not more, a reflection of his realism as of his romanticism.

Ultimately, I think, Scott wanted me, through my reading, to understand and perhaps share some of his basic tenets about existence: that, as Spengler asserted, the Western world was dead (Scott had read Spengler the same summer he was writing *Gatsby* and, as he confessed to Max Perkins, he never quite recovered from it); and that, as he so often told me, there was no such thing as happiness. I was always insisting that happiness was possible, but Scott was adamant it was not. Books, he felt, corroborated his point of view. His most emphatic and eloquent statement on this subject occurs in one of the letters to Scottie, where he defines for her his notion of "the wise and tragic sense of life." As he explains:

By this I mean the thing that lies behind all great

careers from Shakespeare's to Abraham Lincoln's
and as far back as there are books to read—the sense
that life is essentially a cheat and its conditions are
those of defeat and the redeeming things are not
"happiness and pleasure" but the deeper sat-
isfactions that come out of the struggle.

To impress this philosophy upon me and to prepare me for
the reading of Spengler were, then, the ultimate aims of the
education. But to say this was the whole reason for it is
lugubrious. One of Scott's central ideas about education was
that it should be fun—a vibrant, compelling pleasure rather
than a dry, academic exercise.

Also there were more pragmatic reasons for educating me
than to prepare my mind for Spengler. One that we used to
joke about was Scott's notion that I should become a gracious
old lady—the kind that young people love to listen to, and
then I would never be lonely. Hopefully, too, I would attain
this graciousness long before my dotage. We both expected
that by the time of my graduation from College of One in May
1941, I would have the confidence to carry on those intellectual
conversations with people from which I had previously
shrunk. It was the old Pygmalion story with an intellectual
twist—the creation of a socially and, in this case, intellectually
acceptable woman.

I wonder if yet another literary analogy ever occurred to
Scott. For it has recently occurred to me how much I resembled
a character from his own fiction. It is, in fact, not too farfetched
to say that I was a female Jay Gatsby come to life.

Like Gatsby I had rejected my drab inheritance and invented
myself anew. "He sprang from a Platonic conception of
himself. I suppose he had the name (Gatz was his real name)
ready for some time." I too had changed my name from Lily
Shiel to the more aristocratic Sheilah Graham. Then, like
Gatsby, I had moved away from my humble past, concealed it,
and created myself into an image that society would accept
and admire. But also, like Gatsby, I felt inferior in the presence
of my supposed betters, though we both had become success-

ful in our chosen (but not quite dignified) fields—bootlegging and gossipmongering!

The analogies extend still further. Gatsby and I had both tried to obliterate our pasts with a flood of fantasies. He had his photograph taken with some students at Oxford. I had my photograph from my presentation at Buckingham Palace in May 1931 to King George and Queen Mary, and that was as true as Gatsby's picture. After World War I he had spent a brief time at Oxford. To introduce me at court, Johnny, my first husband, had dug up his old society acquaintance from Birmingham, who had been rich and was now poor and was glad of the dress we bought her and the expensive supper at Quaglino's afterwards.

With College of One Scott was thus helping to mold his own Gatsby figure, although I was never as flamboyant or vulgar as his yet likeable protagonist. But I was sometimes socially awkward. And by educating me, Scott was giving me confidence so that my social image would be impressive. What Gatsby did with wealth and lavish parties, I could do with study in our College of One.

Thinking about it, Scott's relationship with me epitomizes his whole ambivalance about society. He admired the rich and condemned the rich. In his line, "The rich are different from you and me," there is envy, admiration, and disapproval. And now here he was in love with a woman who had conned society with even more success than Gatsby had. He admired us for our imagination, energy, and triumph, and there was also a part of him that disapproved of us.

I wonder, too, if Scott ever felt the irony of his and my respective positions in Hollywood. There I was, one of the most powerful syndicated columnists—I could help to make or break a star or director. Scott, on the other hand, was paid bigger salaries than I was, but he was pushed around in the studios, frequently fired, and told in so many words that as far as Hollywood was concerned, he was a flop.

In the education, however, our positions were reversed. Scott was the one who was completely in control. I never questioned his choice of books for me. He was the absolute authority. This was one area of his life in Hollywood where he had no doubts and no competition. Did it ever occur to him that by virtue of his power over the columnist, he regained a kind of indirect authority over the industry that had failed to appreciate him?

If such a thought ever did cross Scott's mind, he never asserted his superiority over me unkindly—except in one instance inadvertently. Scott was discussing a scene from one of Shakespeare's plays, and I confessed to not being familiar with it. "But *everyone* knows that," he said. I was deeply hurt. "You mustn't make fun of me," I replied, close to tears. "You see, I'm so vulnerable." He apologized and never did again, even with my most stupid questions. He realized that the questions were part of the education.

After I published *College of One*, I received dozens of letters from people who believed they could attain culture by following Scott's lists and methods. And the Countess of Dudley, former film actress Maureen Swanson, told me when I was querying her about something else, "I bought all the books on your reading lists I could find." She had gone into a career of dancing at the age of nine, so I doubt if she had had too much regular schooling. I did not ask her if the books Scott had chosen for me had made her more educated. Of course, reading them would be helpful, but I hated to tell her that she was missing the most important factor in College of One—the guidance of Scott. There would be no one to inspire her and carry her over the difficult parts, to discuss with her what she had read as Scott did with me every evening. He was as essential to College of One as the two hundred books that made up the curriculum, books he had found the money to buy for me even when he couldn't afford the exotic food he liked or a new shirt. It was Scott's enthusiasm that kindled mine, and my desire to please him that drew me into the unaccustomed heavy titles until I grew to love the reading for itself. The education, throughout its eighteen months, was inseparable from my involvement with Scott and I still do not see it as something that could come to life without him.

Nonetheless, I presented it in *College of One* as a plausible two-year liberal arts course, and this is how many of the reviewers of the book chose to judge it. As such, it is not perfect. Scanning through the twenty-five pages of my courses with my objectivity of today, I can understand why some of the critics—female especially—who had been to Vassar, Radcliffe, Bryn Mawr, Oxford, or Cambridge, were somewhat skeptical of the books chosen for me and questioned that they added up to a proper liberal arts education.

Certainly there were glaring gaps in the College of One curriculum. There was no math, science, or languages, as Scott, himself, knew very little in these areas. And if the fiction and poetry courses were impressively full, those in history, economics, religion, philosophy, art, and music were fairly skimpy. But one must keep in mind that the two-year course was never meant to be more than an introduction, a key to the door of higher learning. There would be more advanced courses after my first F.S.F. diploma. Meanwhile, Scott was happy to spend most of our time on the books which had been his favorites at Princeton and in the years after when he was educating himself. (He had two thousand books in storage, and he had read them all.) He was careful to choose books that he knew I would enjoy, especially at first, in order to make the education lively and fun.

Scott knew that I loved Dickens. So the first novels in my fiction course were *Bleak House* and *A Tale of Two Cities,* followed by Thackeray's *Vanity Fair, Henry Esmond, Pendennis,* and *The Virginians.* All these were books I couldn't put down—they were as compelling and easy to read for me as the penny weekly *Peg's Paper* magazine from my childhood—stories in which the millhand always married the owner's son after the wicked foreman had tried and failed to seduce her. I think it is fair to say that the works of Dickens and Thackeray combine artistic excellence with the same popular appeal.

The notion that good literature could be fun was not entirely new to me. I had told Scott of my taking a course in English at Kings College, London, to be given the saucy *Moll Flanders* as my first book. Moll was a sexy character and used her men to the limit. If this was good literature, I had thought, how delightful! Scott further encouraged me in what I now see as my rather naïve response—identifying with Moll Flanders or Becky Sharp, suffering for David Copperfield, play-acting scenes from Proust's *Remembrance of Things Past* and many of the other books. It was harder, I told Scott, for me to write an opinion on a book, to dissect it analytically as my daughter can do with her Ph.D. training. I enjoyed my reading. That was enough for me and also enough—at least for the time being—to satisfy Scott's expectations of me.

Perhaps my M.A. course would have included the study of character development or narrative technique, but Scott was very concerned not to load too much onto me at the beginning. He trod oh so carefully on the delicate carpet of my mind. There should be nothing too difficult or I might give up. But who would drop out after reading *Alice in Wonderland* and *Through the Looking Glass?* I had read the first when I was a child in the orphanage, but without understanding the satire and meaning, which Scott now explained to me.

He would not allow me to read the later books of Henry James or Tolstoy because he believed they would bore me. It was enough that I found the earlier works by James so engaging—*Roderick Hudson, The Europeans, Portrait of a Lady, Daisy Miller.* But his other novels were too belabored and slow, Scott said, and the later works of Tolstoy were too mystical. Scott could be sure, on the other hand, of my enthusiasm for *War and Peace* and *Anna Karenina.* I could identify with Natasha's energy, longings, and confusions and feel for poor Anna who, in the society of her day, knew the consequences of leaving her husband and son and running off with Count Vronsky. *War and Peace* was one of Scott's great favorites as well. He always reread it before setting to work on one of his own books.

Another novel excluded from my curriculum was Joyce's *Finnegan's Wake.* Scott debated whether he should give it to me, but I took one hasty glance through the strange reading and said a firm "No." I was interested, however, in the last chapter of *Ulysses* where the woman keeps saying "Yes, yes, I will. Yes yes." I would repeat this when we were feeling amorous. *A Portrait of the Artist* was easy for me to read as were Joyce's short stories in *Dubliners*. "The Dead" in particular I liked as once again I could find a point of personal identification with it. At the beginning of the story, Joyce describes the rain falling on everything in the country. I had been in Ireland and knew this feeling of the rain that he captures so beautifully.

Scott's choice of books for me was also guided by his own literary enthusiasms. Before he wrote *This Side of Paradise*, for example, he had read Compton McKenzie's *Youth's Encounter* and *Sinister Street*. He admitted to me that these novels had influenced him, though not to the extent some critics asserted. Still, he continued to regard them with affection, and they were on my list. I know that they are no longer required reading in college English courses, and I doubt that many other Americans have read them in the past forty years.

Another writer who impressed Scott was Dreiser, and three of his works were on my lists—*Sister Carrie*, *The Financier*, and *The Titan*. My favorite was *Sister Carrie*. Her story reminded me of my own struggle to rise from humble beginnings.

Scott also admired Frank Norris and his brother Charles, whom he said had influenced his attitude against big business. Scott despised businessmen as a group and once quoted someone else's remark, "I wouldn't care to meet any of them in the hereafter." My reading included *Salt*, *The Octopus*, and *McTeague*.

An even more important mentor was Joseph Conrad. I read two of the short stories, "Youth" and "Heart of Darkness" plus a number of the novels. I was enthralled by *The Nigger of the Narcissus*, with its atmosphere of foreboding evil. Scott talked to me about Conrad's aim to make the reader "see," an aim that he, himself, had in his own fiction. Scott also told me that he had learned greatly from Conrad about how to tell a story, using a narrator within the tale to piece things together —like Marlow, or Nick Carraway.

Scott had once met Conrad—or at least been within earshot of him. When Conrad was staying on Long Island in 1923 or '24, Scott and Ring Lardner danced outside his bedroom window until they were removed by the servants. It seemed that when Scott admired another author, he always had to do something about it. So in one drunken escapade or another, he had brought Dreiser an unwanted bottle of champagne, offered to jump out the window in deference to James Joyce, and offended the sensibility of Edith Wharton (whose *Custom of the Country* was on my lists). But all these pranks occurred years before the time of College of One. When he knew me, Scott's more sober concern with these authors (and with Gertrude Stein, Willa Cather, Sherwood Anderson) was that I should be familiar with the work of the generation that had preceded and influenced his own.

He also had me read his contemporaries. I enjoyed Thomas Wolfe's *Look Homeward, Angel* though I agreed with Scott that it was overlong and undisciplined. As for Hemingway, I was never much impressed with his books, though perhaps I was swayed by my resentment at his treatment of Scott. "The Snows of Kilimanjaro," with its reference to "poor old Scott," was conspicuously absent from the curriculum. In fact, I read only two books by Hemingway—*A Farewell to Arms*, which Scott thought was excellent, and *The Sun Also Rises*, which he didn't care for too much. Lady Brett Ashley struck him as a very harsh character, and he thought the whole tone of the novel too cynical. I also enjoyed *For Whom the Bell Tolls*.

I have been talking only about novelists. But as much as the fiction courses, I enjoyed our study of poetry. Once again Scott's stress was on appreciation rather than analysis. He picked out immortal sentences for me to remember: "The hare limped trembling through the frozen grass/And silent was the flock in woolly fold" from Keats' "St. Agnes' Eve"; and from "Ode on a Grecian Urn": "Fair youth beneath the trees/Thou canst not leave thy song/Nor ever can those trees be bare," and "Little town forever wilt thou silent be and not a soul to tell why thou art silent can 'ere return"; Shakespeare's "Hid in death's dateless night"; Blake's "Tyger tyger, burning bright,/In the forests of the night;/What immortal hand or eye,/Could frame thy fearful symmetry?" and from T. S. Eliot, "A current under sea/Picked his bones in whispers." And so many more eternal images. If you repeat them over and over to yourself, the truth and meaning of the line suddenly bursts open like the sun racing up from a dark horizon.

Scott also used the poetry course to translate Rimbaud's poem, "Voyelles." In France he had refused to learn French like so many American men whose wives trotted happily off to their lessons. But still, translating freely, he could write the following lovely poem:

> A black, E white, I red, U green, O blue vowels
> Some day I'll tell you where your genesis lies,
> A black velvet swarm of flies
> Buzzing above the stench of voided bowels,
>
> A gulf of shadow; E where the iceberg rushes
> White mists, tents, kings, shady strips,
> I purple, spilt blood, laughter of sweet lips
> In anger—or the penitence of lushes,
>
> U cycle of time, rhythm of seas,
> Peace of the paws of animals and wrinkles
> On scholars' brows, strident tinkles
> On the supreme trumpet note, peace
> Of the spheres, of the angels. O equals
> X-ray of her eyes; it equals sex.

Our other courses—the study of religion, history, economics, art, and music—were somewhat skimpier, though Scott, himself, was keenly interested in history and economics. A number of books on these subjects were on my curriculum—Lafargue's *Property*, H. G. Wells' *Outline of History*, Plutarch's *Lives*, Hitler's *Mein Kampf*, Karl Marx's *The Working Day*, and Morton's *People's History of England*, which changed me from a conservative to a liberal in one week. How sorry I was that Scott was not alive to hear *Wat Tyler*, the British opera, when it was performed in London. Wat, the working man fighting the nobles, was no longer the villain I had believed he was; he was a betrayed hero as Scott had insisted.

What a difference one good book can make, and when you read two hundred, you cannot remain the same ignorant person. Before my history and economics courses I had been amazed that some of the highly paid Hollywood writers cared about the poor and fought for better salaries for the lesser paid in the industry. The books and Scott's discussions tore the blinkers from my mind. And in fact I became so interested in politics, asking questions all the time about communism and capitalism that in the Red-baiting days of McCarthyism, I was actually accused of being a sympathizer of the party. I never went that far, perhaps because of my natural leaning to caution. And while Scott had flirted quite seriously with communism, its insistence on a certain conformity did not appeal to him. As he explained to me, "I could never join the party. I'm not a joiner. A writer must be free."

Scott's interest in history and politics stretched from our proposed study of "the political development of the Graeco-Roman world" (which he outlined for me but we never got to it) to a lively involvement with current events. Scott wasn't well when André Malraux came to Hollywood to raise money for the Spanish Civil War, but he dragged himself out of a sick bed to attend the meeting in Robert Benchley's bungalow at the Garden of Allah. Likewise, he voted in the Screenwriters' Guild referendum for who should represent them although he was trembling and only just over a drying out period. I was so imbued with his political instruction that he knew I meant business when I threatened, "You'll go to vote if I have to carry you there."

The Screenwriters' referendum was in 1938. Then in 1939 and 1940 a great many of our hours together were spent assessing the war in Europe and also the new contest for the presidency between Franklin Roosevelt and Wendell Wilkie. Naturally we were for Roosevelt, and how delighted we were when Wilkie lost his voice. "If he can't control his larynx," Scott chortled, "how can he control the country?" The night of the election was almost unbearable in its excitement for us as we listened to the radio with the lists of the states on our laps, ticking off the numbers for each party.

I consider Scott's education of me a success. Though I never became a *bona fide* intellectual, I am at ease in discussions with people who are, confident that my opinions and knowledge are valid. And also, because I have such confidence, I'm no longer afraid to say, "I don't understand, please explain."

The dictionary definition of education is "the act or process of imparting or acquiring general knowledge and of developing the powers of reasoning and judgment." My general knowledge is sound both because of my time in College of One—in addition to most of the poetry, which I can still recite from memory, a residue of what I learned has stayed with me—and because of my continued interest in reading good books and keeping up with current events. As for my powers of reasoning and judgment, I feel that I can distinguish good literature from trash and worthwhile people from those who are not. I also know how to judge a painting or a piece of music and to relate today's history and economic upsets and continuing wars with the past. The result is that I am not so frightened by what is happening. I know that we have survived the dangers of past history and that we will probably survive the disasters and inflation of today.

If I still feel unschooled in any way, it is that I lack self-discipline, and I wonder if this might have been corrected with further education. Scottie and my daughter, both of whom had the advantage of attending a top Eastern college, are more disciplined than I am. I find myself thinking, if my courses had not been interrupted, I might have learned that too. Yet Scott, who had great mental discipline and considerable knowledge, had only little success in controlling his personal appetites.

Well, I am not claiming that College of One was or ought to have been a panacea. But I look back on it as one of my life's highlights. I loved to please Scott, and he *was* pleased, knowing that his education for me was successful, that I was soaking up knowledge at such a rate that sometimes he was pressed to keep up with my reading, that I was the best student in our College of One, and that one day I would be as educated as his intellectual friends. Had Scott lived, perhaps the last hope would have been realized. One of my deepest regrets at his death was a selfish one—that I would be deprived of further education under his marvelous aegis.

11.

THE LAST YEAR

I ALWAYS COUNT the last year of Scott's life from the time he stopped drinking. Actually, it was a year and three weeks—from the end of November 1939 to December 21, 1940, and it was the most satisfactory period of our three and a half years together.

For almost the first time, Scott was happy with what he was writing in Hollywood—the film script of "Babylon Revisited"—and he was going full steam ahead, albeit in short spurts, with what the reviewers were to say might have been his best novel, *The Last Tycoon*. Also we were both deriving pleasure from the education plan he had set for me, which, for me, was like an eighteen-hour-a-day university. I believed I would soon be able to hold my own with Scott's friends.

He was no longer making the perilous visits to Zelda that had usually ended in disaster for them both. Scottie was doing well at Vassar and was spending her vacations with the Harold Obers or with friends in Baltimore. And, as often happens with close relatives, distance lent some enchantment to their regard for each other. His letters to her were no longer filled with dire forebodings of the woman she might become. He was no longer stopping her allowance for minor misdemeanours, although he sometimes found it hard to find the $30 a month.

Money and his health were his most persistent worries, but neither of us quite realized the extent to which his health had deteriorated. There were more night sweats, and he was much more easily tired. Still, he was optimistic about the future and fully confident that he had one. His book, he was sure, would give him back his position as an important American writer. He was like a gentle invalid, trying to do as much as possible in the race against time. But I don't think he anticipated that his death would be soon, although there was that one line in his notebooks, "Do I look like death?" which made me shiver when I read it later. At the time we were too content with each other to think of dying.

It was a two-minute walk from my apartment to Schwab's drugstore, and we would go there of an evening to buy the morning papers, flip over the magazines, and drink a chocolate malted milk sitting on the high stools at the counter. Scott laughed when I said, "Imagine, here we are, supposedly sophisticated people, and the highlight of our day is a chocolate malt at Schwab's!" If they could see him now, I used to think, remembering his wild pranks of the 20s and early 30s. He was now the mature Dr. Jekyll. The past was a million miles away. Mr. Hyde, it seemed, had vanished forever.

Sometimes in that last year of tranquility, and I hate to admit this even now, I was restless, wishing for a little more excitement in our lives. But I knew that this quiet existence was good for Scott and his work, and it was a good change for me, whose life had been a series of high and very low points. I was somewhere now in the middle, where psychiatrists, I learned much later, try to put their patients. For the first time for both of us, we were leading average lives, working by day, reading or walking in the evening after the same dinner prepared for us every night by our shared housekeeper, a thin T-bone steak (at 35 cents a pound!), a baked potato, peas, and a grapefruit jelly. We'd make small bets on whether she would ever vary the menu. She never did. We'd sometimes get hysterical over this.

We found so many ordinary things amusing, even the gossip in the studios. It was fun being two busy people, completely fulfilled with our work and happy with each other in the evening. My restlessness was only at the beginning of his last year. I remember it occurred early in 1940, as I drove over Laurel Canyon to the house in Encino—Scott was there until May—where everything was blooming in the premature heat. Before my time with Scott, there had always been several men delighted to take me out to dinner or to the theater or to special events, or to flirt with me. And just as it had taken me some time to settle down for long stretches with the reading (but now in our last year there was never enough time for it), it was the same with our new quietude. My restlessness was fitful and short-lived. After a while I became as quiet and tranquil as Scott seemed.

There was not much money for weekends at expensive places and hotels as in the earlier years, but it was more restful to stay, first in Encino, then, after Scott moved, in Hollywood, talking, sometimes making love or reading a great deal at my apartment or on the balcony at his. In the summer of 1940 we did go to the San Francisco Fair. It was a drive of five hundred miles and we were both exhausted, with Scott driving so slowly, increasingly feeling the strain, and refusing to let me take the wheel. We stopped for a Coke and a sandwich at one of the small huts sprinkled along the coastal highway. At Bakersfield we took the train for the rest of the way and that is when we heard on someone's radio that the British army had escaped from Dunkirk. Everyone cheered.

Humphrey Bogart was at the Fair with his then wife, Mayo Methot. I had visited them in their home in the Hollywood hills—a rather primitive, really the only word is shack, with, I seem to see looking back, a tree growing in the living room, with its roots in the ground and its branches pushing through the roof. Bogey was then complaining about the secondary roles—mostly portraying villains—that he was given at

Warner Brothers. He had made a fine start in pictures, repeating his stage role as the gangster in *The Petrified Forest*, and then came the usual trash. Dark and scowling, he wasn't the leading man type. Or so people thought, until George Raft refused to play Sam Spade in *The Maltese Falcon* and John Huston substituted Bogart.

Another trip Scott and I took in the summer of 1940 was to Monterey, two-thirds of the way to San Francisco. Again the drive seemed long and when we arrived at the two-bedroom bungalow we had booked, Scott immediately rested on his bed while I changed into my red and white polka dot playsuit. I sat in the sunshine and watched the swimmers, but I was also tired and I doubt whether I swam. I didn't realize how much Scott's condition had worsened. Except for our first months together there had usually been something the matter with him, including the fracture on his shoulder—falling down when drunk—when the Alabama football team came for the Rose Bowl game, the ineffectual fights with stronger men that had always landed him on the floor, and the bouts of TB. How careful he was that I should not use the same china, glasses, or spoons, knives, and forks that he did. "TB is easily caught," he explained. But this did not seem to apply when we were kissing and making love.

In any case, ever since becoming a working adult I had been strong. I had eaten well, with little drinking and no smoking. If the liquor hadn't weakened Scott's heart, his smoking would have. In those days there was no warning about cigarettes causing cancer and heart attacks. But knowing this today, I also know that Scott could never have given them up. Smoking, as I have already discussed, was one of his most important crutches, especially after he gave up drinking, along with the coffee, the Cokes, the benzedrine, the digitalis. I would not have wanted to examine Scott's inside, with not only all the above but also the strange food that he ate—sometimes just fudge and crab soup, in that order. He was eating a little more in that last year, lots of cookies, candy, and cake to compensate for the sugar in the alcohol. He was

ng a small pot which, like the balding area on his
was careful to ignore.

y before Scott relinquished the house in Encino, he
_____ me friends over for lunch and to spend the afternoon.
To help him out he still had his beautiful black housekeeper.
Her husband, Gaylord, had one time gently pushed Scott to
the floor in the former time of fighting-drinking, but they both
loved Scott and I think they liked me. She could cook
anything, but I especially remember her iced tea with lemon,
honey, and mint leaves. It was a poem.

Our guests were Eddie Mayer, the Perelmans and his
in-laws, the Nat Wests. "I am leaving this Elysian haunt in two
weeks," Scott had written the Perelmans.

May 13, 1940

Dear Syd and Laura:

This is a love missive so do not be alarmed. I am not
giving a tea for either the Princess Razzarascal or
Twoticker Forsite. *But* I am leaving this Elysian haunt
in two weeks (the 29th to be exact) and sometime
before that nonce I wish you two would dine or
lunch. I know Sunday isn't a good day for you
because of the dwarfs and Saturday next I'm going to
Maurice Evans and Sunday I'm engaged (now you
know, girls, isn't it *won*derful?)

—but any other day between now and the 28th
would be fine. I *want* to see you and very specifically
you, and for the most general and non-specific
reasons. The days being at their longest it is no chore
to find this place up to 7:30 and perhaps the best idea
is dinner. We could either dine *à quatre* or add the
Wests and some other couple—say the Mannerheims
or Browders, and afterwards play with my model
parachute troops. At any events side arms will not be
de rigeur.* Sheilah will be with me just as merry as can
be, to greet you on the porch with a julep. I have just
re-read "Crime and Punishment" and the chapters

*Outer boom or gaff on an old New England square-rigged ship.

on gang labor in "Capitalist Production" and am meek as a liberal bourgeoise lamb.

Call me up on the party line or drop me a note. The only acceptable excuse is that you're going on vacation or have empetigo because I want to see you.

With spontaneous affection,

Scott

5521 Amestoy Avenue
Encino, California
phone: STate 4-0578

Everyone seemed pleased to find a sober Scott—he was so much more interesting discussing politics, literature, when he was not drinking. Scott, who was so shy when addressing large groups or talking to people he did not know, was a brilliant conversationalist with his close friends, and with me especially. Like most intellectuals—although few people then believed that he was one—he spoke simply and you understood what he was saying. Similarly, I had been amazed at the simplicity of Edmund Wilson's writing.

After lunch the Perelmans and Eddie took a walk around the grounds, while Scott brought out his scrapbooks to show Nat and Eileen. She thumbed scornfully through his mementoes, the blonde and brunette curls of young loves tied with pink ribbon, the dance cards with little pink pencils, and the small lace handkerchief he had retrieved at a long ago adolescent party in St. Paul's. She accused him of only loving the rich and I wanted to belt her one on the mouth. How dare she belittle him. I believe she had been a member of the Communist Party, or at least a fellow traveler, and she despised such a show of bourgeois recollections.

My attitude was so hostile toward Eileen—although previously we had been friends—that she took her husband away early from our small party. I was annoyed when she dared to die with Nat in a car crash near Encino within the same twenty-four hours as Scott. They would be going into the unknown together, and if anyone went with Scott, it should have been Zelda, or me—more me I thought at the time, but now I would say Zelda.

There were to be no more parties for Scott. He had neither the strength nor the money to entertain on any scale. The ebbing energy was given to his work—there was the last job at 20th Century-Fox, the Emlyn Williams play, *The Light of Heart*, plus *The Last Tycoon* and my education. Each of these projects had about an equal share of his time. I wonder again if I had known he would die near the end of the year, would I have persuaded him to drop the education and concentrate only on his writing? Perhaps, but I don't think so. He could only write a few hours each day, and teaching me was a rest for his brain.

Living in Hollywood was less exhausting for Scott than the long drive over the canyons from town to Encino. He missed the spaciousness of the Encino home but he had lived in smaller places than the apartment on Laurel Avenue on the third floor I found for him. The street was next to mine on Hayworth Avenue. Some of the neighbors were noisy, which harassed him, and the furniture was rather dreary—vomit green as he described the settee—but it was new and clean and there was a small open balcony adjoining the living room. It was our favorite place on weekends for reading and wondering about the young men and their girls who flitted in and out—but not like the whispering moths of Gatsby's parties on Long Island. These voices were loud.

Pretty Joyce Matthews was an apartment away from Scott. Later she would marry Milton Berle, then Billy Rose, and abandon her precarious movie career. Another neighbor was Lucille Ball, who had not yet married Desi Arnaz, and it seemed she was always begging him to visit a little longer. We made bets on whether she would succeed, which was not often. At this time, Miss Ball, whom I had first noticed in the chorus line-up of the *Goldwyn Follies*, starring Eddie Cantor, was rated as a starlet. Translated, this means extra girl, with maybe a line to speak. It was not until the summer of 1944 that she became famous. That is when I took my husband, Trevor Westbrook, who was seeing his two-year-old daughter

Wendy for the first time, to the CBS television station in Hollywood to view the filming of the "I Love Lucy" pilot. As you know, the show became a tremendous hit and transformed Lucille into a superstar.

We never entertained in Scott's apartment or mine, neither of which fitted into Scott's idea of grandeur. But we were occasionally invited for dinner to the homes of his friends—Dorothy Parker, Eddie Mayer, Buff Cobb—and it was a relief to get away from the T-bone steaks, delicious though they were. We usually ate out when we would be attending a film preview, but not in the expensive restaurants we had patronized in the early eighteen months. I wanted to pay for my share but Scott would not hear of it. I never questioned where his money came from, it would have hurt his feelings.

In this last year he seemed to accept me totally. I was his dear face, dear heart, dear Sheilo, or Presh, or Sweetheart. I had nicknamed my first husband Ma Fois, I had called Donegall Don, but there was never a nickname for Scott, although his writer friends would sometimes call him Scottie.

In addition to the Hollywood writers group, we had some unusual friends. One was the spastic man who sold newspapers opposite the Beverly Hills Brown Derby. After dinner there we always crossed the road to buy the morning newspapers from him. Scott was interested in the members of his family and the pair of them chatted, or rather Scott did, about the headlines of the papers which in 1940 were full of the disasters of the war in Europe. After Scott's death I made a point of buying my papers in the evening from this man, and he was so sorry that Mr. Fitzgerald had died. Later when his son took over he told me he had heard a lot about Scott and me from his father. We were friends to the day I left Hollywood.

There was also the waiter at the Derby. Previously, in the drinking times, Scott had been rude to him. But now they were friendly. The then young man is now the Beverly Derby's head captain, and he takes good care of me when I lunch there for the great corned beef hash. He looks at me as though we are two old-timers who have survived.

In that last year, Scott was always writing letters to his

friends in the East, mostly sad letters exaggerating his hatred of Hollywood, and one a week to Zelda, always with the Dearest prefix. I was somewhat taken aback when I read the correspondence with her in the collection of letters. The last letter was written on December 19, only two days before he died. But whereas his early letters from Hollywood were hopeful that they would get together again, there was no written suggestion of this during 1940. He knew then that they could never resume their marriage. He had realized that together they would be misfits in the new decade, that Zelda had been broken by the past, but that he had the chance of survival and new fulfillment.

I'm not sure when Edmund Wilson's first novel, *I Thought of Daisy*, was published, but in those last months Scott talked a great deal about his friend. Earlier he had written to Bunny suggesting he should try writing a novel, but after *Daisy*, he told me with a small amount of smugness, "He can never be a good novelist. But as a critic, an essayist, and a keen judge of historical events, he's the best. No one comes near him." Scott particularly admired Wilson's *To the Finland Station*, the account of Lenin's journey via Finland after the first chaotic stage of the Russian Revolution (the Kerensky government was vulnerable) to take over the country and to steep it in communism, with Marx as his bible.

Scott talked a great deal, too, about Hemingway, whom he still admired but wouldn't see again, he told me, until after the publication of *The Last Tycoon*, and only, then, if the book was the hoped-for success. He wondered whether Ernest's talent was "thinning out."

I don't remember too many boxes of flowers in this last year—in any case, I didn't want or need them as a reminder of his love. But he managed to scrape up $85 for the silver jug he gave me for my birthday in 1940. It is still my most treasured possession.

One evening, after a film preview, we were strolling on Hollywood Boulevard to the car park when we saw a small shop that advertised "Make your own records—hear yourself speak." We went inside and Scott recorded four readings—I remember best Keats' "Ode to a Nightingale" and something from Shakespeare's *Othello*. When he presented it to me, I wrote on the center, "A new and better Barrymore." Many years after his death when I played it, I was surprised at the deep professorial tone of his voice, much lower than it was in real life. Perhaps even then he was speaking for posterity—he knew I never lost anything that I liked. But he might have felt self-conscious and intent on not sounding frivolous.

The record was in the material Scott had given me, which I had presented to the Princeton University Library in 1959. Perhaps a student or researcher substituted it with a copy, because the record no longer bears my written statement, "A new and better Barrymore." Some of the two hundred books Scott gave me were stolen from me which is one reason I gave the rest to the library.

Scott, in that final year, was encouraging me to write more short stories. I remember one, "Ostrich," about a debutante whose grandmother was very ill. She dreaded receiving a telegram saying that Granny was dead, and then she could not go to the deb party that evening. I borrowed this incident from Proust's *Remembrance of Things Past,* where the Duchesse de Guermantes made sure she did not hear of the death of a relative because she was going to a party.

I wrote a story titled "Janey," about a father and a rebellious girl, who was Scottie to the life—to her creamy dipped-in-milk complexion, the wide-apart blue eyes, the perfect teeth. My character was seventeen, the daughter of a middle-aged professor who in the early 20s was the literary mouthpiece for flaming youth. Scott was amused when I showed him the plan, but thought I should have changed it a little from the actual people so they would not be so instantly recognizable. I also wrote a story about Barbara Hutton, whom I had seen playing tennis at the Beverly Hills Tennis Club, with not a hair ruffled on her sculptured locks. Also the first "Beloved Infidel," and "Not in the Script," about my fight at a studio with Connie Bennett who was then a superstar (See Appendix.)

We were both so busy and yet we had so much time for each

other. I relegated much of my gossip-gathering to my British columnist friend, Jonah Ruddy, and some of his work got me into hot water with the studios, but I didn't care. The column was an interim activity until I could take a chance on fiction, which Scott was teaching me to write.

Recently, Warren Beatty, a great admirer of Scott, said to me, "In a way Scott was bad for you as a writer. You knew you could never write as well as he did and this prevented you from developing in your own right." This is not entirely true. Edmund Wilson, after reading my *College of One*, told me I was a good writer. I knew, of course, that I could never be as good as Scott, but to have such close contact and guidance from a fine author could help me stretch to the end of my limitations. Scott would be pleased that I have done well with my published seven books. This is the eighth, including the novel *Gentleman Crook* I wrote in England before settling in the United States.

In that last year with Scott, everything was going so well for us that I refused another lecture tour that would have given me a few thousand dollars. I did leave Scott for two days—it was early November 1940—to attend the premiere in Dallas, Texas, of the Gary Cooper film *The Westerner*. But I hated going, though I was still thrilled by Gary, who was so handsome and so charming. He had been my second interview in 1936 (Charlie Chaplin was the first). My car had crashed on my way to Paramount, but I had picked up my shattered nerves and rushed on. Now I asked the press agent to be sure to put me in the same plane with Gary, partly to get an interview, but mostly to be close to my hero—there were two planes for the stars and the press.

Mack Millar, the publicity agent who was arranging the junket, said at the airport—in Scott's hearing—"I did as you asked. I have put you in the same plane as Gary." I looked guiltily at Scott. Would he think I would be unfaithful and start drinking again—airports had been unlucky for us. But his face was bland and if he had heard he must have realized that my feeling for Mr. Cooper was pure fantasy, which it was.

I never told Scott of the one moment in Dallas when I could

have translated the dream into reality. I had arrived first and was washing up in the bathroom of the big suite in the hotel where the after-film party was to be held. When I came out, Gary was in the bedroom. His smile at me was a question mark. He held my hands and looked down deeply from the top tower of his eyes into mine. I don't know how long this would have lasted, but remembering Scott, I giggled and pulled away.

Scott was at the airport when we returned and there was not a drop of liquor on him. I thanked God. I introduced him to Gary, who until then had been protective of me—I had been airsick and after Gary had lifted me into my top berth he had wanted to rub my stomach, but this would have been disastrous!

Gary smiled somewhat sheepishly as he and Scott shook hands. They were of the same generation and knew about each other. As Scott drove me to my apartment, I told him about the lunches and dinners that had been given for us. I had ridden horseback in the parade headed by Gary down the main street and wore the brown felt cowboy hat especially made for me by Rex, the best hatmaker in Beverly Hills. I told Scott I felt glamourous and important as I had when I substituted for the star in Mr. Cochran's London Revue *One Damn Thing After Another* in 1928.

If Scott was jealous of this gaiety in which he had no part, he did not show it. He was too pleased to have me back. "I missed you," he said, "You must never go away again." I promised I would not. Neither of us realized then that he would be the one to go away.

12.

THE DEATH

As I REMEMBER it now, December 20, 1940, was a trying day. Scott was restless and irritable. I was also nervous because I had an appointment at M-G-M to see Spencer Tracy. Sometimes he'd be in a jovial mood so that I could get a good interview. But more often he was morose and made me squirm with his hostile stare as though daring me to ask silly questions.

After the first heart attack late in November 1940 at Schwab's drugstore on Sunset Boulevard, the doctor had forbidden Scott to climb stairs. His own apartment on Laurel Avenue in the street next to mine had been recently built. Ceilings were higher then, and there were more stairs to climb. I had a spare bedroom on the ground floor in my apartment on Hayworth Avenue, so, of course, I asked him to use it until his secretary or I could find a similar apartment for him in the same neighborhood.

I found something that I thought would suit him, but there were four steps to the front door and he wouldn't take it. I remember I was somewhat exasperated. As I have mentioned, when Scott was sober he was a hypochondriac, and I was never sure whether he was shamming or really ill. Scott had forbidden me to question his doctor in his absence, but the doctor had told me in Scott's presence that the attack had damaged his heart. "How much?" I asked. "Twenty-five percent," he replied. And this had alarmed me. Why he did not hospitalize him for the usual six weeks flat in bed, I'll never understand. He was a good doctor, so maybe he did ask this of Scott who, I think, would have gone mad during a long hospital stay. But he was resting in my spare bedroom many hours during the day.

During the night of December 20, he slept badly. I had awakened to hear him walking around from the bedroom to the living room and kitchen. He was unhappy when I saw him in the morning. "It's the chapter," he explained, his voice revealing his anxiety. "I can't make it hang together."

It was Chapter VI of *The Last Tycoon*, where Monroe Stahr was to meet Mr. Brimmer, a member of the Communist party. The encounter resulted in Stahr's drinking heavily, the first time in the book that Scott mentioned a drinking problem for the frail producer. By the sixth chapter, Stahr was already becoming Scott Fitzgerald, who would have started drinking as he would have been nervous at meeting Brimmer. In his youth, Stahr had been a scrapper which Scott was not. That came later, after he began drinking. So the now Scott-Stahr challenged him to a fist fight. Brimmer knocked him out. Looking at the prone producer, the Communist marveled that this crumpled heap was where all the capitalist power lay.

After Scott had his breakfast, which consisted usually of orange juice and coffee (he would have a bigger lunch), he returned to bed with a dozen Cokes to wrestle with Chapter VI, on the writing board he had brought from his apartment. It was no use. "Where's Frances?" he demanded peevishly. "She's not coming till noon," I reminded him. "She told you she had an appointment with her dentist."

I had to leave for the studio. "Look" I said, "why don't you try to sleep and when you wake up I'm sure Frances will be here." He acquiesced, and I took away the board and the pencils and paper and closed the Venetian blinds. He was still grumbling about Frances not being there when he needed her, but he lay back on the bed with a deep sigh and closed his eyes.

When I returned—Spencer Tracy's mood had been good—Scott was working with Frances. And after she left several hours later, he came beaming into the living room with its Barker's basement second-hand furniture that we had bought together, and announced, "I've been able to fix it." He was exhilarated as he always was after writing to his satisfaction. "Baby, this book will be good. It might even make enough money for us both to leave Hollywood." I smiled like Ruth mid the alien corn, who said to her mother-in-law, where thou goest, so go I. That was me all right.

He dressed and we went to celebrate the completion of the chapter over dinner at Lyman's, a restaurant-delicatessen on Hollywood Boulevard near a theater—I think it was the Pantages—where we were to attend the preview of *This Thing Called Love*. It was a comedy starring Rosalind Russell and Melvyn Douglas. I can't remember what we ate, but some of the names on the menu—knishes, knadlich, latkas—it was a Jewish restaurant—amused him. He laughed trying to pronounce the strange words.

During the showing of the film he was very quiet, but I was not worried because he usually studied the plot to help him master the technique of "the strange medium of the flicks" as he called it. But when the lights went up and we started to leave, he almost fell. He's lost his balance, I thought, looking around and hoping no one had seen. They would think he was drinking again.

I held Scott's left elbow and steered him slowly to the door. He was breathing somewhat heavily and drew deep draughts of air when we were outside. He seemed all right as he drove me slowly home. "I had the same dizziness as that time in Schwab's," he told me. I was worried. "Shall I get the doctor tonight?" "No, he's coming tomorrow. Don't worry, Sheilo, I feel much better." He took more than his usual number of sleeping pills. When he was finally asleep, I tiptoed into his room every now and then to make sure he was all right. One time he awakened and kissed me and said sleepily, "Go to bed, I'm all right."

He seemed much better in the morning, and I was sure that the new cardiogram would prove that his heart had almost repaired itself. We were both in good spirits, though he was still sleepy from all the pills and didn't dress until about noon.

Scott talked a great deal about Scottie and about Zelda, who was with her mother in Montgomery. He was pleased with them both. Scottie was doing well scholastically and socially at Vassar. The doctors were hopeful that Zelda had reached a plateau where she could function fairly well for the rest of her life, though they had warned that when the stress mounted, she might have to go back to Highlands for brief periods. Scott was very short of cash. But something always turned up at the last minute, and I knew that he would probably soon be receiving another $5,000 from Max Perkins at Scribners, which included the $2,000 I was planning to send to Scribners that day.

I went to Greenblatt's, the delicatessen on the corner of Sunset and Hayworth, for some sandwiches and a Hershey bar that I would eat later. It was a lovely day, and the sun was pouring into the living room through the open Venetian blinds. I settled into the sofa with a biography of Beethoven—I was in the middle of the music course. To reinforce the book, I asked Scott if it was all right for me to play the *Eroica* on the record player he had bought me at the start of the course along with all the thick cases of records—there were no long-playing discs then.

Scott smiled and sank into the dark green armchair with the latest *Princeton Alumni Weekly*, focusing on an article about football. Every now and then he would look up with a faraway expression, perhaps dreaming of the glory he had wanted for himself on the football field.

Earlier he had dictated the letter I was writing to Scottie to go with the clothes I was sending her—I remember a long black velvet evening gown with short puff sleeves and a heart-shaped neckline which I had bought a few months earlier for the Dallas premiere of Gary Cooper's film, *The Westerner*.

Scott stood up and said, "I want something sweet, I'm going

to Schwab's for some ice cream." "But the doctor is coming soon," I reminded him. "I'm sure he'll have good news about your heart. Will a Hershey bar do?" I went to the drawer in my bedroom where I had put it for later munching and gave it to Scott. He savored it slowly while, as I found out later, writing down the nicknames of football heroes of his class opposite their names in the magazine. We both looked up at the same time and smiled at each other while he licked his fingers, and then we settled back to the reading.

A few minutes later, while the *Eroica* shrilled its prophecy, I half saw Scott jump to his feet and clutch the mantelpiece as though to steady himself. He would often stand up suddenly when he had an idea for some writing. Or was it the dizziness again? Before I could reach him, he fell to the floor, spread-eagled on his back. His eyes were closed and he was breathing heavily. I was sure he had fainted.

What do you do when someone faints? I had only fainted twice in my life—once after an operation, and another time when I was punishing my mother by refusing to eat. I had seen girls who had fainted on stage or in the dressing room. Someone had usually sat them up and put their head between their legs. But I wasn't sure I could do this for Scott. Brandy. I had a small bottle in the kitchen. But he hadn't had a drink for so long, would the taste start him off again? If only he would move and open his eyes. Brandy. Nothing mattered except to wake him up. His teeth were clenched and when I poured the liquor into his mouth it spilled all over his chin and neck. I was embarrassed. I felt I was taking advantage of him. But what should I do? And why didn't he regain consciousness? I must get help.

Harry Culver, for whom Culver City had been named, was the owner of the apartments and lived there. I ran to his apartment. He was in and came back with me. Scott was still motionless. Mr. Culver felt his pulse and listened to his heart. He stood up slowly. "He's dead," he said quietly. No no, he couldn't be. He'd been alive and smiled at me a few minutes before. Oxygen. The fire department. "Someone has fainted and can't wake up," I told the man who answered. "We'll be right there."

They seemed to arrive almost before I put the phone down. They put a mask over his face and tried to revive him while I watched as though in a dream. Could death come so swiftly, alive one second, dead the next? And if he were dead, would there be a scandal? I was flooded with all my early feelings of guilt. Thank God it was afternoon and not the middle of the night. But would my reputation be ruined? I was writing a syndicated column for important papers all over the world. These thoughts flashed through my mind while I dialed doctor after doctor, but it was a Saturday afternoon and those I called were out.

Then Scott's doctor arrived, and the firemen, looking glum and shaking their heads, stood aside. It was true. Scott was dead. Suddenly the room was full of familiar faces—among them Frances, Pat Duff, my secretary, Buff Cobb and her husband. I didn't know who had sent for them. Perhaps I had.

Why does death always attract a crowd? It had happened when my mother had died when I was alone with her in our two-room flat in the East End of London. I didn't cry then and I didn't now. But I shook uncontrollably and went into the kitchen to be alone. When I returned to my living room I found they had taken Scott away. A strange sound came from my mouth. Then Buff and her husband, Cameron Rogers, drove me to the house in Santa Monica where they lived with her father, Irvin Cobb, the humorist.

Strange, even now, to call Scott "the body." In an odd way I also felt important—so many people were concerned about me. I remember thinking that Scott would be pleased that his friends were caring for me. And the education, what would become of that fine enterprise? It was so near the end; could I finish it alone? Mostly, I was numb. Of course, I was in shock. Nature shields us from madness at such times so that the impact of what has happened does not strike at once.

The half-hour drive with the windows wide open brought me back to a sort of reality. When I arrived at the house, I telephoned Harold Ober, who had been Scott's agent for so long and asked him to break the news to Scottie. I knew I couldn't do that. I was talking fairly normally, or so I thought, to Buff and her family when the telephone rang. It was Scottie, full of sympathy, and my voice didn't break even when she asked me how it had happened and I told her. I realize now it was a shock for her, but her voice was calm as she said, "Of course I will leave Vassar and get a job." "Oh no," I replied, "You must graduate from Vassar, that was your father's dearest wish." "We'll talk about that another time," she replied.

And then in her eighteen-year-old voice: "Sheilah, you know you can't come to the funeral." "I know," I replied, and said, "Good-bye." That is when I wept, loud weeping that wouldn't stop. I weep now—more quietly—remembering the sudden realization that Scott no longer belonged to me, he belonged to his family, and he might have wanted it that way. I hadn't intended to go to the funeral—I've only been to one funeral in my life and that was by mistake. I prefer to remember those I love as I have seen them alive, not being lowered into the ground or in an incinerator.

And as it turned out, the doctors thought the funeral would be too great a strain for Zelda, who took Scott's death more calmly than anyone had dared to hope for. Her reaction came several months later when she had to return to the sanitarium.

Buff turned over her bedroom to me and gave me two sleeping pills. I slept fitfully, although I had never taken pills before. It was a few days before Christmas, and Mr. Cobb insisted that I stay with them until it was over. I loved them for their kindness, and if Scott's other friends were going to be as kind to me, I thought, perhaps I'll be able to cope with the loss of Scott. I might even become a member of the intelligentsia, and Scott would like that. But I had the feeling of standing over a huge chasm with nothing to hold me up; and if I didn't strain to stay up, I would fall in.

There was a feeling of airiness in my head; nothing was very real except the demands of my daily column. Robert Benchley offered to write some for me, but I knew I had to do it myself, that I would lose my reason unless I immersed myself in work to blot out the image of Scott on his back, lifeless, in my living room. I still don't understand why, but the columns I wrote then were full of humor.

I remember attending a Paramount Studio preview in Van Nuys for a film starring Madeleine Carroll and Sterling Hayden—later they would marry. At the end someone died—it might have been Sterling—and he lay seemingly lifeless on the ground. I started to cry and rushed out of the theater down the boulevard as far as Encino. They'll be looking for me, I thought—I had driven there with Bob Gilham, head of Paramount publicity—so I walked back and managed sufficient composure to get silently into the car. Bob was a friend and he understood.

A few days after Scott died, Dorothy Parker and her husband visited me after going to the Hollywood funeral parlor where his body had been taken. There she had spoken the famous line from *The Great Gatsby*—"the poor son of a bitch." I was in bed, clutching a hot-water bottle to my stomach and drinking a small glassful of gin—the best cure for cramps. It was also Scott's favorite tipple. I recited "Beloved Infidel," Scott's poem to me, over and over, and Dottie said it was beautiful and especially liked the lines that included "And when I join the ghosts who lay beside your flashing fire." "Flashing fire," she repeated, and for a second I felt very desirable. And then I said, "I must find someone like Scott." Later she told Gerold Frank, "That had class." Nonetheless she slaughtered *Beloved Infidel* in her review for *Esquire*.

Just before New Year's Eve and after I had broken down at a party at Dorothy's, I suddenly decided to go to New York. I hadn't minded living in the place where Scott had died. "Why should I?" I asked the friends who wondered that I could. "This is where Scott is." But it was unthinkable to see in the New Year with crowds of Hollywood people as a substitute for Scott, even though we had not been together the previous December 31. The year before he had been with Zelda, but that was different. He was then *alive*.

I learned on the train that Scott's body was also on it, being shipped to Baltimore where he would be buried, so in a way he was still with me. Sydney Perelman was also on the train, accompanying the bodies of Nat West and West's wife, Eileen, who had died in a car crash, several hours after Scott had died.

And it all seemed rather gruesome. There were other people I knew on the train, and I ate my meals with them and looked forward to spending some time in New York, which I had liked so much when I first came to America.

Also I could hold on to Scott for a little longer, by seeing some of the friends he had loved. My first call was on Frances and Albert Hackett. I went straight to their apartment without calling them first. I made the excuse for the visit that I was bringing them the small verse Scott had written after he had been called from their party to work with the producer, Hunt Stromberg, on a script. They already had the verse but accepted mine as though it was the first time they had seen it.

> Sing a song for Shielah's (wrong spelling as usual)
>   supper,
> Belly void of rye,
> Gone before the cocktail, back for the pie.
> Stromberg sent for Poppa, though Poppa hadn't et,
> To do what Jesus couldn't—
> Save Marie Antoinette . . .

It was New Year's Eve, and they were going to a party and invited me to come with them. I went but should not have. I could not be part of the gaiety. I smiled when people talked to me, but I could not bear it and asked Frances if she would mind if I took a taxi back to my hotel. I was full of loneliness and self-pity, and angry with Scott. Why had he done this to me? Why had he taken every part of me into the grave with him? It wasn't fair. I had never given myself so completely to anyone before. Life stretched drearily before me.

My dear friend Margaret Brainard was in the hospital after a minor heart attack. Her doctor had insisted on six weeks flat on her back. I visited her every day that I was in the city. Her other constant visitor was a former actor friend, Richard Gordon, who married her when she was recovered.

When the New Year excitement was over, I phoned the Murphys. My voice was quite steady when I told them I was in New York. Gerald at once invited me to lunch with them. It had been a great loss for them, too. They had always loved Scott and Zelda, and they liked me because they believed I had helped Scott and he had told them good things about me.

We lunched at the French restaurant in Rockefeller Center. They asked me what my plans were, and I told them I wanted to go home, and home for me was England. "I have friends there," I said, and they nodded sympathetically. I was doing fine until Jock Whitney stopped at the table and said how sorry he was. I clenched my teeth or I might have broken down.

I had many meetings with Scottie, whom I liked now for herself, not only because she was Scott's daughter for whom I had acted as a buffer against her father's irritation. I told her of the cable I had received from Lord Donegall after Scott's death, saying how sorry he was and would I settle all my business in America because he would not allow me to return. "You must marry him," Scottie advised delightedly, "and I will visit you in your castle." She was so like her father: his enthusiasm, his smile, his broad forehead, the same eyes. I couldn't have enough of looking at her. I had already made a will leaving her everything I possessed. It wasn't much. The $11,000 in my savings account included Scott's $2,000.

I saw my North American Newspaper Alliance boss, John Wheeler, and he tried to discourage me about England. The war against England was getting hotter with so much of Europe in the hands of Hitler. He said he admired me for wanting to be in a country at war but that I might get killed in an air raid or a German invasion. He told me I was being foolish.

To be killed did not seem such a disaster, but I had too much energy to really want to die. Perhaps I could do some good for England if I wrote sympathetic stories about the fine people of my native land and how they were coping. Perhaps I could do my small bit to bring America to join Britain in the war. But it wasn't until May, several months after I had returned to Hollywood, that I finally received permission to go.

I had cabled Lord Beaverbrook, who I knew admired initiative, to help me obtain an exit visa from England. This was Mr. Wheeler's stipulation, as I was still a British subject, and he feared, he said, that once in England I wouldn't be able to leave. The visa magically appeared.

Then I wanted to fly to England in a bomber. American war planes were flying at a great rate across the Atlantic to replenish the R.A.F., which had lost so much during the Battle of Britain the previous September. Scott was then alive and for the first time since the war had started in the fall of 1939, he believed that the British might win. Dunkirk and the Battle of Britain had convinced him. Before that he had said, "They don't have a chance," and I had hotly argued with him. "For one thing you don't know the British, and for another you don't like them." "Present company excepted" said Scott, smiling.

I wished he had known that Hitler, instead of invading England as expected, had turned his armies and the Luftwaffe against Russia, his supposed ally. How Scott had been shocked when Stalin had signed the infamous treaty with Hitler which paved the way for the invasion of Poland. Now he would never know that it had been a cynical marriage of convenience for both. But I knew I must stop thinking about what Scott would have thought about this or that. To survive, I must push him far back in my mind and not talk about him. Only Donegall and our friends in Hollywood knew about my years as Scott's girl. There would be so much to do, I wouldn't have time for the sterility of self-pity.

I returned to Hollywood to sell the furniture in my apartment. Mr. Culver allowed me to break my lease, and in June, I was on the Super-Chief train for New York, to fly a few days later by Pan American clipper to England via Bermuda, the Azores, and Lisbon. There I changed to a British plane for the air base in Poole, Dorsetshire. I didn't know it then, but I was flying to a new life in which Scott would still play an important role.

13.

THE REBIRTH

BEFORE FLYING TO England in July 1941, I spent several days with Edmund Wilson and his wife, Mary McCarthy, at their home in Wellfleet, Massachusetts. Mr. Wilson had written me the good news that Max Perkins thought so highly of Scott's unfinished novel, *The Last Tycoon*, that they were planning to publish it in a volume with *The Great Gatsby* and he would be putting it all together. He needed my help, he wrote, on some of the notes Scott had made for the rest of the book.

I was somewhat nervous about staying with Scott's "intellectual conscience" and Mary who, with her vast intellectuality, had somewhat intimidated me when Scott and I had visited them in New York eighteen months previously. The journey to their home was tiring, first by train to New York, then a plane to Boston, and a bus to Wellfleet. Bunny and Mary met me, and were both so kind that I relaxed.

Early every morning, Mr. Wilson led me to his study, a round turret, with, up a flight of stairs, a completely windowed room. This is when I first saw the notes and the plan for *The Last Tycoon*. I felt important explaining everything I knew about the six written chapters and the plan. After a few hours, we'd pick up his little son and drive to the nearby beach. It was strange and dreamlike.

Back in New York, although the United States was not yet at war—that would come six months later—the machinery for war had started. All over the city there were men in uniform: army, navy, marine, and air force. The hotels were full of rich refugees from Europe. There was a frenetic gaiety; the theaters and restaurants were jammed with big spenders. I wondered whether London would be like this, and strangely it almost was. Live it up today because tomorrow, who knows.

I telephoned Johnny, my ex-husband, as soon as I arrived in London. He was in the Army and posted near the capital, and he came to see me the next day. He had been a major in the first world war, and had enlisted as soon as the second started. This time he was a captain, still elegant in his Savile Row uniform. But Johnny in his fifties was too old for active service, and soon after I arrived he was mustered out.

Scott had been amused by Johnny's letters to me—they were always so full of hope, for me and for himself. But in *my* letters to Johnny, I never mentioned Scott, except to write that "a very nice man was helping me with my reading." And, as I elaborated, "I wish I had spent all my time in getting an education instead of going to parties. I wish I'd had the sense to want to educate myself when I lived in London near all the big museums. I suppose that when one is young, one has too good a time to think of developing the mind."

When I saw Johnny, he asked me about "the nice chap." It was Scott Fitzgerald, I told him. He had heard the name. "Oh yes, the Jazz Age fellow," he said. I couldn't tell Johnny about my love for Scott. He would have felt pushed into the cold. But I talked to him a great deal about the education and the books Scott had written. And sometimes while I talked I forgot that Scott was dead. Everything he had done for me was alive and satisfying.

At other times my work helped me to live on the surface of my mind. I interviewed George Bernard Shaw on his eighty-fifth birthday, I broadcast my impressions of England at war from the BBC underground in Cavendish Square where it still is, and I saw a great deal of Donegall.

Because of Scott's painstaking education of me, I was in a

better position to marry Don. I would make him a wife he would not have to apologize for. I liked him enormously. There was the same gentleness that Scott had when he was not drinking, and some of the same Irish anger when he was. But Scott had taught me more than I could read in books. Since loving Scott, I was not weighing "what can this do for me?"

It was too soon after his death for me to be in love with anyone and I believed I would not marry again unless I was. Four years earlier, I had been in love with the idea of being a Marchioness and having a husband who moved in the best British circles, but I had been too much in awe of the situation—orphanage girl marries Marquess—to let myself yield enough to find out if I could be in love with him. Now I knew that I wasn't.

Don asked me wonderingly why I had wanted to share the dreadful conditions prevailing in England. But, in fact, London was gay. Don was a member of the Home Guard and regaled me with hilarious stories about his unit. Everyone I met had funny stories to tell about the bombings. It would have made Scott laugh, but I deliberately didn't think about him too much in the six weeks of my 1941 summer in England.

The Paul Willerts had me for lunch—Paul had known Scott in America when his father was in Washington as the correspondent for the London *Times*. And Paul and I had met in Hollywood when he came to help raise money for the Spanish Loyalists. Now he introduced me to a calm, square-faced man with a name like Brada—he had been a spy for the Loyalists, infiltrating into Franco's army. Caught by the Fascists, he had escaped shortly before he was to be shot. What a story Scott could have made of that!

And then Jack Bergen of Grumman Corporation arrived in London in one of his aircraft. Jack had tried to get me a seat on a bomber flying to England, but couldn't. Now he invited me to a cocktail party at his suite in Claridges, where he had several bottles of liquor, nylon stockings, and lipsticks for his English friends.

It was Jack who introduced me to Trevor Westbrook, who had just returned from the Mideast to report to Churchill on the situation there. Trevor had been Lord Beaverbrook's right-hand man when he was Minister of Air. I liked him at once and when, driving me back to The International Sportsman's Club where I was staying, he said he had never read a book, I liked him even more for his honesty and the fact that he was poles apart from Scott Fitzgerald. He would help to blot Scott from my mind.

I was on the point of getting a visa to the Russian battlefront—Quentin Reynolds was already there—when I received a cable from Mr. Wheeler to return to the United States to cover the first visit to Washington of the Duke and Duchess of Windsor since their marriage.

I dreaded returning to America with all its memories of Scott. I would never return to Hollywood, I decided. That was impossible. If I had to live in America I would be a roving reporter with a New York base, and I arranged this with Mr. Wheeler.

Back in the States I realized, as the weeks lengthened into months, I was not in love with Trevor and that I could not marry a man who did not read books. He had given me an engagement ring before I flew back to Lisbon, the Azores, Bermuda, and New York. And yet, because I felt bereft and lonely, I pretended to myself and others that I was still going to marry him.

I had written some pieces on wartime England for *Variety*—the best articles I have ever written and for no pay!—and the editor, Abel Green, asked me to lunch at the '21' club. He knew about Scott, and I didn't want to be pitied. So I talked a great deal about Trevor and about my intention to marry him. My vehemence seemed to irritate Abel (who with his wife, Grace, became good friends of mine) and he said, "If you love him so much, why are you waiting to marry him? Why don't you go back to England?" I was appalled at the impression I had created, especially as I had decided that I did not want to live in England again, and that I was not in love with Trevor. And would not marry him.

I went to Washington and wrote some stories about the Duke and Duchess. I went to Montreal to interview some of the pilots who were ferrying planes to England. I went to various other cities on the Eastern seaboard—to Baltimore to interview Glenn Martin, whose company was churning out war materiel in vast quantities. And I thought I was beginning to cope with the loss of Scott. But as the weeks came closer to December 21, 1941, the first anniversary of Scott's death, I unexpectedly became panic-stricken. I was like a crazy woman, pacing from my apartment bedroom to the living room in aimless strides.

I had a black cleaning woman from Jamaica, who watched me sympathetically. "I don't know what to do," I kept repeating. She put her strong arm around me and said, "Don't worry, honey, something's sure to turn up." Something did. Pearl Harbor. And soon after, Trevor came to Washington with the top members of the British cabinet, the Army, the Navy, and the Air Force, to consult with President Roosevelt on how best to utilize combined war power in the fight against Hitler. Trevor was one of the experts on aircraft.

John Wheeler was sending me to Washington to cover the big story. He hoped I would get some scoops from Beaverbrook, who had given me stories before. Meanwhile, Trevor called Mr. Wheeler and tracked me down to a chair at my dentist's. I told him of my assignment. It was fate, he said. We would get married before he returned with the rest of the experts on the new battleship *King George V* that had brought them. And so we were married across the bridge in Arlington, Virginia, the day of the 21st had passed, and I had survived.

On the plane back to New York, I kept looking at my platinum wedding ring, and wondering what Scott would have thought. I was sure he would have understood my anguish and the need to obliterate the anniversary of his death. But he might have been jealous, and after I became pregnant, I fantasized that Scott had spoken to the powers that be and said, "Don't let her love him, but for God's sake give her a baby." He knew how much I wanted a child, but because of my association with Scott I had accepted the fact that I would probably never have children.

And now this miracle. I remember Roland Young, the

veteran actor, coming to my apartment in the Shoreham Hotel and saying, "It's marvelous that you are pregnant with a child from Scott." "If I was," I replied, "that would be a real miracle." Wendy was born in the fall of 1942. Scott had died in December 1940. I had wanted a boy, to name him Scott (though I knew I was being unfair to Trevor); I compromised by giving Wendy the middle name of Frances—the F at the beginning of Scott's name was Francis.

The year 1941 also saw the birth of *The Last Tycoon.* When I passed Scribners Book Store on Fifth Avenue, with the big window full of Scott's half-finished novel, I hoped that somehow Scott would know. And how pleased he would have been with the reviews, most of which believed that this might have been his best novel, that he had captured the essence of Hollywood better than anyone else. If the book were a success, he had said, we would leave Hollywood. It was wartime and where would we have gone? And what about Zelda? Even if they were divorced she would always be there. What a weird threesome we would be.

I had vowed I'd never return to Hollywood with its memories of Scott. But with my own child, the remembrance, while I could not talk about it, was more bearable. I now had someone that no one could take from me. The winter would soon be coming and I wanted to leave New York. One place I could go to was England where my husband was, but I didn't want to take the baby into the dampness and the blackouts and the bombs.

So I went back to Hollywood and my daily column for NANA. The nanny, Wendy—six weeks old—and I stayed at the Garden of Allah where Scott had lived when I first met him, but even that did not depress me. I was exhilarated that I was walking on the same oddly shaped stones where Scott and I had gone to his upstairs apartment. Errol Flynn was in the bungalow next to mine, and I remembered how jealous Scott had been of him. Nothing really mattered now except the sweet bundle I held in my arms.

In 1950 Budd Schulberg's book about Scott, *The Disenchanted,* was published, telling of the Dartmouth Winter Carnival, where Scott had been in disgrace and fired by the producer of the film, Walter Wanger, because of his drinking. This was one time when I hadn't reproached Scott. He should never have gone there with a temperature of 102°. But he needed the $1,500 a week he was being paid.

The Disenchanted came in the wake of growing interest in Scott's writings and his not-so-private life. About a year later, Arthur Mizener published *The Far Side of Paradise*, the first full-length biography of Scott. He didn't mention me by name because I had not yet revealed my association with his subject.

Edmund Wilson had advised Mizener to contact me for information about Scott's last years. He did not come to Hollywood to question me, as Andrew Turnbull did later, but sent a long list of queries, which I promptly answered, never dreaming that later I would be accused of borrowing from him!

This started a shower of books about Scott: biographies, collections of his letters, studies by Professor John Kuehl (on Scott's reading and the letters of Scott and Max), Professor Dan Piper, and Professor Matthew Bruccoli who has edited the *Fitzgerald Newsletter* for 10 years and the *Fitzgerald/Hemingway Annual*, and with Scottie and Joan Kerr recently co-authored a photographic book on her father, mother, and friends, including some of my mementos. Bruccoli recently published a biography of John O'Hara, and I was glad to give him information. I had known O'Hara well.

All this, however, is getting ahead of the more private rebirth. Back in Hollywood with my baby, I drove home fast from the studios to cuddle Wendy and take innumerable photographs of her—in her canvas bathinette, on the bed, on the floor, sitting up, lying down. I bought all the paraphernalia for taking pictures—lamps, a tripod, an expensive camera—and I used a doll as a stand-in. Having a baby was wonderful and I was zealously maternal. Recently I showed Wendy her baby book, and I thought she would throw up, reading sentences like, "When will you speak to me, my darling." Today I can almost join her and say Ugh. But as a baby she was a good substitute for Scott Fitzgerald. And life became yet more complete when I gave birth three years later to my son Robert Trevor Westbrook.

The "Robert" was for Bob Benchley, who had insisted on

being the godfather. He died shortly before my son was born, but I called him Robert anyway. I had liked Mr. Benchley, as Dorothy Parker always called him, very much. He had sometimes made fun of me, but always, I thought, liked me. He was living with a very charming girl who married after his death and lives in Europe.

With two children to take care of—Trevor had insisted on a divorce when I refused to return to England—I decided I would make lots of money to give them everything I had been denied as a child. If you want something badly enough, you get it, and I was a success. I was paid $5,000 a week for the Sheilah Graham Show on Television in 1955. I still have the card that opened the show with the view of Hollywood pierced with searchlights. There were about 160 newspapers taking my column, including the *New York Mirror* and the *Hollywood Citizen News;* I had a weekly radio show (no hard gasping this time); and I wrote monthly articles for several magazines, including a bi-monthly piece for *TV Times.*

I was busy and happy, and ten years after Scott's death, I thought I could talk about him calmly. I was having lunch at Romanoff's with Jean Dalrymple, the brilliant producer for musicals and ballet at New York's City Center, and when she asked me about Scott, I launched confidently into our story. But when it came to speaking about his death, I burst into tears.

I didn't discuss him again until 1957 when an editor of *The Woman's Home Companion* called at the house in Beverly Hills, 607 North Maple Drive, that I had bought ten years previously. He wanted me to write my life story for his magazine. I said, "What you really want is an account of my time with Scott Fitzgerald." "No," he assured me, "we want *your* story. Of course—[casually]—anything you write about Fitzgerald will add to the interest."

It took me one week to talk it all into his tape recorder, but when he left the magazine soon after and I asked for a copy of what I had said, there were some problems, and I had to buy the tapes back from him. Holt supplied the cash because now they were going to publish *Beloved Infidel.* The book made a considerable sum of money and enabled me to send my children to the best schools in the East, and then to leave Hollywood and live in New York City and Connecticut, yet without giving up my job. Jonah Ruddy supplied me with news of filmland and I also made frequent visits there to fill the column I was still giving a Hollywood dateline. Busy as I was in the East, I even filled in for Walter Winchell's column and radio show for several weeks, while he was unable to work because of an infection in his jaw.

I was on top of the world where I would not have wanted to be if Scott were alive. I was not ambitious for myself during those years with him. But, after that, as Julia Foster, the British actress who portrays me in the excellent TV documentary, *Scott Fitzgerald in Hollywood*, says, "I made a name and found a place for myself in this country."

I'm not sure that Scott would like the woman into whom I evolved. An English friend of mine told me in 1934, when he came to New York, "You seem tough on the outside, but you are soft inside." Now I am soft outside and tough inside. I've had to be. I grew to believe with Scott that I am valuable. Before knowing him, while I seemed confident and sure—I was pretty and this helped—I was in reality unsure, and despised myself for all the trickery I had used, at first to survive and later to be successful in my area. But now I realize I am no worse than anyone and sometimes better. At least I hope so. And now that I feel stronger about myself, I can see Scott, whom I earlier adored so unquestioningly partly out of the sense of my own inferiority, much more objectively. I can view him today by the standards that he set for me.

14.

THE LAST PARTY

MARCH 23, 1974, almost thirty-four years after Scott's death. It was party time again—with a difference. Scottie, who had kept in touch with her relatives much more than her father ever did, had invited a whole bunch of them to celebrate the new expensive film version of her father's most popular novel, *The Great Gatsby*. She provided them with plane and train tickets and fine lodging at the Waldorf Astoria on Park Avenue. There were three of cousin Ceci's four daughters, Mrs. Hume Taylor, Mrs. Conrad Little, Miss Virginia Taylor. Also Mrs. Daniel Vaughan, the daughter of Scott's sister, Annabel. Scottie told me that she was very fond of Aunt Annabel and she could not understand why her father didn't like her when they were adults. I found Mrs. Vaughan a delightful, sweet lady.

While Scott had ignored most of them during his lifetime, and some had not yet been born when he died, they were all here to pay him homage. About twenty cousins, mostly Abels and Taylors, and two of Scott's granddaughters, Cecilia and Bobbie—who married eighteen months ago and has produced twin boys (one has Scott for his second name). And Scott's twenty-five-year-old grandson, Jack Lanahan, Jr. Also several of Scottie's classmates at Vassar, with their husbands, and Professor Matthew Bruccoli, Alexander Clark, in charge of the Fitzgerald papers and others in the Rare Books Library at Princeton, his assistant, Wanda Randall, Scottie's first and current husbands, Samuel Jack Lanahan and Clinton Grove Smith, and my son Robert Westbrook, who was to meet me in the party room—a small ballroom at the hotel.

While I waited for him I mingled with the guests on a personal tour of inspection. Perhaps I would find Scott again among the faces of his relatives. I would have liked to meet Ceci Taylor, his favorite cousin, but she had long ago passed away.

I searched their faces but there was little trace of Scott. None of Scottie's children from her marriage to Jack Lanahan resembled their grandfather. They were again charming to me as they had been during the times I had visited their parents in Washington, D.C. I was trying not to feel as I imagine the Duchess of Windsor had when, after the Duke's death, she was finally invited to Buckingham Palace and Windsor Castle. But there was no need to. All the relatives were accepting me with great kindness, some with a dash of well-bred curiosity. I was comfortable with them. They were part of Scott, although there was only a momentary glimpse in the faces and voices of the man whose work they had come to honor.

But there was one young man, Charles Abels, a grandson of Cousin Ceci, who arrested my search. He had Scott's shaped head, the same nose and mouth, and the rain-washed eyes, but the total of the features just missed being Scott. Perhaps I was hoping for too much.

It was a lovely party with the best food and drink the hotel could supply. The voices were subdued, with now and then a sudden rise when a guest was greeted. My son and I sat at the table with Professor and Mrs. Bruccoli, Mr. Alexander Clark, Mrs. Randall, and a Mr. and Mrs. Frazer Clark, while Scottie walked among the tables making sure her guests were comfortable. There was no brashness and no shyness. Scottie has always been her own person, and she had the situation well in hand.

Scott would have been proud of his daughter. But if he had been there it might have been a totally different affair. Not necessarily difficult, but he would have taken it over, getting the guests involved in various activities, games, and tricks. He would probably have taken a drink or two, and then anything could have happened. He might have been a very bad brownie.

It was time to go to the theater. Scottie tinkled a spoon on a glass, commanding attention, and told us of the arrangements to get us there. Buses were outside the Park Avenue entrance to take us to our theater. There were two *Gatsby* film premieres that night, and the money raised from the lot was to go to a Boys Club charity. The theater chosen by Scottie for herself and her guests was not the main one on Broadway, where such notables as Mrs. Henry Ford and Mrs. Gloria Vanderbilt Wyatt were photographed sweeping inside in all their finery. Ours was also on the West Side but in a quieter street.

Scottie had seen the film before—Paramount had given her a special showing in Hollywood—and while she had tactfully praised it on radio and television, she had found it, as the critics did, far too drawn out. (But she was delighted to find *Gatsby* was still showing in London when she visited there last year.) I was sitting next to Mr. Lanahan and his second wife and I could see that they were as restless as I was at some of the stretched-out sequences.

Scott himself would have been the first to say, "Cut some of it." But they never do—as Henry King, the director of *Beloved Infidel*, said when I complained that the film dragged, viewing it at a Long Beach preview in 1959, "I love every foot of it, I won't cut anything." I believe it was chopped a bit for television, which is perhaps why it seemed better on the small screen.

Strangely I had felt nothing while watching *Beloved Infidel*. But the recent ABC-TV documentary, *Scott Fitzgerald*, moved me to the point where I couldn't speak as I ran out of the projection room before the lights went up so that no one could see that I was crying. It's the best so far of anything about

Scott, who is difficult to translate into film. Tuesday Weld as Zelda is superb. She will finally receive her long-awaited due as a dramatic actress. Jason Miller, who played Scott, is nothing like him in looks and at first I was disappointed, but he evolved into the character so well that before the end he was completely the man he was portraying. Julia Foster, the young British actress who played me, was great, and I thank her for making me seem so admirable, so worthy of the respect for which I have always longed.

There was another party the night of the *Gatsby* premieres, given by David Merrick, the producer, and Robert Evans, Paramount's head man (the studio had financed the film). David and Bob had been at odds over the cast and script and were barely polite to each other but this did not affect the general gaiety. This party had a 20s atmosphere—people dressed in the period, champagne flowed, bands blared the songs of the time—"The Sheik of Araby," "In the Morning, in the Evening, Ain't We Got Fun," "Charleston, Charleston"—there was extravagant food: caviar and pheasant under glass, and so many gatecrashers that some of Scottie's guests were unable to find seats at the hundreds of small tables. I watched while Scottie tried to seat them in that bursting crowd, and when I saw her looking for a seat for herself, I beckoned her to come to the table where I was sitting with my son, near the exit—why do people never sit at the nearest tables but wander into the center?

The press found it a piquant situation, Scottie and I sitting together, and obviously enjoying each other's company. An Associated Press girl reporter knelt on the floor between us and said, "It's strange that you two are such friends, when you"—looking at Scottie—"were Fitzgerald's daughter, and she"—inclining toward me—"was . . ." Scottie would not allow her to use the obvious word. She jumped to her feet and said indignantly, "Why shouldn't we be friends? Sheilah was my stepmother. She prolonged my father's life. I love her." I didn't know whether to cry or kiss her. Of course I did both.

APPENDIX

This Appendix consists of an unpublished play—*Dame Rumor* (Act I: Scenes I and II)—written by Sheilah Graham and F. Scott Fitzgerald.

Also included in the Appendix is a short, short story written by Miss Graham, and corrected by Fitzgerald. This presentation, also unpublished, is a facsimile of the original manuscript—with all corrections in Fitzgerald's own handwriting.

Dame Rumor

CHARACTERS
(In Order of their Appearance)

Act I.
Scene 1.

ENGINEER
MARTHA, maid
MISS MINNS, secretary
CHRIS MCMANN, director
JUDY JOHNSON, columnist
GABRIEL, news gatherer
(On telephone) ROBERT ACTON, Great Lover

ACT I.   45 minutes (25-20)
ACT II. 55   "   (15, 20, 20)
ACT III. 25   "

Plot is that radio commentator's broadcast brings to climax long brewing resentment against her and her kind. She loves a director who has fallen into the clutches of a woman psychiatrist, is put in the position of sentencing her. She is about to be pilloried, but circumstances demonstrate that her removal

236

takes the very life and humanity from people who pictured her as their enemy. She is as much or necessary part of the industry as any other element—more, she is the only real person in a world of marionettes.

As for the love story, the director sees that the psychiatrist encourages the unreality and phonies in characters—which Judy frankly castigates and concludes that she is the healthier influence—and particularly for himself.

CHARACTERS

ACTON VAN CLEVE, ventriloquist
CONSUELLA VAN CLEVE, his wife
JOY, child star
JOSIE RITCHIE, singer-screen star
JOHN RITCHIE, her husband-manager
HOLMQUIST, masseur
CARESS, young actress
MICHAEL, young actor
LEFTY, tennis pro
JUDY JOHNSON, columnist-commentator
CHRIS MCMANN, director
DR. ANNA SLAGLE, psychiatrist
JOY's mother
ARNOLD LIGGETT, radio sponsor
GABRIEL, news gatherer
Secretary
MARTHA, maid

ACT I

SCENE I

Living Room of Judy's house in Beverly Hills—6:15 of an August evening. The house rents unfurnished for $150 a month. The living room has cretonne curtains, and comfortable furniture. A low bookshelf runs all around the room on top of which are knickknacks and photographs, not of film stars. There is a large desk down stage at right—on it is a small vase with two roses and a microphone, and before it a swivel chair. In the center of the stage is a small table with a typewriter and a telephone—sheets of paper have fallen from it to the floor. The aperture on the back wall is an impromptu window drilled into the serving pantry. This has been glassed in so that the kitchen can be used as a control room. One door leads to outer hall and stairs—the other to the kitchen.

> (*As the curtain rises, Martha, maid of all work—thirty-five, fresh complexioned, hair tied German fashion—sits in front of the microphone, clutching it with both hands. Her face is serious, slightly frowning. Bending over her, making adjustments to the microphone, is a young radio engineer.*)

RADIO ENGINEER: (*Straightens up and says in bored voice*) When I give the signal, you talk into this in your natural speaking voice—understand?

> (*Martha, a determined, solemn expression on her face, stares at him silently*)

RADIO ENGINEER: (*Impatiently*) You understand, don't you?

MARTHA: (*Slowly, with a German accent*) What I say?

RADIO ENGINEER: Oh, anything—let's see—say something about your boss, Miss Johnson.

MARTHA: But don't know anything about her—I only came work here last Friday.

RADIO ENGINEER: (*Looks at his watch with exasperation*) "Jesus—it's 6:15, in 45 minutes we go on the air and I've got to test this set-up. Where is Miss Johnson?

MARTHA: She in some studios. She say anyone come say she back six o'clock.

RADIO ENGINEER: She's fifteen minutes late. If she doesn't hurry one million listeners are going to be very disappointed not to hear 'Dame Rumor' dishing the dirt. And I'll get the blame. And I don't think her sponsors will like it. Look—you're Miss Johnson (*as Martha gapes*)—Yes, you're not, I know. But you will be just for a few minutes—to please me. (*Martha shrugs her shoulders in bewilderment*) You've heard her on the air, haven't you?

MARTHA: Sure. Last month when I work Mrs. Ritchie—she's opera singer—she always listen Miss Johnson—sometimes she say 'I no go dinner until that *MM* come on.' (*There is no doubt what the MM stands for*) And Greta Garbo—I work for her two months ago—she listen Miss Johnson. Everyone listen Miss Johnson—they hope perhaps she say something terrible about their friends.

RADIO ENGINEER: That's fine. Now just keep talking.

MARTHA: (*Beaming*) I talk all America? Yes? Want speak brother Berlin. Yes?

RADIO ENGINEER: No. Now just talk. I go listen control room. Jesus, She's got me doing it now. (*Exits into kitchen, while Martha looks fearfully at the microphone. His face appears at glassed-in window and his voice booms suddenly into the room, frightening Martha*)

RADIO ENGINEER: Now say something—just like before.

MARTHA: Who I talk about now?

RADIO ENGINEER: Look, I wouldn't strain your brain like this—only I'm new to the job, too. This is the first time I've fixed a radio in a private house—and I hope it's the last. Just answer my questions. Is Miss Johnson married? No, don't turn round—answer into the mike.

MARTHA: (*Holding the mike like a telephone*) She is, she not.

RADIO ENGINEER: That's fine.

MARTHA: No, not fine. I no like work for woman no man in house. (*Now warming up to her subject*) Her secretary say Miss Johnson marry young. I no know what happen—I think he—(*she turns to engineer and makes motion of drinking. He shakes his head and motions her to turn back to the mike.*) She divorce. Now, see this man, that man.

(The telephone bell rings and Martha jumps to answer it)

MARTHA: Hallo—yes—what? No—this 1530 Prince Road, Beverly Hills. Who you want speak? Yes, this Miss Johnson house. You want speak her? Who speak? Yes, this Miss Johnson house. Who? Mr. Boxstead? Foxtead? Jones? Acton? Oh, Mr. Acton. (*The radio engineer gives up and comes back into the room*) No, she not here. Message? All right, I say you call. (*Repeating slowly*) Mr. Robert Acton —tank you—you welc'm.

(*From the hall, a stately, dyed, somewhat affected woman of forty comes languidly into the room*)

MISS MINNS: Who was that, Martha?

RADIO ENGINEER: Miss Johnson?

MISS MINNS: (*Arranging hair*) No—I'm only her secretary. You're the radio man? (*He nods*) Is everything ready?

RADIO ENGINEER: Okay.

MISS MINNS: (*To Martha*) Who was that on the telephone?

MARTHA: (*Slowly*) Mr. Robert Acton.

MISS MINNS: (*Waking up*) Really? Hm! Miss Johnson *IS* going up in the world. Public Lover number one.

RADIO ENGINEER: That sap! I can't see what my wife sees in him. I bet he puts glue on his hair. Does he? You ought to know. My wife tried to get me to look at her like he looks at dames. (*Gives a terrifying imitation*) He must have a crook in his neck all day.

MISS MINNS: He's only been here once. He was probably calling about something he didn't like in her column. She has a lot of that to deal with. One day she and her friends are thick as thieves—I don't really mean thieves—you know what I mean—and the next day they won't even come to the phone when she calls them. What time is it?

RADIO ENGINEER: Time Miss Johnson was here. It's 6:17—she goes on the air at 7:00.

MISS MINNS: Oh, she'll be here. She always is—sometimes only 10 minutes before the broadcast. She's out collecting the very latest gossip—what with her column to do as well, she's on the go all the time.

RADIO ENGINEER: I once had the pleasure—(*sarcastically*)—of hearing Miss Johnson. Don't tell her I said so, but I don't go for this gossip about the stars. Who cares whether Marlene Dietrich sleeps in her pajamas or her birthday suit? And I don't care if Clark Gable's going to marry his grandmother. I put in a radio for him last year and there's one swell guy. But why should some dame yap about his private life?

(*The door bell rings.*)

MISS MINNS: (*A little dithery*) That's Miss Johnson.

(*Judy bursts into living room. She is in her middle twenties, slender, attractive, with quiet vivacity. She is well dressed—hat by Lily Daché, a conservative model; dress by Magnin's—also conservative. She speaks with a rather British intonation though her original Nova Scotia vocabulary is full of Americanisms.*)

JUDY: (To radio engineer) Good evening. Everything ready?

RADIO ENGINEER: (*Nodding*) But I'd like to run through it with you once—if you don't mind. (*He speaks humbly and stares at her unbelievably. He had expected a middle-aged homely woman.*)

JUDY: Look, I've still got 35 minutes and I want to rest. I'll be ready in ten. (*She takes her hat off, loosens hair, gives hat to Martha*) Would you like a drink while you're waiting, Mr. ———?

RADIO ENGINEER: Kopfki. Thanks, I never drink on duty.

JUDY: (*Absently*) Fine—give him a drink, Martha.

(*Kopfki and Martha exit right*)

(The phone rings and Miss Minns starts for it)

MINNS: Mr. Acton called twice—if it's him again, are you in?

JUDY: He promised to get me an interview with Solita Dino. (Considers) No, today I'm not in.

MINNS: (At phone) Hello . . . Who is this please? Oh, Mr. McMann. (Hand over mouthpiece) You don't want to speak to Mr. Chris McMann, do you?

JUDY: Oh, heavens! Yes. (Goes to phone)

MINNS: Well, I didn't know.

JUDY: (At phone—starts to speak enthusiastically, stops herself, takes a deep breath and continues in a languid voice) Hello, Chris. (Then with more heartiness) I mean hel*LO* Chris . . . You can't—Oh . . . No, of course I'm disappointed, but it doesn't matter . . . (her face tightening) No, not tomorrow—I'm tied up this week. You see three times I'd put people off and three times . . . No, Please DON'T, I'm broadcasting—hello . . . (She hangs up the phone and turns around to Miss Minns) He's coming over. (Suddenly, half unwillingly, she smiles.)

JUDY: (Surprised) Well, that was effective. Usually that 'either or' thing is only good with weak specimens. And I never thought of Chris McMann being weak.

MINNS: Me either. I had a bit in one of his pictures and I stood near him all afternoon. Five hundred extras and Chris McMann never raising his voice or losing his head.

JUDY: One's private and public personalities.

MINNS: What's that?

JUDY: Well, me for instance. Isn't the general impression that I'm as tough skinned a little she-cat that ever came to Hollywood?

MINNS: Well, I wouldn't say—

JUDY: And underneath I'm as timorous a female as—

MINNS: You have character, Miss Judy.

JUDY: Have I?—Is that what it is when you're more afraid to stop than to go on?

MINNS: You have character—something we actresses never have—(Complacently)—We only have other people's characters.

JUDY: I'd trade with anybody—character, profession, person and all.

MINNS: You don't like—exposing people.

JUDY: I don't mind that. That's an honorable profession that goes back to Cato and Junius. But there's so little to expose. These people haven't the time or the brains or the stimulous for doing anything very bad or very good.

MINNS: Eddie Cantor is very charitable.

JUDY: Yes, and Fatty Arbuckle was very indiscreet. But Miss Minns, here's the awful secret (lowers her voice)—There isn't an actress in Hollywood whose private life could make second page of the New York Times—unless she was an actress. I'm an *imag*inative writer—that's what I am—

(Chris McMann enters left. He is—description here—a little out of breath)

CHRIS: I came right in.

JUDY: Hello, Chris.

MINNS: (Nervously) You have just 20 minutes, Miss Judy.

JUDY: All right. (Miss Minns goes out)

JUDY: Well, Chris . . .

CHRIS: I had to see you—you seem in a mood. I'm—

JUDY: I am. I'm in the mood—(weighing her words)—where chasing you seems scarcely worth the effort.

CHRIS: I wouldn't say you've been chasing me.

JUDY: I have been. Or I've stood pretty still when you were chasing me.

CHRIS: (Trying the spoiled child) Oh, I feel badly about the whole thing.

JUDY: All right, you sit and feel badly. Only today I won't be sorry for you, Chris. Because I feel a little sorry for myself.

CHRIS: You do?

JUDY: I feel a bit alone—just before these broadcasts—one girl against an industry—that sort of thing. When I go to that mike about 1000 people and their syncopants and admirers are waiting to see what I dare to say.

CHRIS: You ought to get a guard like Winchell.

JUDY: I'm not afraid that way.

CHRIS: No, you're not afraid. That's why I need you.

JUDY: Doesn't your lady psychiatrist help?

CHRIS: Yes—and no. Judy, I hate her.

JUDY: (Cynically) Yes? That's why you're having dinner with Dr. Anna Slagle tonight.

(Phone rings)

CHRIS: I swear I'm not—I'm going to the Ritchie's and she won't be there. I wanted to see you but she's got me so mixed up—

JUDY: —that she wouldn't let you have dinner with me.

(Miss Minns comes in door)

MINNS: Mr. Acton again. Same message?

JUDY: Same message. (To Chris) The Great Lover is trying to enter my life.

CHRIS: *Re*-enter your life you mean. You told me that was over. (annoyed) You, a hardboiled newspaperwoman, to fall for that. (walks a few steps) I don't see how that fellow could do it without an audience.

JUDY: You're indecent. I like Acton—*he* thinks I ought to be *in* pictures instead of writing about them. What do you think? (joking) Haven't I got it on most of your stars. Why don't you give me a test for 'The Last Blonde.'

CHRIS: (Absently) You said you had a screen test in Nova Scotia.

JUDY: I did—I won a contest and it got me a job in New York. The City Editor sent for me—he said I was just the type but he didn't say what for. He took me out to dinner and next day I was a newspaper woman. (*Chris nods knowingly*) Not what *you* think? And not what *he* thought. He gave me the job because it was cheaper than paying my fare back to Nova Scotia.

CHRIS: (*Gloomily*) I'm stingy—I can understand.

JUDY: A new fault—I hate stingy people. (*She sighs*) Chris, you represent everything for which I have the most sincere contempt. And I love you—perhaps because you're the only honest man I've ever known.

CHRIS: Not even that—I haven't told you everything about Anna Slagle.

JUDY: (*Ironically*) Don't shock me. Did you think I thought your nerves were the only bond between you?

CHRIS: Judy, she's older than I am. She has a son. God, how I hate that boy. Just the thought of having him call me papa doesn't bear thinking of. Fine thing to be telling you.

JUDY: You'll never find me so interested in anything again.

CHRIS: It all began with my mother complex—that's why I'm good in war scenes.

JUDY: I don't quite follow.

CHRIS: Well, my mother fed me till I was three, so I can't sleep above the second floor and—

JUDY: Wait a minute. Go back to war scenes.

CHRIS: Well, mother hated war, see—so when I'm directing a war scene—

JUDY: You can't do it above the second floor.

CHRIS: It's easy to sneer at all this—but half the people in America believe it. And the other half soon will.

JUDY: Sometimes I think this country ought to go to bed—as one man. But that's my Nova Scotia birth.

CHRIS: It'll reach Nova Scotia, too.

JUDY: No, no, let's keep it right here in Los Angeles. Honestly, Chris, I'm not sneering—I'm nearer crying. What about your mother, what has it got to do with me?

CHRIS: Judy, I've been married three times. Each time I marry I make my wife into my mother and go to someone else for love because I *have* to get away from my mother.

JUDY: That's not so good.

CHRIS: It's awful—the very words of the marriage ceremony do it—I've heard it three times—I pronounce you man and—mother.

JUDY: And Dr. Slagle is going to cure you.

CHRIS: In six more months. If I stick to her six more months I'll be through with it forever. Then I'm yours if you want me. I'll have something to bring you.

JUDY: If you knew how unattractive that sounded. Are you a sissy—just under the surface?

CHRIS: (*Laughs*) That's the last thing I am—and you know it. I'm a neurotic—and most of the important work of the world is done by neurotics.

JUDY: I don't mean your work—your work's fine—I think you're the best director in Hollywood, except maybe Lubitsch. But I want somebody to love me, and you're not anybody—you're a stock company with a lady doctor holding over half the shares. Let me alone for six months—I'll be here—probably.

CHRIS: What do you mean probably. Judy, I'm mad about you. I've got to have you. I couldn't bear to think of your being with other men. If I had my way I'd marry you tomorrow.

JUDY: You once told me you always had your way.

CHRIS: I do. By God, I do! I'll marry you and Dr. Slagle can cure me afterwards. Or if she won't I'll get somebody else.

JUDY: (*Tenderly*) You don't need a doctor. You need to love someone outside yourself.

CHRIS: And that's you, Judy. What you do to me never has been done before.

(*The kitchen door opens. Radio engineer appears, says apologetically*)

RADIO ENGINEER: It's 20 minutes to broadcasting time. We'd better run through your material.

JUDY: Oh, my God! (*She calls*) Miss Minns—my script. (*Secretary comes in from kitchen and stares at her open-mouthed—slowly*) The broadcast—get me the broadcast.

MISS MINNS: You didn't give it to me. I thought you had it—

JUDY: (*Impatiently*) Of course I did—that stuff you typed this morning.

MISS MINNS: (*Weakly*) Oh, that? Oh, dear, or dear! (*Miss Minns collapses onto the sofa. And now it is Judy who stares at secretary.*)

JUDY: Very good stuff, Miss Minns. What ails you? I've got 19 minutes to the broadcast. Where's the material?

MISS MINNS: (*Weakly*) I thought it was for your column, Miss Johnson. I thought it was your column. I wired it off to New York for the morning papers.

JUDY: My God! (*She sits on edge of sofa*) I haven't any program.

MISS MINNS: Why can't you use it anyhow?

JUDY: In some cities it's on the sheets already. I'll just have to get another program together quickly. Get me that contract list quickly and I'll try to round up something. (*Turning to Chris*) Chris, what do you know that I could use?

CHRIS: I only know what I read in your column and hear on your broadcast.

JUDY: This isn't the time for joking.

(*Martha has come to the door and stares at the scene impersonally. She stares for a couple of seconds, then says phlegmatically*)

MARTHA: You want skins potatoes or insides tonight dinner?

JUDY: (*Still calm*) Not now, Martha, not now. (*As though talking to a child*) Go back to the kitchen and I'll tell you about the potato skins after the broadcast—(*As Martha turns slowly back*) Oh, just a minute, Martha. You've worked for Garbo—you've only just left Josie Ritchie—can you think of anything unusual that happened while you were there? (*The telephone rings. Miss Minns answers it—while Martha's face gets blank as she tries honestly to think*)

MISS MINNS: Oh, Mr. Gabriel—Miss Johnson's very busy now. Will you call later—yes.

JUDY: Don't put that receiver down—(*takes it just before Miss does so*) Oh, he's rung off—get him, Miss Minns. (*Miss Minns dials*)

MARTHA: (*Hesitantly*) I don't know—perhaps this good—but when I work for Miss Garbo—no, don't think any good.

JUDY: (Still keeping calm) It might be, Martha. Just tell me, then I'll decide.

MARTHA: No, it no good.

MISS MINNS: (*Almost screaming*) Oh, Martha, what is it, for heaven's sake! I'm going crazy—No, Mr. Gabriel, I'm not going crazy, I mean I am—Oh, I don't know what I mean—Miss Johnson wants to talk to you.

JUDY: (*Taking phone—talking quickly*) Have you anything exciting I could use for the broadcast? Yes, tonight's broadcast; yes. I know you gave me some items this morning. I want some more. Why? Oh, Gabe, please, this is a crisis. My broadcast has gone—never mind where—oh, think of something, please—Oh, I knew I could rely on you. All right, come over—but write the items on the way. (*Turning to others*) Call NBC, Miss Minns, tell their lawyer to stand by—I'll have a new program to read to him. (*Miss Minns dials*) Now, Martha, what was that about Miss Garbo?

MARTHA: (*Twisting her apron*) She say she tank she go home Denmark Sweden.

(*Chris roars*)

JUDY: You're a fine one to laugh—while I'm about to be ruined. What about *your* new picture, Chris? We ought to get something out of that.

CHRIS: You've sucked that dry in your column. You've interviewed everyone in it—from Josie Ritchie to the prop man.

RADIO ENGINEER: (*Poking his head out*) You only have 15 minutes, Miss Johnson.

JUDY: Oh, wait a minute. Why don't you go into your cage—(*waves vaguely in direction of glassed-in compartment*) I'll have it all ready soon.

MISS MINNS: (*On telephone*) Yes, Mr. Butcher, Miss Johnson will call you in five minutes—it's very innocuous this week—so there won't be any trouble. All right, then, in three minutes. You'll hold on—well—yes, I suppose that's all right. (*She puts earpiece down and puts finger to mouth.*) Sh! We'll have to be quiet—the NBC libel lawyer is on the phone.

RADIO ENGINEER: (*From control room—his voice always booms into room*) I've got something you can use—about a year ago when I put in that radio for Clark Gable—he called up Carole Lombard while I was there—I think he's in love with her. That's good, isn't it—unless you think it's too old?

JUDY: (*Smiling politely*) No, of course not. Thanks very much. (*Out of the corner of her mouth to Minns who is waiting to type the items*) Forget it.

(Gabriel rings doorbell. Judy opens door. Sound of whispering in hall)

GABRIEL: (*Breezily*) What's all the trouble? (*Gabriel is short, stocky, very dark—speaks with ultra cockney accent—he is an Australian. He does not see Chris, who is reading paper in corner of room. He brings out his notebook*) Miss Minns, takes this dictation. Dr. Anna Slagle, well known psychiatrist, and Mr. Chris McMann, the famous Hollywood director, are planning a Yuma-igration—(*at this point he sees Chris—doesn't falter*) Oh, hello, old chap—let me be the first to congratulate you. (*Chris goes on reading paper*)

JUDY: (*Coldly*) Cut that one—but keep on dictating. (*She is looking down list of names in her hand*)

GABRIEL: (*To Chris*) Pardon me, sir, but isn't Solita Dino in your new picture? Gad, she's a lovely creature—almost as lovely as Johnson. Any item about her is news—surely you can think of something.

CHRIS: (*Getting up*) You'd better leave Miss Dino out of this. I don't want anything to upset her. You know what she is about keeping her private life private.

GABRIEL: (*Penitently*) Sorry, sir—I only thought that in these trying circumstances, well—how about Josie Ritchie—she's in your picture, too, isn't she?—and she likes publicity—or why does she give all those parties, because she likes the press?

CHRIS: (*Really trying to think now*) Let's see, what can I tell you about Josie Ritchie—well, she has terrific lung power—equal to a man's. (*Miss Minns takes this busily*) She broke a couple of recording instruments when she sang into it a couple of days ago. They wanted to take a picture of her showing her lungs and the broken records—but she refused—said it would destroy the illusion of fragile femininity the studio had built around her.

JUDY: That's good, Chris. I'll use it—if you think it won't hurt you with the picture.   ·

CHRIS: Well, don't say you got it from me—that's all. I'm going there for dinner tonight, so be careful.

GABRIEL: And Robert Acton—he's your leading man, isn't he? I have an item about him. They tell me he's drinking again—or rather that he never stopped. How about something like this—Robert Acton, the Great Lover of the Screen, has been at the bottle again, which is why he will soon be a has-been lover of the screen. Damn funny, what!"

JUDY: A—it's not funny; B—it's not true; C—it's libelous; and D—it's not funny. I'd sooner use something about you, Chris—give your picture a boost.

CHRIS: (*Casually*) Just as long as you don't say it's a bad picture.

JUDY: (Dictating to Miss Minns) My scouts inside the studio inform me that 'The Last Blonde' is a near future candidate for Academy Honors. A brilliant cast will enact the scintillating story—check their names, Miss Minns—No less a personage than the great Solita portrays the title role. Of course, her beautiful red hair will be dyed blonde for the picture.

MISS MINNS: I thought her hair was dark brown.

JUDY: It is—(*repeats*) beautiful red hair—it was red for her last picture, wasn't it? (Miss Minns nods, typing)—will be dyed blonde. Playing opposite her and fighting for the hero's love, is Josie Ritchie, that famous song-bird from the New York Metropolitan Opera House, who will make her picture debut in this wonderful film. Robert Acton, the male lead, tells me that never before in his screen life has he had a role that fits him so well—and you know what that means, girls—

MISS MINNS: (*Sighs blissfully*) Yes. (*Radio Engineer looks bored and shakes head in disgust*)

JUDY: But best of all, 'The Last Blonde' is directed by that famous veteran of the screen, the man who put sex into screen love-making—the man who made the movies move—who was there to guide the stars over the first talkie hurdle—

CHRIS: (*Softly*)—And to catch them when they fell—

JUDY: —That brilliant megaphonist responsible for the success of half the actors and actresses in the business, who has always put art before money, but has made money pay for art. I refer to that old in experience—youthful in years —handsome, Chris McMann.

CHRIS: (*Getting up*) My God!

JUDY I can't help it, Chris.

CHRIS: Don't overdo it. I'll listen to you at the Ritchie's. (*He kisses her*) Goodbye, darling. We'll have dinner tomorrow.

(*He goes out*) "Buck up, old girl—time is jolly well passing, you know."

JUDY: (Absently) "Yes." (Still looking after Chris, she sighs a little and comes back to center of stage.) "All right now, let's get going." (Reads names on list) "Joy—oh yes, Little Joy—I saw her in a downtown cafe yesterday with Philip Jones."

GABRIEL: "She's only about ten years old. Or is she? I had a cable from Australia a few days ago saying my paper had definite proof that Joy Dawkins is really about 25."

MISS MINNS: "Yes, I've heard that, too. No child could act the way she does—and her language—well, I don't know how or where any child could hear the things she says."

JUDY: "How do you know?"

MISS MINNS: "Mr. Gabriel keeps telling me—"

GABRIEL: "Yes, my dear, it was excrutiatingly funny. When I interviewed her, she gave me a highball and flirted like hell. Asked her mother if she could sit on the knee of the 'nice mans' as she couldn't hear very well. Doesn't sound like a child, does it?"

JUDY: "It sounds like a lie to me."

GABRIEL: "All right, belittle me. I'm only trying to help."

JUDY: "Of course you are, Gabe. Forgive me. I'm nervous."

GABRIEL: "I understand, old dear."

JUDY: (To Miss Minns) "What do you think is the better item —that the child wonder of the screen is really a woman of 25, or that she had a date with Philip Jones, who's 16, if he's a day."

MISS MINNS: "I'll take romance."

GABRIEL: "That settles it. Use my item." (Miss Minns and Gabe glare at each other—and audience understands they dislike each other.)

JUDY: (To Gabe) "Yes, I think yours is more sensational—and that's what the sponsor wants. Now let's get something on an M-G-M star. What about Greta Garbo?"

GABRIEL: "I saw her talking to Harpo Marx in the studio. They both ran when they saw me."

MISS MINNS: "Who wouldn't?"

JUDY: "They went to a preview together according to the Reporter. I think I'm safe in saying they are thinking of getting married."

GABRIEL: "Harpo Marx is already married."

JUDY: (Sighs) "Yes, I knew that wouldn't really work. Well, I'll just say—"(and here dictates to Miss Minns)—" 'Greta Garbo will shortly elope with a well known comedian who plays a harp and has never yet spoken on the screen.' That'll disguise him."

GABRIEL: "Here's something about Solita Heber. I happen to know the people who live next door to her house. And they say she's gone—or going—crazy. She talks to herself all the time. She sometimes laughs, they've even heard her cry. She's going crazy! I think that's a wonderful item."

JUDY: "It's not bad, but I've got to be careful. That libel lawyer at NBC won't pass it—I don't think he likes me. Besides, she's in Chris' picture. The last thing I want to do is make him sore. Let's see, 'Solita Heber is so excited about her role in 'The Last Blonde' she rehearses her part night and day.' No, that wouldn't thrill a high school girl. This is it—'Solita Heber is so bored with her self-imposed solitude, that she has taken to talking to herself—so I'm informed by her neighbors.' "

GABRIEL: "Good."

JUDY: "Or 'Things look bad for the number one recluse of Hollywood,' and then the rest. Now there ought to be something to say about Robert Taylor—let's see—everyone knows he's got hair on his chest."

GABRIEL: "But not as much as I have, by Jove." (Bares his very hairy chest.)

JUDY: "Gabe!" (Judy stares at chest in fascinated horror) "You never told me about this! I'll use it." (Dictates) " 'Mr. Dan Gabriel, Hollywood scribe, challenges Robert Taylor to a hair-on-the-chest competition. Judges to be a hand-picked beauty chorus. The winner gets a date with Solita Heber.' "

RADIO ENGINEER: (Almost hysterically) "You've only got 10 minutes, Miss Johnson."

JUDY: (Showing nerves for the first time) "I'd better take a drink now. I'm getting awfully nervous."

MISS MINNS: "It's the aspirin you take for your nerves—the drink's to pep you up. Martha, get two aspirins for Miss Johnson." (Martha goes upstairs)

JUDY: (To Miss Minns) "NBC is still waiting? Tell them to keep the line open. And Martha—" (shouting upstairs) "bring down my lozenges—my throat's getting dry—I don't think I can speak."

MISS MINNS: (Shouting) "And bring some aspirin for me—I can't stand this any more. We've only got three pages done —you need another two."

RADIO ENGINEER: "Six more minutes."

JUDY: "Loretta Young—anything new on Loretta Young?"

GABRIEL: "Well, she's not going to marry Joe Mankewicz or Tyrone Power or Charlie Chaplin or Eddie Sutherland or David Niven or Jon Hall or Jimmy Stewart or Wayne Morris or Cesar Romero or George Brent or Brian Aherne."

JUDY: (Slightly feverish) "Good, I'll use that—say something about 'Loretta Young being a confirmed celibate, will not marry Joe Mankewicz or Tyrone Power or Charlie Chaplin or Eddie Sutherland or the rest of Hollywood's bachelors.' That should take up a minute."

GABRIEL: "Katherine Hepburn flew East yesterday."

JUDY: "To see Howard Hughes?"

GABRIEL: "I don't know—she didn't tell me."

JUDY: "Fine. We'll say she's going around the world with Hughes in his plane. First, of course, they will be married by the pilot—they're like captains of ships—and can marry people."

GABRIEL: "No. I don't think so."

JUDY: "They do where I fly from."

RADIO ENGINEER: "Five minutes, Miss Johnson. I've got to send the station the Okay signal."

JUDY: "Well, send it—I'm ready—practically. Look, Gabe—you take this stuff upstairs and telephone it to Mr. Butcher of NBC—the line's open." (Gabe takes it from Miss Minns) "And tone it down as much as possible when you talk to him. Say a messenger is on the way with a copy." (Gabe is out of the room during half of the conversation) "Now what else." (Judy scans contract list) "Er—the Ritz Brothers—the Ritz Brothers—No, I'm not that hard up." (Turning page to Warners' list) "Er—Kay Francis—Miss Minns, what would you like to know about Kay Francis—pretend you're the listening public and I mention Kay Francis' name. What would interest you most to hear about her?"

RADIO ENGINEER: "That she's quitting the screen."

MISS MINNS: "Oh, how could you! I think she's wonderful. Looks so fragile and helpless. I can't think why she doesn't marry."

JUDY: (Repeating) "Why she doesn't marry." (Shouting upstairs) "Gabe, when you've finished on that phone tell me why doesn't Kay Francis marry."

GABRIEL'S VOICE: "I guess she hasn't met her ideal man yet."

JUDY: (Dubiously) "It's weak—but I'll have to use it." (Looking at list again) "Errol Flynn—Errol Flynn—he's always good for a war trip or something." (Calling upstairs again) "Is the Spanish War still going on, Gabe?"

GABRIEL: (Shouting) "Yes!"

JUDY: "Then I can't send him there."

MISS MINNS: (Thoughtfully) "We've sent him on cruises to South America, the South Seas, and India."

JUDY: "All right, he's going to South Africa in his boat because he doesn't like the looks of the peace situation there and will fight for the side that is right."

GABRIEL: (Coming into room) "NBC didn't like your item about Joy going out with Philip Jones—said it might give ideas to the youth of America."

JUDY: "Oh. Then I'll use the other item about her—I'm sure she's older than her mother says she was. Yes, it's a better item anyway—write it down the way I said it before." (Miss Minns types)

RADIO ENGINEER: "Two more—"

JUDY: "Stop saying that, please! I know, I've got two more minutes. How many pages, Miss Minns?"

MISS MINNS: "With your review of the week's pictures, it's the right length."

JUDY: (Collapsing weakly into chair) "Thank God! I wouldn't go through this again for all the money in Louis B. Mayer's bank."

GABRIEL: (Always in a very tough voice but with precise English) "Well, I presume I can go now, Johnson. I have a date with a gem of a girl. We are going to make love." (Rather coyly) "She promised to give herself tonight. Toodle-oo. I'll listen to the broadcast in my car. Best of luck, old top." (He goes)

JUDY: (Wearily) "Better telephone those last items to NBC, Miss Minns—upstairs. Leave the duplicate with me." (Miss Minns goes—Judy scans copy—murmuring some of the notes aloud.) "Hm—not bad—but not awfully good—I wish I had something startling—I'd like a baby." (Radio Engineer coughs into the microphone—but Judy is oblivious to it) "I've never had a baby except once—and that didn't come off."

MARTHA: (Who has been at door most of the time, interrupts) "You no tell me—how potatoes done—skins—inside?"

JUDY: "I forgot to tell you, Martha, I'm dieting—no potatoes at all. And—" (as Martha starts to talk)—"I'm very busy —the broadcast—I'm going to broadcast" (slowly) "Martha, I talk America—" (Martha makes another motion of talking)—"Look, why don't you go into your bedroom, turn on your radio, and listen in?"

MARTHA: (Slowly) "A'right." (Leaves the room)

RADIO ENGINEER: "Stand by, Miss Johnson. I'll give you a 30 second signal at the end—so you can cut or go slow if you're too long or short." (Judy, making pencil corrections in copy, nods.)

MISS MINNS: (Half-way downstairs in a stage whisper) "It's all right, Miss Johnson—but they want a copy right away." (During this stage whisper, Martha has come into room again)

JUDY: "Oh, Martha, Martha—what is it?" (Moans softly)

MARTHA: (Whispering at sign from radio engineer) "Baby —what you say want baby—remind me something." (The radio engineer does a silent 'sh') "Josie Ritchie—the one I work last week—she going have baby—big secret. She no know I know. But me know those things."

JUDY: (Snatches piece of paper and writes furiously while saying to Martha) "Remind me to give you $10 after the broadcast."

MARTHA: (Looking blank) "What you say?"

RADIO ENGINEER: "Stand by for the commercial, Miss Johnson."

JUDY: (Looks trapped for a second—clears throat—finds it not clear) "My lozenges" (she whispers to Martha—Martha rushes upstairs, brings them down during middle of commercial. Judy puts one in mouth, sucks furiously —swallows before beginning. The commercial which lasts one minute, is heard.)

(First a bar of spirited martial music)

("The makers of So-Good Chewing Gum bring you"—here another bar of music—" 'Dame Rumor'—on a coast to coast hook-up." Another ta-ra of trumpets. "Dame Rumor, the nom de air for that beautiful brilliant reporter of the Hollywood scene—Miss Judy Johnson —brings you good news, exclusive news—and new news. Her column is syndicated from Hoboken to Honolulu, from Montreal to Malibu. Her delicious tid-bits of Hollywood gossip are brought to you every Tuesday at this hour by the makers of 'So-Good Chewing Gum.' Incidentally, we do not necessarily agree with Dame Rumor's opinions. But we like them and you will. Of that the makers of So-Good Chewing Gum are confident. . . . Before introducing Dame Rumor, we will do our weekly slenderizing exercises. Have you all got your package of 'So-Good Chewing Gum' ready, ladies and gentlemen? All right—place two lumps in your mouth. Yum—Yum. Tastes good, doesn't it—but there is better to come. Now, while I beat time with the music, chew, using the back teeth only—opening the mouth as wide as possible." Judy unconsciously begins to chew and open mouth—with the lozenges Martha has just given her—the audience can see how very nervous she is. Music starts like that Margaret had—one-two-three—open, open, wider, wider, etc. "There, did you feel a surge of circulation through your entire body? Of course, you did. And good circulation is good for dissolving the cells of fat that too often mar the female form divine—and the masculine. Now once more—" (here repeat)—"And now here is Dame Rumor in person—and while you listen to her chew the rag—don't forget to chew So-Good Chewing Gum." A loud trumpet call. "DAME RUMOR!" Judy's voice is now beautifully modulated, soft and clear—no nervousness after the first convulsive gulp.)

JUDY: "Good evening, listeners of the United States—and Nova Scotia. This is Dame Rumor in the living room of her home in Hollywood bringing you the latest and most authentic" (here makes a slight grimace) "—news of the stars." (Here I will use my funniest real star item.) . . . (Black out and—

CURTAIN.

ACT I.

Scene II.
(short scene)

Short scene, ventriloquist's house.
7:55 P.M. Same night.
Atmosphere: Comedy and eerie.

Actor Van Cleve
Joy
Mrs. Consuela Van Cleve.

Plant time.
Little girl's fascination with ventriloquist and dummy.

Hollywood wife bored.

Broadcast about child, no effect.

Broadcast about ventriloquist, great effect, ending with hint of his madness.

Child's mother takes her away, worries about ventriloquist.

ACT I.

SCENE II.

The drawing room of the Ritchie's house in Beverly Hills.

Over the fireplace is a portrait of Josie Ritchie in a white very picturesque dress, with barbaric jewelery on her wrists and throat and a white gardenia in her hair. The walls are painted in apple green and a somber painted screen covers where a fire would be if it were winter. The walls are decorated with good prints showing a canal in Venice, a Doge's Palace in Florence. One side is practically covered with a tapestry showing the harbor at Naples. At the far end of the room is a very large grand piano, on which is much stacked music. On a table stand inscribed photographs of prominent opera stars. Two large sofas in cream satin face each other by the fireplace with small low tables in front of them. The drapes are drawn, showing the dusk of a California summer evening. The cream parchment lamps are lit.

When the curtain goes up, Tom Ritchie, in a dinner jacket, sits at the piano playing very softly. He is dapper, short, with scanty black hair brushed very carefully back over his high forehead. His eyes are his best feature—large and dreaming. His wife, Josie Ritchie, dressed exactly like the portrait over the fireplace, is lying on the sofa beneath the light holding a script, humming from it as her husband plays. She is very attractive in a spectacular way—her red hair is a startling frame for her pale handsome face; her lipstick is the same shade as her hair. One foot, in a silver shoe, taps in time to her humming.

RITCHIE: (*After playing a few bars of the song which is a compromise between the classical and popular.*) If you were a torch singer, you could sing this. But for your glorious voice—it's just funny.

JOSIE: Speak to Rossoff.

RITCHIE: No, he's only the music director—this is too important—it's the title song of the picture. Rossoff can't do anything without Chris . . . Don't look so worried.

JOSIE: I'm not, Tom. You always fix everything.

RITCHIE: Of course it's hardly the picture I'd pick for your debut—Josie Ritchie between the trained seals and elephants—it's—it's illegitimate.

JOSIE: Solita Dino isn't a trained seal—or an elephant.

RITCHIE: How D'ye know? Have you ever seen her?

JOSIE: (*Somewhat ironic*) Has anybody? But you forget there's also Joy to keep me company. She and her mother are coming to dinner tonight.

RITCHIE: My God! And we haven't a high chair. Did you invite the seals?

JOSIE: They're probably studying their roles. (*Turning pages of thin script*) They don't seem to have left much to me.

RITCHIE: (*Coming over and putting his arm round her*) Will you stop worrying? You worry all the time lately. Chris is a good director—the best. You mustn't expect too much—this is Hollywood—not the Metropolitan. And fifty thousand for three songs. A hundred dollars a note. (*He sighs*) But sometimes I wish we were back in the old days in Florence.

JOSIE: We were happy then. You were going to be the best pianist in the world.

RITCHIE: You were so sure I would be.

JOSIE: I still think so. Remember the day I fainted because I'd had nothing to eat for 36 hours?

RITCHIE: Yeah—life was pretty wonderful in those days. Sure, we didn't have any dough—but we had other things. (*Comes toward her sentimentally*)

JOSIE: Oh, Tom—please—you promised.

RITCHIE: (*Humbly*) I'm sorry, darling. I know. You can't give everything to the millions who worship your glorious voice and have anything left for your husband. But you're so lovely—it isn't so easy.

JOSIE: Tom, don't—I can't stand this sort of thing. When the season is over, we'll go away somewhere. Tom, you mustn't forget it was you who taught me that music comes first. Remember Martha Sorel.

RITCHIE: That's different. She boasted of having had a hundred affairs before she was 21. And God knows how many afterwards. But Constinelli—(*Looks at her and breaks off*) oh, I'm sorry, darling. I know it upsets you when I talk about him.

JOSIE: (*primly*) Constinelli was a tenor—that's different.

RITCHIE: Forgive me, Josie. I'm sorry. I'm just a big, ugly brute at heart, I guess. Come on—let's dance. (*He pulls her up from the sofa*)

JOSIE: They'll be here in a minute. It's after seven. (*He looks at wristwatch*)

Ritchie holds her in his arms. She towers above him.

RITCHIE: Better take your shoes off.

Josie kicks them off. They dance a bad rhumba cheek to cheek. Ritchie draws himself up to his fullest height with a very proud and yet humble look on his face as he presses his cheek against Josie's.
The bell rings very softly, but they do not hear it. A child's

laughter rings out by the door as Little Joy Terry comes in with her mother. Joy is about 12 years old—rather thin, but with masses of golden curls. She wears an organdie party dress. The mother is like a freshly painted doll, her round eyes move like a doll's; what she says has a doll's range and mechanical sound. They stand in doorway until Josie sees them and stops dancing. The Terry's come down center.

JOSIE: (*Very sweetly*) You're little Joy, of course. How d'ye do. (*Shakes her hand*)

JOY: *To her mother.* Dolly—this is Mrs. Ritchie. She's going to sing in my picture.

JOSIE: *Looking for her shoes.* Please sit down, Mrs. Terry.

JOY: *To Josie.* D'ye always dance without your shoes? You'll get cold. *Looking at her mother.* Dolly has a cold from watching me on the set.

RITCHIE: Will you have a drink, Mrs. Terry? *Butler is now handing them canapes.*

JOY: Have a stiff one, Dolly. It'll do you good.

Robert Acton enters, strides into the room. Englishman, handsome, a young 40.

ACTON: *He crosses room to radio.* Hello, everyone. Am I in time for Judy Johnson's broadcast? *Twiddles with switch of radio.*

JOSIE: Yes—it's just seven.

ACTON: *Still twiddling with knobs.* What's new on our picture?

RITCHIE: Nothing. I wish we had a director who knew more.

ACTON: What station is she on?

JOY: KFI. *To Ritchie.* I heard that Mr. McMann can't read.

JOSIE: Oh, yes he can read. I know. He just likes to have his scripts read to him.

JOY: Maybe we could get my school teacher to give him lessons on the set.

ACTON: Sh—

ANNOUNCER'S VOICE: Before introducing Dame Rumor, we will do our weekly double-chin reducer. Have you all got your package of Wendell's Chewing Gum ready, ladies and gentlemen? All right—place two sticks in your mouth. Yum—Yum. Tastes good, doesn't it—but there is better to come. Now while I beat time to the music, chew, using the back teeth only—opening the mouth as wide as possible.

People in the room unconsciously begin to chew and open mouths—music starts.

ANNOUNCER'S VOICE: One-two-three, open, open, wider, wider. There. Did you feel a surge of circulation through your entire body? Of course you did. Good circulation is good for dissolving the cells of fat that too often mar the line of the chin. Now once more—

Everyone in the room chews—even the butler who comes in and stands in the door. Behind him comes Chris McMann and, seeing him, Ritchie turns off the radio.

CHRIS: Hello, Josie. How are you? Hello, Joy. Mrs. Terry. Well, if it isn't my old friend, Acton. Hello, Tom.

Ad lib greetings.

JOSIE: How's everything with you?   .

CHRIS: Everything? Everything's perfect.

JOSIE: Since when?

CHRIS: Josie, darling, I'm in love. She's wonderful—wonderful. I tell you—wonderful.

JOSIE: I get it. She's wonderful.

CHRIS: Everything I've always wanted in a woman. Yes, it took me by surprise, too, but wait till you meet her.

JOSIE: But I have—and she's coming for dinner tonight.

CHRIS: Tonight? But I've just only left her and she was up to her eyes in work.

JOSIE: When I called her this afternoon, she said she wanted to surprise you.

CHRIS: Funny, she didn't tell me.

JOSIE: Anna always does things her own way.

CHRIS: Anna? Josie, you don't mean Anna Slagle? *He laughs.* I wasn't talking about her!

JOSIE: No?

CHRIS: *Emphatically.* NO! *He laughs.* It's Judy Johnson.

ACTON: *Hearing the last four words.* I wish someone would get Judy Johnson's program.

JOSIE: *To Chris.* Oh-h-h! She's nice.

RITCHIE: I don't like newspaperwomen. They make me nervous. They twist everything you say into something they've got already written.

JOSIE: Not Miss Johnson, Tom. She seemed most intelligent. *To others.* She had lunch with me here last week. I thought she was very charming.

RITCHIE: She was just like the rest of them—didn't know an A minor or a B flat.

JOY: She promised to buy me a rabbit. I don't like rabbits—but I like her.

ACTON: I can't complain—she's always done very well by me. *Humming softly with a far-away look in his eyes.* In fact, I once named her as one of the ten most attractive women in Hollywood.

JOSIE: *To Chris.* I promise to call her and invite her for dinner one night—as a friend, not a newspaperwoman.

RITCHIE: You can't trust reporters. They think in headlines. There isn't one of them who wouldn't sell out his best friend for an inch of space in his paper.

CHRIS: You don't know Judy. I've told her things that would ruin me if she ever used them—I'd tell her anything.

RITCHIE: They're a menace to the industry. I know a lot of picture people here who won't let her get inside their homes.

CHRIS: It's her business to print things about the movies. And she does a good job. That's what they pay her for. Here, let me at that radio. *Goes to radio and turns switch.*

Major Crandall comes in.

JOSIE: *Going to him.* Major Crandall! Do you know everyone here? *To others.* Major Crandall.

Crandall ad libs greetings.

Dr. Anna Slagle comes in. She is dark-haired—fairly slender but rather big busted, about 38, fairly good-looking, little makeup. Chris doesn't see her. His back is to the door—until she speaks.

JOY: *Who sees her first.* Good evening, Dr. Slagle.

JOSIE: Hello, Anna. Come on over. We're listening to Judy Johnson.

SLAGLE: *Coldly.* No, thanks. I'll stay here. *Josie gives Chris an embarrassed look. Chris smiles at Anna feebly and waves his hand.*

DAME RUMOR: *Over radio.* So "The Last Blonde" is at last in production. And now for some scoops about the members of this brilliant—*she clears her throat*—cast. *They look at each other meaningly—Chris smiling—Robert Acton self-consciously tugging at collar—Mrs. Terry beaming. Joy with nonchalance, Ritchie with a vague sneer. Dr. Slagle seats herself near the door.* Neighbors of Solita San Martin are complaining about her new habit of talking to herself. Can it be that self-imposed solitude is breaking her down? It'll be too bad if her illness causes a postponement of "The Last Blonde."

JOSIE: Oh, dear, I hope not.

JOY: Sh—I want to hear the rest. *Chris' smile fades.* Dr. Slagle gets more interested.

DAME RUMOR: *Continuing.* Now here's an item that will surprise you as much as it surprised me. Little Joy Terry—*Joy gets very excited, holds her mother's hands and looks round triumphantly at others.* She is not the little girl you have been led to believe. She is a young woman of 27. I hate to say this because I love Joy just as much as you do—but the little sweetheart of America is the same age as your Dame Rumor. But this doesn't mean that young Joy—or should I say "old" Joy?—should stop portraying the child roles she has made so famous.

MRS. TERRY: *Very indignantly, but with confusion.* Well!

Chris gets less amused and Dr. Slagle more—the others are a mixture of being startled and amused with Josie registering sympathy for all of them.

DAME RUMOR: *Continuing.* And now for the scoop of the week. *They all lean forward expectantly.* Josie Ritchie, who was brought here from New York for the top singing role in "The Last Blonde" is preparing a bassinette for the little stranger she is expecting in February. That will be all this week, except—

When the word "all" has been said, Ritchie turns off the radio.

RITCHIE: What did I tell you? That girl's a malicious liar. Josie going to have a baby! Why, it's the most outrageous thing I ever heard! The girl is crazy!

JOY: She can't do that to me—and get away with it!

RITCHIE: We were so nice to her. Treated her like one of the family. I even got Josie to sing for her. And all we get for thanks is a baby!

JOSIE: *Weakly.* I think I'll have a drink.

JOY: My, how pale you are, Mrs. Ritchie.

RITCHIE: Darling, you're not going to let this silly story upset you, are you?

Across the room, Robert Acton faints to the floor.

RICHIE : *Ad lib. In perplexity.* What the hell—! He's fainted! Get water! Slap him on the back! Put him under a shower! Get a doctor!

JOSIE: *A little frantically.* Do something! Take him into the den —the big couch.

RITCHIE: Yes, dear, of course. *To butler.* Here—give me a hand. *They half carry, half drag him out of the room.*

CHRIS: *Sitting dejectedly on sofa.* I could have sworn Judy would never do a thing like this. I'd have trusted my life with her.

JOSIE: Tom was right, Chris. I'm through with reporters. I'll never give another interview as long as I live.

SLAGLE: She's smarter than I thought. When did she say the happy event takes place, Josie?

JOSIE: This is not the time for kidding. Can't you see I'm very upset?

SLAGLE: That's just it. Why don't you come to my office tomorrow? Maybe I can reconcile you.

JOSIE: *Stiffy.* No, thanks. I'm sorry—I know you mean well —but—. *Anna shrugs shoulders and goes over to picture censor.*

SLAGLE: I'll call you in the morning.

BUTLER: Mr. Thater calling, Mr. McMann.

CHRIS: *Jumping up.* Solita's manager.

SLAGLE: *Maliciously.* Take the call here, Chris.

CHRIS: *On phone.* Yes, I know it was terrible . . . Of course not

. . . Why should the studio give out that item? What do you think we are—on Judy Johnson's payroll? . . . Well, we're not! Look, put Solita on the phone. Let me talk to her. . . . Yes, I know she's upset—so are we all.

JOY: I'm not a bit upset. *They shush her—all wanting to hear Chris.*

CHRIS: Solita, hello . . . Yes, awful . . . But no one will believe it . . . I suppose you *have* got a case for slander—but those things are always unpleasant—you'll have the rest of the press on your neck. . . . You want her run out of Hollywood tonight. *He laughs, without enthusiasm.* Of course you're joking, Solita. *To others.* She hung up on me. *Puts receiver down with dejected air. It immediately rings again. Chris lifts it hopefully—but expression changes to gloom.*

CHRIS: London calling—for Mrs. Terry.

JOY: Let me take it, Dolly. Hello, the Daily Express? This is Joy . . . Is it true? Dolly, they want to know, is it true? *She laughs shrilly—then into phone.* What do YOU think? *Puts phone down.*

JOSIE: Poor Joy. We'll get out of this mess somehow. Even if you are a midget—it isn't your fault.

Butler enters.

BUTLER: The Josie Ritchie Fan Club would like to talk to you, Mrs. Ritchie.

JOSIE: My God! Where are they—outside? *Butler silently hands her receiver. Josie braces herself and in her most sugary tone.* No—it isn't true. Yes, I'm sorry too. . . . Oh, that was very sweet of you . . . Yes . . . *Grimly.* Yes, I promise if I have one I'll let you know first . . . Yes, goodbye. *To the others.* They want to organize a Josie Ritchie Baby Fan Club.

RITCHIE: *Coming agitatedly into room.* Bob's sitting up, but he's still very weak. He wants to talk to you, Josie.

JOSIE: The poor boy—this has been a terrible shock to him.

Excuse me. *To her husband who is following her out of room.* Let me go alone.

RITCHIE: I'm coming with you.

Josie shrugs her shoulders—they exit.

CHRIS: *Disgustedly.* We have a great cast with one star crazy —the other going to have a baby, and—*sinks his voice*—Joy a midget.

Joy and her mother have been whispering aside. They come down left together.

JOY: Dolly, I'll lay you five to one we can do it.

MRS. TERRY: It sounds so risky.

SLAGLE: What's on your mind, Joy.

JOY: Nothing, Dr. Slagle, nothing. I'm only going to call on Judy Johnson tomorrow—and scare the living daylights out of her.

MRS. TERRY: When we're finished with her she'll be sorry she ever heard the word 'midget.'

JOY: Don't tell them, Dolly. It's a secret, remember. Let's go look at Mr. Acton. I've never seen a fainted man. *They exit to den with Crandall.*

Dr. Slagle comes over to Chris, puts her arm around him. He takes no notice.

SLAGLE: Now, Chris, take a toe-hold on yourself.

CHRIS: *Very tersely.* I resent the implication.

SLAGLE: Look. I've been giving you psycho-analysis for three years now. I think I can claim to understand you better than anyone else, don't I?

CHRIS: I suppose so.

SLAGLE: And I've helped you, haven't I?

CHRIS: I suppose so.

SLAGLE: You don't sound very convinced, Chris. You look almost as desperate as when you first came to me for help three years ago. You'd been to other psychiatrists and they weren't able to help you, were they?

CHRIS: Yes, yes.

SLAGLE: You'd just been divorced for the second time.

CHRIS: Oh, why bring that up.

SLAGLE: *Passionately.* Because you're headed for the same mistake again. You were only 19 when you married that girl in Texas. Now you're thirty-seven. For seventeen years you've been fighting the love your mother imposed on you when you were a little boy.

CHRIS: I didn't tell you that. All I said was that my mother didn't wean me until I was three.

SLAGLE: *Ignoring the interruption.* You married a sweet little girl. You loved her—she loved you. And immediately she became your wife you began deceiving her. And why? Because directly she was your wife, she became your mother.

CHRIS: Yes. Yes, that's right.

SLAGLE: Then you marry your mistress, and how long were you faithful to *her*, Chris?

CHRIS: Quite a long time—about a month.

SLAGLE: That's practically a lifetime considering the sub-conscious forces that were tearing you apart. A month after your second marriage, you have an affair with your script girl.

CHRIS: Well?

SLAGLE: You manage to keep this affair from your wife a long time—at least two months. But she has you watched.

CHRIS: She'd been having affairs, too—

SLAGLE: What did you expect her to do—enter a nunnery?

CHRIS: No, I didn't.

SLAGLE: That's when you came to see me. The script girl wanted to marry you.

CHRIS: I'll always be grateful to you for getting me out of that.

SLAGLE: She preferred the cash anyway—Now tell me, how much are you in love with Judy?

CHRIS: At this moment, not at all.

SLAGLE: *Judiciously.* She's young and I suppose some people would call her pretty. And she's very much in love with you—of course, for what she could get out of it.

CHRIS: She's not a gold digger.

SLAGLE: You can't judge that. I'd have given you a week at the most to have an affair with a woman you could regard as your sweetheart.

CHRIS: I thought I was cured.

SLAGLE: It's obvious that you're not. But it's also obvious you don't need me any longer.

CHRIS: *In wild alarm.* Anna, darling, I'm sorry. I didn't mean to hurt you. Look—be reasonable. I love you. I need you. You can't run out on me now—just as I'm almost cured. Anna, you can't go—I'd go crazy without you.

SLAGLE: Goodbye, Chris. *She moves toward the door.*

CHRIS: Anna, don't be silly. *Goes over to her—tries to take her in his arms. Then desperately*—I'll kill myself, I swear it—if you give me up. I hate Judy Johnson. I'll never see her again. I need you so, Anna, please, please, don't go.

SLAGLE: *Who now sees she has him where she wants him and can afford to torment him.* I don't know, Chris—you're so unstable.

CHRIS: I know I am—that's why I need you so. Anna, marry me—now BEFORE the picture starts. I wouldn't be able to make the picture anyway—if you run out on me.

SLAGLE: *Taking off her coat.* You know I couldn't abandon you, darling. You're such a fine person, I want so much for you to find yourself in life.

CHRIS: Then you'll marry me?

SLAGLE: Yes.

CHRIS: Thank God! We'll buy the ring tomorrow. *He kisses her cheek. The others are heard coming down the stairs.*

Ritchie, Acton and Josie are the first to come into the room. Acton is still very pale and Ritchie is supporting him.

ACTON: *Testily.* I tell you, I'm all right now. *Ritchie lets go and Acton staggers slightly. But recovers, walks to fireplace, and leans against mantelpiece.*

SLAGLE: Chris and I are getting married.

JOSIE: *Watching Acton anxiously and hardly hearing.* I'm so glad. *Double-take.* What! *Chris avoids her eyes.*

SLAGLE: Yes. *She lights her cigarette with fingers that tremble a little.*

JOSIE: Oh, how wonderful. *To Acton.* How do you feel, Bob?

ACTON: I'm all right, Josie.

RITCHIE: I'm going to that Judy Johnson and push her face in.

JOSIE: No, she might get more vindictive and say I was going to have twins. Maybe Bob will speak to her—he has a way with women that's irresistible.

ACTON: *Weakly.* Thank you, dear. I'll do my best.

SLAGLE: *To Josie.* Don't let it get you down, Josie.

JOSIE: I'm not—but how would you feel—it would be the happiest day in my life, if it was true.

RITCHIE: *Quietly.* And mine, Josie.

BUTLER: *In doorway.* Dinner is served.

JOY: Poor Mrs. Ritchie. Don't worry about Judy Johnson. She'll be leaving Hollywood tomorrow. I'm going to fix her good.

All exit to dining room except Ritchie and Crandall.

CRANDALL: I'm glad this happened tonight—these radio commentators and newspaper columnists have been carrying their dirt dishing too far. My office will take strong action. Tomorrow morning every studio will put Judy Johnson on the black list.

He exits.

Ritchie is now alone on the stage.

JOSIE'S VOICE: Tom, are you coming?

RITCHIE: Yes, dear. *Leaves room looking very worried.*

CURTAIN.

A SHORT SHORT STORY

Not in the Script

By Sheilah Graham

1443 N. Hayworth Avenue
Hollywood, California

Here, ~~you find it -- I can't.~~ Yeah -- Judy Martin's column. ~~I suppose~~ I'll be blamed for it as usual. That's what ~~a supervisor --~~ I ~~mean producer's for. Say,~~ After this I'm going to keep track of who likes who -- and who doesn't. Maybe after this it will be better if I don't go on the set at all. I always knew Bonnie ~~Burton~~ was no good, but the way she picked on Judy Martin was ~~not only the silliest but~~ the ~~dirtiest,~~ lousiest thing she's ever done to me. And she's done plenty, ~~damn her baby blue eyes.~~

Pretty gal, that reporter -- and young, too ~~-- say, don't think that's why Bonnie got so sore?~~ Bonnie's 37 if she's a day -- ~~been running around for years. She can't act - never could -- even though we do pay her $2,000 a week. But~~ she's still a good name on the marquee. ~~Who says I'm~~ scared of her? ~~But if I am,~~ It's no disgrace. ~~Everyone else is. Nice the way Judy Martin talked back. She's intelligent, that girl - asked a million questions about the~~ picture. I told you what it's about, didn't I? Well -- it all takes place at the beach -- Bonnie is chased to the South of France by a rich guy and he gets her there in a weak moment and marries her. There's more to it of course, she nearly drowns ~~-- I wish she would --~~ and he saves her and you get the general idea.

Well, Bonnie's been drowning all afternoon, and Judy Martin comes on the set. I see her talk to Sam Destry ~~-- who's~~ the director, and she makes a lot of notes. Then ~~Taylor~~ chips over and ~~waves his teeth~~ at her and she makes some more notes. I reckon it's time she knew the producer, so I give her the big hello and tell her what an expensive production it is and how everything is real -- even the sand -- none of your ~~phoney~~ projection shots, I tell her. She asks me how to spell my name and says she has to rush off and send her column.

"Going so soon?" I say to her. If only I'd kept my ~~big~~ trap
shut.

"I've been here two hours and interviewed everyone - except
Bonnie ~~Burton~~," she says. How was I to know she didn't want to talk to
Bonnie? She should have told me. I thought she was scared or something.
I told you, everyone's scared of Bonnie. But she's been much sweeter
since she was called poison at the box office. So like a ~~big big~~ *Sap* I
offer to introduce her.

She said afterwards that she DID try to stop me, and now that
I think of it, she did say, "No, don't." But anyway ~~as I said~~, I introduce them. Bonnie is having her hair brushed and she turns round
very slowly. A great big grin covers that pasty face of hers when
Miss Martin says, "How ~~dixe~~ do." I smile, too, and wait for Bonnie
to say something nice. It begins to get embarrassing and I'm just
going to break the silence myself, when Bonnie says - so soft and sweet:"

"So _you_ are Judy Martin - _you_ are that little ~~so-and-so~~
~~children, leave the room~~ "You are the ~~so-and-so~~ who writes that
~~filthy lying~~ stuff that's only fit for the garbage ~~pail~~ *Can*. So _you_ are
the biggest ~~so-and-so~~ in Hollywood."

I thought I'd die. I felt so embarrassed, but Miss Martin
pretends that Bonnie is joking. She ~~laughs~~ *smiles*. Nice going, *kid* I thought --
but of course I didn't say it. Then she says, very quietly:

"_I'm_ not the biggest ~~so-and-so~~ say kids, I told you to get
out" *only* — I'm the second biggest ~~so-and-so~~." Not bad for a gal that only
makes $150 a week, eh? No one's ever talked that way to Bonnie before.
And if this wasn't my picture I'd have been tickled pink. I'm afraid
to look at Bonnie. I wait for her to roll on the floor and scream or
walk off the picture or something. ~~Ha! We'd have been in some mess.~~
But she just smiles. The extras all crowd round, enjoying it like hell.
Bonnie's not ~~what you'd call~~ *exactly* popular. I suppose I should have done
something, but what? Besides, they were both grinning and I couldn't

3.

make out if they were quarrelling or ~~not~~ *kissing*. Oh, yes, I did say to Miss
Martin:

"This will probably be the beginning of a beautiful friendship between you two." They both laughed at that -- I felt easier.
Then Judy Martin says very businesslike:

"Sit down, ~~Miss Burton~~ *Bonnie* and tell me all about it."

She was a fool to start it ~~again~~ again. But Bonnie sits
down, still grinning fit to die and offers the gal a cigarette. She
says she doesn't smoke. And a minute later asks me for a cigarette!
The crowd goes away thinking the fireworks are over, but everyone
comes back at double trot when Bonnie says:

"I can't believe that a girl with such a round face could be
such a ---- " and she calls her that name again. Oh, God, I think,
she's started again. That makes ~~Judy~~ *Miss* Martin mad and she says:

"Your face is rounder than mine, so ~~I~~ that makes *still*
you the bigger ---- " I couldn't stand it.

"I wish I'd been struck dead before I introduced you to each
other," I say. That gets them.

"See what you've done - you've upset him," says Judy.

"Oh, you poor darling," says Bonnie. ~~She~~ *and gets up and* rushes into my arms
and kisses me. I'd like to choke her but we're in the middle of a
picture - so I kiss her back and say I'm not upset if they are not.
Sam Dealey ~~calls for Bonnie, And am I relieved! I try and think~~
It gave me a
chance to patch things up
~~of something to say and manage to whisper so Bonnie won't hear.~~

"She's not as bad as she sounds," I whisper ~~to~~ *her Martin*

"It's hot in here," she replies - as if I didn't know. Then
she says: "Sure, she's a very nice woman, ~~Just look at her~~ the
look at her
cold-blooded fish -- acting -- ~~if you can call it acting~~ as though
nothing had happened."

"She's got a lot of control," I had to admit.

4

"I hate her," she says, *lowly,* and I didn't blame her.

"Don't worry, you ~~handled right with her~~ *handled yourself nicely*," I tell her. ~~She~~ *had at that.* ~~cheer her up.~~

"Did I really?" she wants to know. Her voice breaks and she tells me she has a cold. But I know better. She's upset.

"Why don't you go now while Bonnie's acting?" I suggest.

She shakes her head. "And have it said she kicked me off the set? No, I've got to stay, but God, ~~how~~ I hate her."

"Yeah, I see your point," I tell her.

The sequence is over -- too soon -- and Bonnie comes back, still with that ~~Cheshire~~ cat grin on her face.

"What are you so sore about?" Miss Martin asks Bonnie. She's a fool not to drop the subject. Bonnie laughs and says to me:

"Sore - she thinks I'm sore - as if anything she could write could make the slightest difference to me."

"There are a lot of things I could have written - and didn't," says Miss Martin.

"My dear girl, I don't even read your column," says Bonnie, which is a lie. But it stumps Miss Martin. I can see her thinking hard for something clever to say. But Bonnie beats her to it. In a loud screech that everyone hears, she says to me:

"Darling, why do you let ~~such awful~~ *these* strays clutter up the set? ~~It's most disturbing.~~" I had to laugh ~~with Bonnie and the rest.~~ *but we all* ~~We all~~ look at Miss Martin ~~and wait for her to crush Bonnie but she~~ *still* doesn't say anything. Just freezes her mouth into a terrible grin that *She* shows both rows of her teeth *so that she just barely looks pretty. and* ~~when she came in I wouldn't have noticed not of that~~

The director wants Bonnie again and she kisses and cuddles me before going into her scene. ~~I didn't know she was fond of me~~ *when she* ~~comes~~ *runs off* ~~the rest~~. Miss Martin ~~looks like she's going to cry, and~~ says:

"*You* ~~Do you~~ think it's all right if I go now? It won't look as though I were afraid if I want now?"

Not in the Script 281

5.

Here it is!

~~right~~ now before she comes back," I tell her. But she

waits another minute, *takes her time* powdering her nose ~~slowly~~ and putting on some

lipstick. Then she walks slowly to the exit. *almost.* That ~~fool~~ Bonnie ~~shouts~~
~~after her~~ *turns around just in time to see her trip over*

~~"And don't come back -- over." The poor kid trips over a cable.~~ *a cable, and the* *out loud.*
~~Bonnie laughs.~~ But ~~she~~ doesn't turn round, ~~or reply.~~ *Miss Martin* I'm telling you,

it was the most embarrassing afternoon I've ever had in all my life.

Here I'll find the column -- *Listen!*
~~And now,~~ give me that paper. ~~Bloody God, you're right. She is~~

~~the biggest so-and-so in Hollywood. Listen --~~

Poor Bonnie Burton -- persistent flapper of 1919. It isn't
~~is having so much trouble photographing Bonnie Burton's hips as~~
~~had painting them. And by the way, it isn't~~ true that Bonnie's screen *her features*

eclipse has ~~transformed her into an angel of consideration for those~~ *softened her. She* It certainly hasn't *modified*

~~working with her. She is just as difficult as she ever was.~~ Especially

her language. ~~Phew!~~ Really, Bonnie, you made me blush for the children

in your picture who were within earshot during your tirade of temper

when I was on the set last week. Fortunately, the mothers of the

moppets were out of hearing - or I might have had to rescue you from

a very awkward situation. ~~Miss Burton, persistent flame of 1919, has~~ *dont*
~~been symbolically enough cast as a ghost in her last productions."~~ . . . .

~~Get my hat and bag. I'm leaving town for a few years.~~

If So that's that -- or is it? ~~That column runs 356~~

We ~~Excuse my gotdam laughter -- call it relief.~~ *times a year --*

Ha ha ~~Well, I don't know -- call it a draw --~~

~~I think Bonnie got off light.~~

Remind me to send Baby Martin a mink coat for
Christmas. Bonnie got off light.

Index